MW00331879

FREE Test Taking Tips Video/DVD Offer

To better serve you, we created videos covering test taking tips that we want to give you for FREE. **These videos cover world-class tips that will help you succeed on your test.**

We just ask that you send us feedback about this product. Please let us know what you thought about it—whether good, bad, or indifferent.

To get your **FREE videos**, you can use the QR code below or email freevideos@studyguideteam.com with "Free Videos" in the subject line and the following information in the body of the email:

   a. The title of your product

   b. Your product rating on a scale of 1-5, with 5 being the highest

   c. Your feedback about the product

If you have any questions or concerns, please don't hesitate to contact us at info@studyguideteam.com.

Thank you!

SIE Exam Prep 2023-2024

Practice Tests and Study Guide Book for the FINRA Securities Industry Essentials Certification [Includes Audiobook Access]

Joshua Rueda

Copyright © 2023 by TPB Publishing

All rights reserved. No part of this publication may be reproduced, distributed, or transmitted in any form or by any means, including photocopying, recording, or other electronic or mechanical methods, without the prior written permission of the publisher, except in the case of brief quotations embodied in critical reviews and certain other noncommercial uses permitted by copyright law.

Written and edited by TPB Publishing.

TPB Publishing is not associated with or endorsed by any official testing organization. TPB Publishing is a publisher of unofficial educational products. All test and organization names are trademarks of their respective owners. Content in this book is included for utilitarian purposes only and does not constitute an endorsement by TPB Publishing of any particular point of view.

Interested in buying more than 10 copies of our product? Contact us about bulk discounts:
bulkorders@studyguideteam.com

ISBN 13: 9781637759578
ISBN 10: 1637759576

Table of Contents

Welcome

Dear Reader,

Welcome to your new Test Prep Books study guide! We are pleased that you chose us to help you prepare for your exam. There are many study options to choose from, and we appreciate you choosing us. Studying can be a daunting task, but we have designed a smart, effective study guide to help prepare you for what lies ahead.

Whether you're a parent helping your child learn and grow, a high school student working hard to get into your dream college, or a nursing student studying for a complex exam, we want to help give you the tools you need to succeed. We hope this study guide gives you the skills and the confidence to thrive, and we can't thank you enough for allowing us to be part of your journey.

In an effort to continue to improve our products, we welcome feedback from our customers. We look forward to hearing from you. Suggestions, success stories, and criticisms can all be communicated by emailing us at info@studyguideteam.com.

Sincerely,
Test Prep Books Team

FREE Videos/DVD OFFER

Doing well on your exam requires both knowing the test content and understanding how to use that knowledge to do well on the test. We offer completely FREE test taking tip videos. **These videos cover world-class tips that you can use to succeed on your test.**

To get your **FREE videos**, you can use the QR code below or email freevideos@studyguideteam.com with "Free Videos" in the subject line and the following information in the body of the email:

    a. The title of your product
    b. Your product rating on a scale of 1-5, with 5 being the highest
    c. Your feedback about the product

If you have any questions or concerns, please don't hesitate to contact us at info@studyguideteam.com.

SCAN HERE

1

This material is provided for exam preparation purposes only and does not indicate an endorsement of any specific scientific, political, or religious point of view. © TPB Publishing. You have been licensed one copy of this document for personal use only. Any other reproduction or redistribution is strictly prohibited. All rights reserved.

Quick Overview

As you draw closer to taking your exam, effective preparation becomes more and more important. Thankfully, you have this study guide to help you get ready. Use this guide to help keep your studying on track and refer to it often.

This study guide contains several key sections that will help you be successful on your exam. The guide contains tips for what you should do the night before and the day of the test. Also included are test-taking tips. Knowing the right information is not always enough. Many well-prepared test takers struggle with exams. These tips will help equip you to accurately read, assess, and answer test questions.

A large part of the guide is devoted to showing you what content to expect on the exam and to helping you better understand that content. In this guide are practice test questions so that you can see how well you have grasped the content. Then, answer explanations are provided so that you can understand why you missed certain questions.

Don't try to cram the night before you take your exam. This is not a wise strategy for a few reasons. First, your retention of the information will be low. Your time would be better used by reviewing information you already know rather than trying to learn a lot of new information. Second, you will likely become stressed as you try to gain a large amount of knowledge in a short amount of time. Third, you will be depriving yourself of sleep. So be sure to go to bed at a reasonable time the night before. Being well-rested helps you focus and remain calm.

Be sure to eat a substantial breakfast the morning of the exam. If you are taking the exam in the afternoon, be sure to have a good lunch as well. Being hungry is distracting and can make it difficult to focus. You have hopefully spent lots of time preparing for the exam. Don't let an empty stomach get in the way of success!

When travelling to the testing center, leave earlier than needed. That way, you have a buffer in case you experience any delays. This will help you remain calm and will keep you from missing your appointment time at the testing center.

Be sure to pace yourself during the exam. Don't try to rush through the exam. There is no need to risk performing poorly on the exam just so you can leave the testing center early. Allow yourself to use all of the allotted time if needed.

Remain positive while taking the exam even if you feel like you are performing poorly. Thinking about the content you should have mastered will not help you perform better on the exam.

Once the exam is complete, take some time to relax. Even if you feel that you need to take the exam again, you will be well served by some down time before you begin studying again. It's often easier to convince yourself to study if you know that it will come with a reward!

This material is provided for exam preparation purposes only and does not indicate an endorsement of any specific scientific, political, or religious point of view. © TPB Publishing. You have been licensed one copy of this document for personal use only. Any other reproduction or redistribution is strictly prohibited. All rights reserved.

Test-Taking Strategies

1. Predicting the Answer

When you feel confident in your preparation for a multiple-choice test, try predicting the answer before reading the answer choices. This is especially useful on questions that test objective factual knowledge. By predicting the answer before reading the available choices, you eliminate the possibility that you will be distracted or led astray by an incorrect answer choice. You will feel more confident in your selection if you read the question, predict the answer, and then find your prediction among the answer choices. After using this strategy, be sure to still read all of the answer choices carefully and completely. If you feel unprepared, you should not attempt to predict the answers. This would be a waste of time and an opportunity for your mind to wander in the wrong direction.

2. Reading the Whole Question

Too often, test takers scan a multiple-choice question, recognize a few familiar words, and immediately jump to the answer choices. Test authors are aware of this common impatience, and they will sometimes prey upon it. For instance, a test author might subtly turn the question into a negative, or he or she might redirect the focus of the question right at the end. The only way to avoid falling into these traps is to read the entirety of the question carefully before reading the answer choices.

3. Looking for Wrong Answers

Long and complicated multiple-choice questions can be intimidating. One way to simplify a difficult multiple-choice question is to eliminate all of the answer choices that are clearly wrong. In most sets of answers, there will be at least one selection that can be dismissed right away. If the test is administered on paper, the test taker could draw a line through it to indicate that it may be ignored; otherwise, the test taker will have to perform this operation mentally or on scratch paper. In either case, once the obviously incorrect answers have been eliminated, the remaining choices may be considered. Sometimes identifying the clearly wrong answers will give the test taker some information about the correct answer. For instance, if one of the remaining answer choices is a direct opposite of one of the eliminated answer choices, it may well be the correct answer. The opposite of obviously wrong is obviously right! Of course, this is not always the case. Some answers are obviously incorrect simply because they are irrelevant to the question being asked. Still, identifying and eliminating some incorrect answer choices is a good way to simplify a multiple-choice question.

4. Don't Overanalyze

Anxious test takers often overanalyze questions. When you are nervous, your brain will often run wild, causing you to make associations and discover clues that don't actually exist. If you feel that this may be a problem for you, do whatever you can to slow down during the test. Try taking a deep breath or counting to ten. As you read and consider the question, restrict yourself to the particular words used by the author. Avoid thought tangents about what the author *really* meant, or what he or she was *trying* to say. The only things that matter on a multiple-choice test are the words that are actually in the question. You must avoid reading too much into a multiple-choice question, or supposing that the writer meant something other than what he or she wrote.

3

This material is provided for exam preparation purposes only and does not indicate an endorsement of any specific scientific, political, or religious point of view. © TPB Publishing. You have been licensed one copy of this document for personal use only. Any other reproduction or redistribution is strictly prohibited. All rights reserved.

5. No Need for Panic

It is wise to learn as many strategies as possible before taking a multiple-choice test, but it is likely that you will come across a few questions for which you simply don't know the answer. In this situation, avoid panicking. Because most multiple-choice tests include dozens of questions, the relative value of a single wrong answer is small. As much as possible, you should compartmentalize each question on a multiple-choice test. In other words, you should not allow your feelings about one question to affect your success on the others. When you find a question that you either don't understand or don't know how to answer, just take a deep breath and do your best. Read the entire question slowly and carefully. Try rephrasing the question a couple of different ways. Then, read all of the answer choices carefully. After eliminating obviously wrong answers, make a selection and move on to the next question.

6. Confusing Answer Choices

When working on a difficult multiple-choice question, there may be a tendency to focus on the answer choices that are the easiest to understand. Many people, whether consciously or not, gravitate to the answer choices that require the least concentration, knowledge, and memory. This is a mistake. When you come across an answer choice that is confusing, you should give it extra attention. A question might be confusing because you do not know the subject matter to which it refers. If this is the case, don't

 eliminate the answer before you have affirmatively settled on another. When you come across an answer choice of this type, set it aside as you look at the remaining choices. If you can confidently assert that one of the other choices is correct, you can leave the confusing answer aside. Otherwise, you will need to take a moment to try to better understand the confusing answer choice. Rephrasing is one way to tease out the sense of a confusing answer choice.

7. Your First Instinct

Many people struggle with multiple-choice tests because they overthink the questions. If you have studied sufficiently for the test, you should be prepared to trust your first instinct once you have carefully and completely read the question and all of the answer choices. There is a great deal of research suggesting that the mind can come to the correct conclusion very quickly once it has obtained all of the relevant information. At times, it may seem to you as if your intuition is working faster even than your reasoning mind. This may in fact be true. The knowledge you obtain while studying may be retrieved from your subconscious before you have a chance to work out the associations that support it. Verify your instinct by working out the reasons that it should be trusted.

8. Key Words

Many test takers struggle with multiple-choice questions because they have poor reading comprehension skills. Quickly reading and understanding a multiple-choice question requires a mixture of skill and experience. To help with this, try jotting down a few key words and phrases on a piece of scrap paper. Doing this concentrates the process of reading and forces the mind to weigh the relative importance of the question's parts. In selecting words and phrases to write down, the test taker thinks

This material is provided for exam preparation purposes only and does not indicate an endorsement of any specific scientific, political, or religious point of view. © TPB Publishing. You have been licensed one copy of this document for personal use only. Any other reproduction or redistribution is strictly prohibited. All rights reserved.

about the question more deeply and carefully. This is especially true for multiple-choice questions that are preceded by a long prompt.

9. Subtle Negatives

One of the oldest tricks in the multiple-choice test writer's book is to subtly reverse the meaning of a question with a word like *not* or *except*. If you are not paying attention to each word in the question, you can easily be led astray by this trick. For instance, a common question format is, "Which of the following is...?" Obviously, if the question instead is, "Which of the following is not...?," then the answer will be quite different. Even worse, the test makers are aware of the potential for this mistake and will include one answer choice that would be correct if the question were not negated or reversed. A test taker who misses the reversal will find what he or she believes to be a correct answer and will be so confident that he or she will fail to reread the question and discover the original error. The only way to avoid this is to practice a wide variety of multiple-choice questions and to pay close attention to each and every word.

10. Reading Every Answer Choice

It may seem obvious, but you should always read every one of the answer choices! Too many test takers fall into the habit of scanning the question and assuming that they understand the question because they recognize a few key words. From there, they pick the first answer choice that answers the question they believe they have read. Test takers who read all of the answer choices might discover that one of the latter answer choices is actually *more* correct. Moreover, reading all of the answer choices can remind you of facts related to the question that can help you arrive at the correct answer. Sometimes, a misstatement or incorrect detail in one of the latter answer choices will trigger your memory of the subject and will enable you to find the right answer. Failing to read all of the answer choices is like not reading all of the items on a restaurant menu: you might miss out on the perfect choice.

11. Spot the Hedges

One of the keys to success on multiple-choice tests is paying close attention to every word. This is never truer than with words like *almost*, *most*, *some*, and *sometimes*. These words are called "hedges" because they indicate that a statement is not totally true or not true in every place and time. An absolute statement will contain no hedges, but in many subjects, the answers are not always straightforward or absolute. There are always exceptions to the rules in these subjects. For this reason, you should favor those multiple-choice questions that contain hedging language. The presence of qualifying words indicates that the author is taking special care with his or her words, which is certainly important when composing the right answer. After all, there are many ways to be wrong, but there is only one way to be right! For this reason, it is wise to avoid answers that are absolute when taking a multiple-choice test. An absolute answer is one that says things are either all one way or all another. They often include words like *every*, *always*, *best*, and *never*. If you are taking a multiple-choice test in a subject that doesn't lend itself to absolute answers, be on your guard if you see any of these words.

This material is provided for exam preparation purposes only and does not indicate an endorsement of any specific scientific, political, or religious point of view. © TPB Publishing. You have been licensed one copy of this document for personal use only. Any other reproduction or redistribution is strictly prohibited. All rights reserved.

12. Long Answers

 In many subject areas, the answers are not simple. As already mentioned, the right answer often requires hedges. Another common feature of the answers to a complex or subjective question are qualifying clauses, which are groups of words that subtly modify the meaning of the sentence. If the question or answer choice describes a rule to which there are exceptions or the subject matter is complicated, ambiguous, or confusing, the correct answer will require many words in order to be expressed clearly and accurately. In essence, you should not be deterred by answer choices that seem excessively long. Oftentimes, the author of the text will not be able to write the correct answer without offering some qualifications and modifications. Your job is to read the answer choices thoroughly and completely and to select the one that most accurately and precisely answers the question.

13. Restating to Understand

Sometimes, a question on a multiple-choice test is difficult not because of what it asks but because of how it is written. If this is the case, restate the question or answer choice in different words. This process serves a couple of important purposes. First, it forces you to concentrate on the core of the question. In order to rephrase the question accurately, you have to understand it well. Rephrasing the question will concentrate your mind on the key words and ideas. Second, it will present the information to your mind in a fresh way. This process may trigger your memory and render some useful scrap of information picked up while studying.

14. True Statements

Sometimes an answer choice will be true in itself, but it does not answer the question. This is one of the main reasons why it is essential to read the question carefully and completely before proceeding to the answer choices. Too often, test takers skip ahead to the answer choices and look for true statements. Having found one of these, they are content to select it without reference to the question above. The savvy test taker will always read the entire question before turning to the answer choices. Then, having settled on a correct answer choice, he or she will refer to the original question and ensure that the selected answer is relevant. The mistake of choosing a correct-but-irrelevant answer choice is especially common on questions related to specific pieces of objective knowledge.

15. No Patterns

One of the more dangerous ideas that circulates about multiple-choice tests is that the correct answers tend to fall into patterns. These erroneous ideas range from a belief that B and C are the most common right answers, to the idea that an unprepared test-taker should answer "A-B-A-C-A-D-A-B-A." It cannot be emphasized enough that pattern-seeking of this type is exactly the WRONG way to approach a multiple-choice test. To begin with, it is highly unlikely that the test maker will plot the correct answers according to some predetermined pattern. The questions are scrambled and delivered in a random order. Furthermore, even if the test maker was following a pattern in the assignation of correct answers, there is no reason why the test taker would know which pattern he or she was using. Any attempt to discern a pattern in the answer choices is a waste of time and a distraction from the real work of taking the test. A test taker would be much better served by extra preparation before the test than by reliance on a pattern in the answers.

This material is provided for exam preparation purposes only and does not indicate an endorsement of any specific scientific, political, or religious point of view. © TPB Publishing. You have been licensed one copy of this document for personal use only. Any other reproduction or redistribution is strictly prohibited. All rights reserved.

Bonus Content & Audiobook

We host multiple bonus items online, including all 5 practice tests in digital format and our audiobook. Scan the QR code or go to this link to access this content:

testprepbooks.com/bonus/sie

The first time you access the page, you will need to register as a "new user" and verify your email address.

If you have any issues, please email support@testprepbooks.com.

This material is provided for exam preparation purposes only and does not indicate an endorsement of any specific scientific, political, or religious point of view. © TPB Publishing. You have been licensed one copy of this document for personal use only. Any other reproduction or redistribution is strictly prohibited. All rights reserved.

Introduction to the SIE Exam

Function of the Test

The Securities Industry Essentials^{SM} (SIE^{SM}) Exam is an introductory-level exam developed and administered by the Financial Industry Regulatory Authority (FINRA) to assess prospective securities industry professionals' basic industry knowledge. FINRA has designed the exam to be a candidate's first major step toward a career in the securities industry. Questions address topics pertaining to securities such as regulatory agencies and their functions, available products and their risks, capital markets, trading, prohibited activities, and rules. After passing the SIE^{SM} exam, candidates interested in working in the securities industry for a firm must become associated with a firm and pass a qualifications exam, such as the Series 7 exam.

Besides being of the age of 18 or older, there are no prerequisites for taking the SIE^{SM} exam. Test takers may be in school, changing careers, or seeking to demonstrate their basic knowledge of the securities industry to potential employers. Candidates may or may not be associated with a firm; it is not a requirement to sit for the test.

Test Administration

The SIE^{SM} exam is offered via computer at Prometric testing centers around the country. International sites may be available as well. Candidates must first enroll with FINRA; after enrollment, FINRA will provide test takers with a 120-day window within which they are to schedule and take the exam.

Individuals who are currently registered with a broker-dealer as a general securities representative (Series 7) are not eligible to sit for the SIE^{SM} exam, but they should receive SIE credit. As with FINRA's other exams, test takers who do not pass the SIE^{SM} exam are subject to a waiting period that must elapse before they are permitted to retake the exam. This waiting period lasts 30 days after the first and second failed attempts; it increases to 180 days after the third (and any subsequent) failed attempt/s.

In accordance to the Americans with Disabilities Act (ADA), FINRA provides accommodations to test takers with documented disabilities and/or learning impairments. Test takers seeking modifications to the testing environment or administration must complete and submit the FINRA Special Accommodations Eligibility Questionnaire and Special Accommodations Verification Request Form. While test takers may suggest or request any sort of accommodation, FINRA will review the documentation submitted and have the final say. Candidates will receive written notification from FINRA detailing what accommodation(s), if any, can be provided.

This material is provided for exam preparation purposes only and does not indicate an endorsement of any specific scientific, political, or religious point of view. © TPB Publishing. You have been licensed one copy of this document for personal use only. Any other reproduction or redistribution is strictly prohibited. All rights reserved.

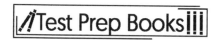

Test Format

The SIE^{SM} exam consists of 75 scored multiple-choice questions and 10 unscored pretest questions scattered throughout, and test takers have 105 minutes to complete the exam. Test takers will not know which questions are the unscored pretest questions. There are four primary domains or sections on the exam. The following table lists the breakdown of the content and questions on the exam:

Section	Percentage of Exam	Number of Questions
Knowledge of Capital Markets	16%	12
Understanding Products and Their Risks	44%	33
Understanding Trading, Customer Accounts, and Prohibited Activities	31%	23
Overview of the Regulatory Framework	9%	7

Scoring

Results are available on the computer shortly after completing the exam, but test takers will also receive a printed copy of their pass/fail status and score report. Score reports for those who have passed the exam provide no additional details. Score reports for those who do not pass the exam also contain additional performance details, such as the overall score and the test taker's success with each topic addressed on the exam, which can be used to inform study preparations for potential retakes.

Points are awarded for each correct answer and there is no penalty for incorrect responses, so guessing is encouraged when the test taker is unsure of the answer. Results of the SIE^{SM} exam are scaled from 0 to 100, and a score of 70 is the minimal score required to pass. The scaling process allows multiple iterations of the test to be compared even with slight variations in the difficulty of the test questions. A test taker's results are valid for four years from the date he or she passes the exam.

9

This material is provided for exam preparation purposes only and does not indicate an endorsement of any specific scientific, political, or religious point of view. © TPB Publishing. You have been licensed one copy of this document for personal use only. Any other reproduction or redistribution is strictly prohibited. All rights reserved.

Study Prep Plan for the SIE Exam

1 **Schedule** - Use one of our study schedules below or come up with one of your own.

2 **Relax** - Test anxiety can hurt even the best students. There are many ways to reduce stress. Find the one that works best for you.

3 **Execute** - Once you have a good plan in place, be sure to stick to it.

One Week Study Schedule		
Day 1	Knowledge of Capital Markets	
Day 2	Understanding Products and Their Risks	
Day 3	Trading, Customers Accounts, Prohibited...	
Day 4	Overview of Regulatory Framework	
Day 5	Practice Tests #1 & #2	
Day 6	Practice Tests #3, #4, & #5	
Day 7	Take Your Exam!	

Two Week Study Schedule			
Day 1	Knowledge of Capital Markets	Day 8	Overview of Regulatory Framework
Day 2	Offerings	Day 9	Practice Test #1
Day 3	Understanding Products and Their Risks	Day 10	Practice Test #2
Day 4	Options	Day 11	Practice Test #3
Day 5	Investment Risks	Day 12	Practice Test #4
Day 6	Trading, Customers Accounts, Prohibited...	Day 13	Practice Test #5
Day 7	Customer Accounts and Compliance...	Day 14	Take Your Exam!

10

This material is provided for exam preparation purposes only and does not indicate an endorsement of any specific scientific, political, or religious point of view. © TPB Publishing. You have been licensed one copy of this document for personal use only. Any other reproduction or redistribution is strictly prohibited. All rights reserved.

One Month Study Schedule					
Day 1	Knowledge of Capital Markets	Day 11	Glossary	Day 21	Answer Explanations #1
Day 2	Market Structure	Day 12	Trading, Customers Accounts, Prohibited...	Day 22	Practice Test #2
Day 3	Offerings	Day 13	Trade Settlement	Day 23	Answer Explanations #2
Day 4	Glossary	Day 14	Customer Accounts and Compliance...	Day 24	Practice Test #3
Day 5	Understanding Products and Their...	Day 15	Books/Records and Privacy Requirements	Day 25	Answer Explanations #3
Day 6	Municipal Securities	Day 16	Prohibited Activities	Day 26	Practice Test #4
Day 7	Options	Day 17	Glossary	Day 27	Answer Explanations #4
Day 8	Packaged Products	Day 18	Overview of Regulatory Framework	Day 28	Practice Test #5
Day 9	Direct Participation Programs	Day 19	Reportable Events	Day 29	Answer Explanations #5
Day 10	Investment Risks	Day 20	Practice Test #1	Day 30	Take Your Exam!

Build your own prep plan by visiting:

testprepbooks.com/prep

11

This material is provided for exam preparation purposes only and does not indicate an endorsement of any specific scientific, political, or religious point of view. © TPB Publishing. You have been licensed one copy of this document for personal use only. Any other reproduction or redistribution is strictly prohibited. All rights reserved.

Quick Reference Sheet

Options

$$Option\ Premium = Time\ Value + Intrinsic\ Value$$

$$Put\ Value = Exercise\ Price - Stock\ Price$$

$$Call\ Value = Stock\ Price - Exercise\ Price$$

Charges

$$Load\ Charge = Initial\ Investment \times Commission\ Fee$$

$$Sales\ Charge = \frac{Public\ Offering\ Price - Net\ Asset\ Value}{Public\ Offering\ Price}$$

Valuations

$$Conversion\ Ratio = \frac{Bond\ par\ value}{Conversion\ price}$$

$$Current\ Yield = \frac{(Coupon\ Rate\ \% \times Par\ Value\ of\ Bond)}{Market\ Value}$$

$$Net\ Asset\ Value = \frac{Property\ Value}{Outstanding\ Shares}$$

Term	Description
Coupon Rate	Is the annual payment from a fixed security
Face Value	Often used interchangeable with par value. Both refer to the value of the bond at issuance.
Basis Point	Equal to 0.01% or 0.0001
Public Offering Price	Is the price new shares of stock are offered on the open market
Conversion	When securities are exchanged for other kinds securities
Yield	Is the measure of the return on a security
Outstanding Shares	Is the number of shares a company has available for sale on the open market
Exercise Price	Is the same as the strike price, which is the price a share of stock can be bought
Intrinsic Value	Is the current value of a security based on cash flows
Call Option	Increases in value when the price of the security to which it is tied increases in value
Put Option	Increases in value when the underlying asset declines in value

Valuations

$$Yield\ to\ Maturity\ (YTM) = \frac{\left(\frac{(Coupon\ Rate \times Face\ Value \times Years\ to\ Maturity)+(Face\ Value - Purchase\ Price)}{Years\ to\ Maturity}\right)}{\left(\frac{(Face\ Value\ at\ Maturity + Purchase\ Price)}{2}\right)}$$

$$Yield\ to\ Call\ (YTC) = \frac{\left(\frac{(Coupon\ Rate \times Face\ Value \times Years\ to\ Call)+(Call\ Value - Purchase\ Price)}{Years\ to\ Call}\right)}{\left(\frac{(Call\ Value\ to\ be\ Received + Purchase\ Price)}{2}\right)}$$

This material is provided for exam preparation purposes only and does not indicate an endorsement of any specific scientific, political, or religious point of view. © TPB Publishing. You have been licensed one copy of this document for personal use only. Any other reproduction or redistribution is strictly prohibited. All rights reserved.

Knowledge of Capital Markets

Regulatory Entities, Agencies, and Market Participants

The Securities and Exchange Commission (SEC)

Purpose and Mission

The Securities and Exchange Commission (SEC) was formed in 1934 by Franklin D. Roosevelt after the stock market crash. It was meant to restore public confidence in U.S. markets and regulate the securities industry. It's an agency of the U.S. Federal Government and is today responsible for "protecting investors; maintaining fair, orderly, and efficient markets; and facilitating capital formation." All broker-dealers must register with the SEC to conduct transactions and are subject to many rules and regulations. The SEC has the authority to file civil and criminal lawsuits against anyone who violates SEC rules.

Jurisdiction and Authority

The SEC was established by Congress in the **Securities Exchange Act of 1934** (commonly known as simply the Exchange Act), not in the **Securities Act of 1933** (commonly known as simply the Securities Act). The SEC is primarily charged with maintaining the integrity of capital markets and capital formation processes so that investor capital can be deployed confidently in support of growing the economy.

The Exchange Act granted the SEC jurisdiction and authority to propose, draft, and enact laws in furtherance of its purpose. The SEC may also draft and enforce regulations and rules to more effectively carry out enacted laws. The SEC consists of several different divisions, all of which are responsible for focusing on different aspects of the securities law regime.

The most prominent divisions are the Division of Corporate Finance (focusing on fair and adequate disclosure of information related to securities), the Division of Trading & Markets (focusing on fair and efficient capital market operations), the Division of Investment Management (focusing on the protection of investors), the Division of Enforcement (focusing on the investigation, recommendation, and prosecution of securities related matters), and the Office of Compliance Inspections and Examinations (OCIE), focusing on the examination of regulated entities to ensure compliance with federal securities regulations.

Self-Regulatory Organizations (SROs)

Purpose and Mission

Self-regulatory organizations (commonly referred to as SROs) are entities created to regulate industry segments within an organization itself and without reliance on an actual governmental authority such as federal and state governments. SROs are sometimes preferred in industries by industry participants because SROs can create regulations without having to endure the lengthy legislative process required by the United States Constitution.

The purpose of a typical SRO is to self-govern more efficiently in a narrow field. The ability to self-govern creates the opportunity for more specialized rules and regulation, as the rules and regulations are often drafted and enforced by individuals with expertise in their field. In the securities industry, the most

This material is provided for exam preparation purposes only and does not indicate an endorsement of any specific scientific, political, or religious point of view. © TPB Publishing. You have been licensed one copy of this document for personal use only. Any other reproduction or redistribution is strictly prohibited. All rights reserved.

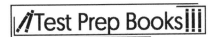
prominent SROs are the Financial Industry Regulatory Authority (commonly known as FINRA) and many of the exchanges that facilitate the trading of securities across the globe.

Jurisdiction and Authority

Cboe Global Markets (Cboe) is a self-regulatory organization (SRO) which owns the largest options exchange in the United States, the Cboe Options Exchange. It was originally established by The Chicago Board of Trade in 1973 as the Chicago Board Options Exchange (CBOE) until rebranding in 2017 as Cboe Options Exchange and offers options on the S&P 500 Index, S&P 100 Index, Dow Jones Industrial Average, NASDAQ-100 Index, and several others. Cboe creates the rules for all options exchanges and has the authority to enforce them. Cboe options contracts are all cleared by the Options Clearing Corporation (OCC). Cboe also calculates the Cboe Volatility Index (VIX) and shares its findings with the appropriate parties.

The Financial Industry Regulatory Authority (FINRA) is an SRO accountable to the SEC. It develops and implements rules and regulations specifically for brokerage firms and their employees and associates involved with securities trading and investments. FINRA also has the authority to settle disputes between customers from the general public and banking firms. All firms trading securities must be registered with FINRA.

Another SRO overseen by the SEC is the Municipal Securities Rulemaking Board (MSRB). The MSRB establishes rules that banks and securities firms must abide by when they engage in buying, selling, underwriting, or recommending municipal securities. Its goal is to promote fair trading and to prevent fraudulent or manipulative practices. The MSRB sets the standards of conduct for all broker-dealers, as well as the standards for banks, financial institutions, and municipal advisors. However, it is not authorized to enforce violations of its rules.

Other Regulators and Agencies

Department of the Treasury/IRS

The Department of the Treasury is the financial arm of the United States federal government. The Treasury is part of the executive branch of the federal government and is headed by the Secretary of the Treasury, who is considered one of the most important governmental figures. The Treasury works closely with the Federal Reserve and the Federal Reserve Chairman to coordinate policies to foster economic growth. This relationship was critically important during the 2008 financial crisis, when the Treasury and Federal Reserve worked together to bring the country out of crisis.

In its simplest function, the Treasury collects taxes from the citizenry and initiates borrowing on behalf of the federal government through the auction of Treasury securities including treasury bills, treasury notes, and treasury bonds. The collection of taxes and proceeds from the auctions provides the revenue used by the federal government to operate. The Treasury does not enact tax laws, which are the province of the legislature. However, the Treasury does adopt rules and regulations in furtherance of the tax laws to ensure tax laws are applied effectively.

The Treasury utilizes the Internal Revenue Service (IRS) to actually collect the taxes.

State Regulators

The North American Securities Administrators Association (NASAA) is an association devoted to investor protection and was created fifteen years before the SEC was created by Congress. NASAA primarily creates "model" securities laws that broadly reach many potential securities regulation issues. NASAA

This material is provided for exam preparation purposes only and does not indicate an endorsement of any specific scientific, political, or religious point of view. © TPB Publishing. You have been licensed one copy of this document for personal use only. Any other reproduction or redistribution is strictly prohibited. All rights reserved.

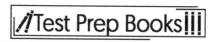

drafts these model acts that many states use as the foundation for the laws actually enacted by the state.

As model laws, the NASAA acts do not have legal authority by themselves. It is up to the states to use the models to draft actual laws governing securities in their own states. State laws of this kind are commonly referred to as "**blue-sky laws.**" Therefore, it is critically important that industry professionals consult the enacted blue-sky laws when making a decision in light of the state's unique securities regulatory regime.

For industry professionals seeking licensing, NASAA provides the basis for FINRA licenses 63, 65, and 66.

The Federal Reserve
The Federal Reserve Board (FRB) plays a pivotal role in determining the state and direction of the economy in the United States. The FRB is a network of regional banks operating under the authority of the federal government. It's responsible for making impactful decisions that affect the stock market and the economy, including setting interest rates and increasing the money supply.

Securities Investor Protection Corporation (SIPC)
The **Securities Investor Protection Corporation (SIPC)** and the Federal Deposit Insurance Corporation (FDIC) protect the interests of investors and bank customers. The SIPC protects clients of brokers and dealers in case of financial failure of the broker. If SIPC funds are not adequate, financial assistance can be provided by the U.S. Treasury. The SIPC is not a government entity and is fully funded by its member broker dealers. In the event of failure of a broker-dealer, the SIPC organizes cash and the securities to be distributed to the clients of the failed member firm.

If cash or securities are unavailable, the SIPC covers up to $500,000 of the equity balance of the customer, which includes up to $250,000 in cash. It also provides guidance when a firm requires liquidation. Some types of individual securities still have their guarantees. Treasuries are still backed by the U.S. Treasury, as are conforming mortgage-backed securities issued by Ginnie Mae, Fannie Mae, and Freddie Mac. Commodity and futures contracts are typically not guaranteed by any organization.

The Federal Deposit Insurance Corporation (FDIC)
The FDIC serves a similar capacity as the SIPC but for traditional bank deposits. The FDIC currently insures a bank account up to $250,000. Member banks pay dues to fund the FDIC. The FDIC also has a $100 Billion line of credit with the U.S. Treasury. The FDIC audits and monitors member banks to ensure that they are adequately capitalized, that they are not taking excessive risk, that they have sufficient systems in place to prevent fraud, and that they follow bank regulations and guidelines.

Market Participants and Their Roles

Investors
Capital markets comprise a variety of different market participants. One of those market participants is the investor. However, the term "investor" can have more specific meaning. In fact, there are many different types of investors. **Institutional investors** can most effectively be described as investors with the backing of immense amounts of capital. The immense amounts of capital are supplied by the constituents or members with their form, depending on the type of institution involved. Some common examples include large financial institutions such as commercial banks, investment banks, insurance companies, pension funds, and hedge funds. Institutional investors are the core drivers of the price of securities in capital markets.

This material is provided for exam preparation purposes only and does not indicate an endorsement of any specific scientific, political, or religious point of view. © TPB Publishing. You have been licensed one copy of this document for personal use only. Any other reproduction or redistribution is strictly prohibited. All rights reserved.

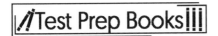

Retail investors can most effectively be described as individuals investing for their future through common vehicles such as mutual funds, exchange-traded funds, and individual stocks and bonds in standard brokerage accounts or retirement accounts such as individual retirement accounts (IRAs) and 401(k)'s. Individually, retail investors have almost no effect on the price of securities in capital markets. Collectively, in times of panic or prosperity, retail investors following a herd mentality may help sustain a movement in price initiated by larger financial institutions.

Accredited investors are a different type of investor as defined in securities-related acts. Accredited investors can most effectively be described as investors with sufficient net worth, annual income, and/or expertise and experience investing such that the accredited investor does not require the same level of protection afforded to retail investors by securities-related laws. Accredited investors are also given the opportunity to purchase and sell unregistered securities. The purchase and sale of these securities is commonly referred to as private equity and are governed by Regulation D of the Securities Act of 1933.

Broker-Dealers

Broker-dealers are financial institutions that affect securities transactions on behalf of individuals and entities or affect transactions for their own accounts. When affecting securities transactions on behalf of others, a broker-dealer is acting in an agent capacity, i.e., broker. When affecting securities transactions for their own accounts, a broker-dealer is acting in a principal capacity, i.e., dealer.

The term "broker-dealer" is often applied incorrectly. For example, the individual who affects the transactions is usually referred to as a broker, but their technical name is a registered representative. Broker-dealers are also often confused with investment advisers. Investment advisers are in the business of providing investment advice for compensation. Investment advisers will often initiate transactions, but when they affect the transaction, they are acting as a registered representative.

Introducing brokers are the futures market equivalent of a registered representative in the equities markets. **Clearing brokers** work for firms that ensure proper settlement of transactions so that investors are ensured that their transaction is completed properly. **Prime brokers** provide many different services to select clients who need more specialized, higher level services. Prime brokers are often used by hedge funds that require sophisticated services to ensure that their funds operate properly and are compliant with applicable securities laws.

Investment Advisers

According to the Securities and Exchange Commission (SEC), individuals who meet the criteria of investment advisers must register with the SEC. Larger advisers with over $25 million in assets under management register with the SEC, and smaller advisers register with state securities authorities.

An **investment adviser** is defined as an individual or employee who provides investment advice, recommends the purchase or sale of securities, issues research reports, or otherwise analyzes securities and is paid for doing so or that is part of their occupation or business.

This material is provided for exam preparation purposes only and does not indicate an endorsement of any specific scientific, political, or religious point of view. © TPB Publishing. You have been licensed one copy of this document for personal use only. Any other reproduction or redistribution is strictly prohibited. All rights reserved.

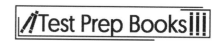

Certain firms and persons are exempt from registering. These include, but are not limited, to the following:

- Certain domestic banks

- Advisers whose business relates solely to obligations of the United States government, such as treasury bonds

- Lawyers and accountants whose advice is related to their profession

- Broker dealer firms who do not receive any special compensation for their investment advice

Municipal Advisors

Municipal advisors are entities that specialize in the intricacies of financing operations of local governments, i.e., municipalities through bond offerings. Raising capital in municipal markets can vary greatly because each municipality has its own laws and processes for creating revenue to finance their local government operations. This level of detail requires specialized knowledge for effective outcomes.

Municipal advisors work with local government officials to help raise funds for critical local functions such as schools, infrastructure, hospitals, parks and recreation, and any other project a municipality decides to complete for the benefit of local citizens.

Municipal advisors are required to register with the Securities and Exchange Commission and individuals acting on behalf of a municipal advisor are required to pass the Municipal Securities Rulemaking Board's (MSRB) MSRB's Municipal Advisor Representative Qualification Examination (Series 50).

Issuers and Underwriters

To raise capital to grow their business, companies often turn to capital markets for funding. In particular, they become issuers of securities in the primary market. As issuers, companies will hire an investment bank for guidance on the appropriate type, amount, and timing of a securities offering. All three factors can have a tremendous impact on the success of an offering for an issuer. So, choosing the best investment bank for a company's offering is critical.

The investment bank will serve as an underwriter for the offering. The exact nature of what the underwriter will do for the issuer depends on what kind of offering the issuer is seeking to place. The two most common types of underwriting arrangements are best-efforts underwriting and firm commitment underwriting.

In best-efforts underwriting, the investment bank is only required to place as much of the issuance as is possible given market conditions. If the underwriter is unable to sell all of the shares for the issuer, then the underwriter is not legally responsible for purchasing any remaining shares itself. This is not ideal for the issuer, but it does protect the investment bank from having to make a purchase of shares that the bank does not desire to purchase.

In firm commitment underwriting, the investment bank is required to purchase the entire issuance of the offering if any shares remain after being offered to the public. The underwriter has a legal obligation to purchase any remaining shares itself. This is ideal for the issuer who is guaranteed that all of its shared will be sold, but it does potentially leave the investment bank holding shares that it would otherwise not desire.

This material is provided for exam preparation purposes only and does not indicate an endorsement of any specific scientific, political, or religious point of view. © TPB Publishing. You have been licensed one copy of this document for personal use only. Any other reproduction or redistribution is strictly prohibited. All rights reserved.

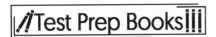

Traders and Market Makers

Most secondary markets have a designated market maker (also known as "specialists"). They maintain fair and orderly markets and make sure there is sufficient liquidity for specified firms that are traded on an exchange. This helps to reduce volatility in the stock price. The maker is a point of contact for the company and keeps them informed as to who has been trading the stock and what trading conditions have been like for the company's stock.

The maker is usually required to provide quotes for a specific percent of the time. Makers must have adequate capital to be approved to trade and provide quotes on an exchange. The primary difference with makers is that they have access to information only after a trade has been placed, so they have the same information as floor brokers, as opposed to having inside information. Makers can't trade for their own account when they have an open order for the same security at the same price on their book. The SEC prohibits broker dealers from using manipulative or deceptive devices to affect short sales (this is where an investor can profit from the decline in a stock's price) or influence swap agreements for their own profit.

Traders, commonly known as **proprietary traders**, are market participants that engage in capital markets for a variety of reasons for their own account. Some traders engage the market for the purposes of hedging. **Hedging** is a process where traders take positions to reduce the risk of other positions. Some traders engage the market for the purposes of speculation. Speculators provide a critical risk allocation component to market mechanics by taking positions based on their perception of future market direction. As speculators can base their market transactions on many factors beyond basic fundamental analysis used by most investors, speculators' transactions can serve as liquidity pools for investor transactions that require a party to take the opposite side of a transaction.

Custodians and Trustees

Custodians and trustees operate in the financial services industry to ensure that securities transactions and securities accounts are processed correctly and to provide confidence to investors that their choice to engage in financial market activity is being handled properly by trained and dedicated professionals. While that is the basic function of custodians and trustees, there are important distinctions. In fact, there are many different types of custodians performing different functions and many different types of trustees performing different functions. The key for investors is to understand that there are many individuals and firms operating behind the scenes to support the securities market function.

In the most common sense, custodians simply hold on to securities for safekeeping. Custodians ensure that the securities that an investor owns are actually in possession of the investor's account. Many of the most popular names in the industry serve a custodial function, including names like Fidelity, Schwab, and the like.

While trustees can also serve a custodial function, they are generally defined by a legal relationship where the trustee—often a bank or other large financial institution—has a legal obligation to act in the best interests of the trustor, who can be an individual, family, or other entity such as a partnership, corporation, or estate. The trustee manages the trustor's property interests "in trust" for many reasons, including proper investment and minimizing tax consequences.

Transfer Agents

Endorsements are when ownership is transferred to another party or when the owner of an asset signs the negotiable contract or instrument. A **transfer agent** is typically a commercial bank that is a client of

This material is provided for exam preparation purposes only and does not indicate an endorsement of any specific scientific, political, or religious point of view. © TPB Publishing. You have been licensed one copy of this document for personal use only. Any other reproduction or redistribution is strictly prohibited. All rights reserved.

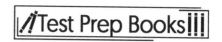
the corporation (or in some cases is the corporation itself) and that maintains records of all equity and bond holders. The transfer agent cancels and issues new certificates and resolves issues with certificates. A registrar coordinates with the transfer agent to keep track of stock and bond ownership. They keep record of the shareholders eligible to receive additional shares during events such as a stock split or stock dividend. The registrar also ensures that only the authorized amount of stock is in circulation at any time. For debts, the registrar ensures that the issuance is a corporation's genuine obligation.

Transfer procedures are the steps governed by the Securities and Exchange Commission (SEC) that determine how stock shares are transferred from one owner to another.

Depositories and Clearing Corporations

The Depository Trust and Clearing Corporation (DTCC) serves as a custodian and clearing entity for a significant amount of all securities transactions across the globe. As a custodian, the DTCC maintains an electronic database identifying the proper owner of securities processed through the DTCC. The DTCC's functions are critical to the proper functioning of the financial markets.

The DTCC also serves as a clearing agent for securities transactions. In the capacity of a clearing agent, the DTCC ensures that all required settlement procedures for securities transactions are honored. Ensuring the securities transactions are settled properly is critical to maintain investor confidence in the orderly function of their investments. If investors could not reasonably rely on the DTCC clearing process, they might be less likely to engage in the financial markets, which would cause serious problems in capital raising in the primary market and the purchase, sale, or exchange of securities in the secondary market.

The Options Clearing Corporation (OCC), which will be discussed again later on, guarantees that contracts on each side of an options contract are fulfilled, which primarily means that the seller or writer of a contract received a premium, and that the buyer of the contract received the underlying security from the seller of the option exercised. The OCC holds about $120 billion in collateral each day and is regulated by both the Securities and Exchange Commission and the Commodity Futures Trading Commission. The OCC has its own board of directors and generates revenue on the fees it receives from settling options transactions.

The OCC is rated by all three major bond rating agencies. The OCC settled options traded on exchanges only until 2011, when it began to settle over-the-counter options trades. The OCC has made changes to its settlement process in recent years. In 2013, expirations moved from Saturdays to Fridays. The OCC has both weekly and monthly expirations that can expire on a consistent and repeated process and is now aligned with global option market settlement schedules.

Market Structure

Types of Markets

The Primary Market

Securities are created on the primary market. Debt and equity are sold, issued, and traded in primary markets (also known as capital markets). Corporations and governments use capital markets to borrow money, raise capital, and finance everything from operations, to forming new companies, to mortgages and loans. The U.S. capital markets are mostly regulated by the Securities and Exchange Commission

This material is provided for exam preparation purposes only and does not indicate an endorsement of any specific scientific, political, or religious point of view. © TPB Publishing. You have been licensed one copy of this document for personal use only. Any other reproduction or redistribution is strictly prohibited. All rights reserved.

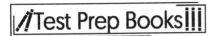

(SEC), but other entities like the Consumer Finance Protection Bureau, the Federal Reserve, and the U.S. Treasury have some level of oversight. Modern capital markets trade on electronic platforms. Capital markets are usually associated with long-term sources of capital as opposed to money markets, where short-term and overnight financing occurs. Capital markets are also different from traditional bank lending (though sometimes traditional banks sell loans to be repackaged and sold in capital markets). Traditional banks are more heavily regulated and require greater capitalization than corporations in the capital markets.

As of 2013, there were approximately $283 trillion in stocks, bonds, and bank assets globally. This is compared to $75 trillion in world Gross Domestic Product (GDP).

The Secondary Market
The secondary market is where previously issued stocks, bonds, and other financial instruments are available to buy and sell. Electronic exchanges are exchanges that bring buyers and sellers together through an electronic trading platform. The NASDAQ is an example of an electronic exchange. The benefits of these exchanges include lower transaction costs, better liquidity, faster trade execution, increased competition, improved transparency, and smaller bid-ask spreads. Some of these exchanges use algorithms to improve trade execution. An auction market establishes a price through **competitive bidding** through brokers (who represent their respective clients and investors). Most auction markets have the following rules:

- The first bid has priority.
- The high bid and low offer "have the floor."
- A new auction begins when all bids at a certain price are exhausted.
- There are no secret transactions.
- Bids and offers must be audible.

Equity markets have specialists and market makers who assure liquidity and market stability for specific equities. To trade on an exchange auction market, companies must meet certain listing requirements. To trade on the New York Stock Exchange, a company must have $1.1 million worth of public shares with a market value of at least $40 million. Companies must have at least 400 shareholders with each share valued greater than or equal to $4.00. They must also have a pre-tax annual income of $100 million aggregate for the last three fiscal years. Most exchanges have trading curbs or circuit breakers. This means all trading is stopped when markets have a significant decline. The New York Stock Exchange sets these breakers on a quarterly basis. Depending on the size of the decline, trading may stop temporarily and resume that same day or stop for the day entirely.

Third Market
In addition to the primary market (new issuances) and the secondary market (market transactions), the third market exists to provide another avenue of facilitating trade in financial markets. Usually, exchange-listed securities are just that—securities that are listed and traded on an exchange. However, in the third market, those exchange-listed securities are actually traded in the over-the-counter (OTC) markets, which is usually where unlisted securities trade.

These stocks are traded through a telephone and computer network rather than on an organized exchange. Smaller companies typically trade OTC because they do not meet the criteria to be listed on an exchange. OTC markets are regulated by the Financial Industry Regulatory Authority (FINRA). An example of an OTC market is what is known as the "pink sheets." These markets usually have daily bid

This material is provided for exam preparation purposes only and does not indicate an endorsement of any specific scientific, political, or religious point of view. © TPB Publishing. You have been licensed one copy of this document for personal use only. Any other reproduction or redistribution is strictly prohibited. All rights reserved.

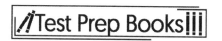
quotes published. Bulletin board stocks are another example of an OTC market. Thinly traded micro-cap and penny stocks trade on this exchange.

Exchange-listed securities are often listed on exchanges for credibility for investors because the exchanges have a rigorous vetting process before a security can be listed and traded on the exchange. On the other hand, institutional investors are sophisticated enough to make a securities purchase or selling decision without relying on the exchange vetting process. Sometimes institutions prefer to trade off the exchange. Institutions can do so in the OTC market. A common reason why institutions might prefer to trade off the exchange is to not adversely affect the price of the security the institution desires to purchase or sell.

For example, if an institution wants to buy a large block of a particular security, the massive size of that order might inadvertently increase the price of the security that the institution desires to buy. An institution can minimize the chance of paying more by trading in the third market with another institution without the current market price being inflated just when the institution desires to buy.

Fourth Market
In addition to the primary market (new issuances), the secondary market (market transactions), and the third market (over-the-counter), institutions may initiate transactions in the fourth market. The fourth market is simply an electronic network utilized specifically and only by institutions. The primary, secondary, and third markets are known as "lit markets," to distinguish them from the fourth market, which is known as a "dark" market or "dark pools" because the transactions are not lit up on an exchange and are instead performed outside of the view of investors.

A common reason why institutions might prefer to trade off the exchange is to not adversely affect the price of the security the institution desires to purchase or sell. For example, if an institution wants to buy a large block of a particular security, the massive size of that order might inadvertently increase the price of the security that the institution desires to buy. An institution can minimize the chance of paying more by trading in the fourth market with another institution without the current market price being inflated just when the institution desires to buy.

Economic Factors

Federal Reserve Board Impact

Monetary vs. Fiscal Policy
In the United States, the economy is deeply affected by government policies. The two most powerful policies affecting economic growth are monetary policy and fiscal policy. These policies are used in conjunction with each other to promote economic growth down a sustainable path.

Monetary policy is primarily concerned with how the money supply can be utilized to maximize economic growth. Monetary policy is administered by the Federal Reserve, its Chairman, Board of Governors, Regional Federal Reserve Bank Presidents, and the Federal Open Market Committee. Using open-market operations, the Federal Reserve can adjust the money supply. Monetarist economists believe that the money supply by itself is the most important factor in determining economic growth. Monetarists believe that an increased money supply will lead to increased economic growth.

On the other hand, **fiscal policy** is primarily concerned with government taxation and expenditures. Typically, increased taxation will lead to less economic growth because there will be less capital to invest

This material is provided for exam preparation purposes only and does not indicate an endorsement of any specific scientific, political, or religious point of view. © TPB Publishing. You have been licensed one copy of this document for personal use only. Any other reproduction or redistribution is strictly prohibited. All rights reserved.

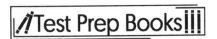

in economic growth. Decreased taxation will lead to more economic growth because there will be more capital to invest in economic growth.

Similarly, decreased government expenditures will lead to less economic growth because the government will be investing less capital for economic growth. Increased government expenditures will lead to more economic growth because the government will be investing more capital for economic growth. Keynesian economists believe that the level of government expenditures will determine the level of economic growth.

Open Market Activities

Open market activities (commonly referred to as **open market operations**) are initiated and executed by the Federal Reserve to affect the money supply and economic growth. The Federal Reserve buys and sells United States Treasury securities from and to primary dealers. The operations are performed by the Federal Reserve Bank of New York.

When the Federal Reserve wants to increase the money supply, it will buy United States Treasury securities on the open market. The purchase of these securities effectively transfers money from the balance sheet of the Federal Reserve to the market economy in exchange for holding the securities on the balance sheet of the Federal Reserve. In other words, there is now more money in the economy and less money held at the Federal Reserve. The increase in the money supply created by this open market operation makes more money available to market participants to use for economic growth such as investing in capital expenditures to grow businesses.

The sale of these securities effectively transfers the securities from the balance sheet of the Federal Reserve to the market economy in exchange for money that will be held on the balance sheet of the Federal Reserve. In other words, there is now more money held at the Federal Reserve, and less money is in the economy. The decrease in the money supply created by this open market operation makes less money available to market participants to use for economic growth activities.

Different Rates

There are four main interest rates to be aware of:

- Federal Funds Rate: The rate that the largest banks charge each other for overnight loans of $1 million or more. This is the most volatile interest rate, and short-term interest rates are linked to the federal funds rate.

- Prime Rate: The rate that banks charge low-risk customers (namely corporations) with excellent credit. This rate fluctuates based on the money supply set by the Federal Reserve Board.

- Discount Rate: The interest rate that the FRB charges to Federal Reserve Banks when the bank is issuing short-term loans.

- Broker Loan Rate: The rate that banks charge brokers and dealers when lending money for a customer's margin accounts. It's also known as the call loan rate or the money rate.

An important thing to remember about the discount rate is that any changes can have significant effects on the economy. When the FRB lowers the discount rate, it costs banks less to borrow money from the Federal Reserve and other banks, so banks can charge a lower interest rate to customers. This prompts many individuals and companies to start borrowing more money. When the FRB raises the discount rate,

This material is provided for exam preparation purposes only and does not indicate an endorsement of any specific scientific, political, or religious point of view. © TPB Publishing. You have been licensed one copy of this document for personal use only. Any other reproduction or redistribution is strictly prohibited. All rights reserved.

it costs banks more to borrow money from the Federal Reserve and other banks, so they charge customers a higher interest rate. This can discourage people and companies from borrowing money.

Reserve Requirements are a set of ratios established by the Federal Reserve System that specify how much of a customer's deposit a commercial bank must keep in its reserves versus lending out. This gives the Federal Reserve greater control over the money supply since it can change interest rates at any time.

Business Economic Factors

Purpose of Financial Statements

The four primary statements companies provide on an annual and quarterly basis are: an income statement, a balance sheet, a cash flow statement, and a statement of retained earnings. Companies typically provide schedules on debt maturities, stock issuance, lease schedules, earnings estimates, cash reserves, and other schedules to help investors and analysts evaluate the financial status of the company. The **income statement** shows the revenues and expenses of the company over a period of time and calculates a net profit or net income number (net of expenses, interest, taxes, etc.). Usually, this statement is reported using the accrual method, which means a line item like revenue represents money that's been billed but hasn't been received. The income statement provides significant information for investors, but it also includes additional footnotes and disclosures about accounting methods, depreciation, intercompany transactions, purchases and sales of securities, and other information that investors must read when taking into account the reported information.

The **cash flow statement** is reported with the income statement and represents cash flows from investing, operating, and financing activities. The statement represents operating results and changes in the balance sheet. Healthy companies typically generate their cash flow from operating activities, which represent the cash flow from day-to-day business activities and the company's core business. The cash flow and the amount of cash on the company's balance sheet are good indicators of how solvent the company is. Adjustments to the income statement are used along with the cash flow statement to help investors value a company's stock price.

Business Cycle

Understanding business cycle stages can help investors and brokers make timely decisions. There are four key phases of the business cycle:

- Phase 1 – Expansion: Business conditions are good and economic indicators remain strong. During this phase, stock prices, house prices, and wages are high, and job opportunities are plentiful.

- Phase 2 – Peak: The high point of the expansion phase when economic indicators tend to be on the downswing. During this stage, there's less investing and spending activity.

- Phase 3 – Contraction: Commonly identified as a recession or, in extreme cases, a depression.

- Phase 4 – Trough: Downtrends begin to level off and then stop, which sets the stage for a new cycle of expansion.

This material is provided for exam preparation purposes only and does not indicate an endorsement of any specific scientific, political, or religious point of view. © TPB Publishing. You have been licensed one copy of this document for personal use only. Any other reproduction or redistribution is strictly prohibited. All rights reserved.

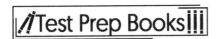

Indicators

Economists use a number of tools to analyze the market and determine what business cycle or phase the market is in. The leading indicators of the market based on certain signals (e.g., a high number of homes under construction or recent stock market activity) help to predict where the economy is headed.

Coincident indicators reflect the state of the economy at any given time and are tied directly to economic shifts. Lagging indicators are signals that the economy is either improving or declining. These might include higher or lower than normal profit reports of Fortune 500 companies, significant increases or reductions in wages, or a change in debt-to-income ratios among consumers.

Effects on Bond and Equity Markets

Economists also use yield curves to forecast economic changes. These represent interest rates for bonds of the same credit rating with different maturities. One of the most commonly used yield curves compares U.S. Treasury debt for maturities of three months to thirty years. This particular yield curve can be used as a basis to compare other bond yields.

Inflation decreases the purchasing power of currency by lowering the value of the future cash flows of a bond. To lower this demand, investors typically require a higher bond yield or more attractive interest rates to justify the purchase.

Reviewing yield curves can provide an indication of current market conditions because it's based on how bond markets are performing. Yield curves illustrate the relationship between bond interest rates and maturity dates. In a healthy economy, the yield curve appears to be "normal," which means interest rates increase along with the bond's maturity, so the curve has an upward slope.

An inverted yield curve typically signifies a future recession since bonds with longer maturity dates have a lower yield rate. Flat yield curves are indicative of minimal to no difference between short-term and long-term yields.

When reviewing equities markets, it's important to recognize shares of stock that are extremely sensitive to fluctuations and changes in interest rates. According to the capital asset pricing model, these stocks have large "beta factors." Understanding the different types of industries that make up the market can help predict which businesses will be the most profitable and identify worthwhile stock investments.

Defensive industries are economy sectors that sell products that are in high demand regardless of the state of the economy. Two of the biggest defensive industries in today's economy are food and tobacco products. Since the demand for these products is predictable, investing in companies in these industries is usually safer. However, expecting large earnings or profits from these investments is unrealistic since people usually don't buy more than their basic needs.

On the opposite side of the spectrum from defensive industries, cyclical industries are comprised of companies that tend to perform extremely well during a bull market but poorly during a bear market. Cyclical industry companies sell luxury goods, automobiles, or raw materials that produce high-end goods, so their stock values are dependent on whether customers are in the market to buy more expensive items.

This material is provided for exam preparation purposes only and does not indicate an endorsement of any specific scientific, political, or religious point of view. © TPB Publishing. You have been licensed one copy of this document for personal use only. Any other reproduction or redistribution is strictly prohibited. All rights reserved.

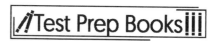

Economic Theories

To gain a better understanding of current market conditions, many economists also turn to history and these economic theories:

Keynesian Economic Theory: This theory was named after economist John Maynard Keynes who taught continued demand is what supports the economy, since increased or steady demand for certain products or services naturally leads to more businesses being created. These conditions result in more jobs, rising wages, an increase in loans, etc. According to this theory, the federal government must sustain the economy by spending tax money on projects that stimulate certain sectors or the economy as a whole.

Monetarist Economic Theory: This theory was developed by economist Milton Friedman who taught that inflation and deflation are the direct result of the available money supply. If there's not enough money in circulation, prices fall. When there's too much money in circulation, prices rise. According to this theory, the federal government must regulate the money supply and stay out of the market. The only way to keep demand for goods and services steady without risking inflation is to gradually increase the money supply.

International Economic Factors

U.S. Balance of Payments

The balance of payments (BOP) is more comprehensive than the balance of trade (BOT) for a country because it tracks all the inflows and outflows of the country over a given time period. This includes intangible exchanges, the dollar amount of all imports and exports, and records of all financial transactions between different countries. A positive BOP indicates a net inflow of money while a negative BOP indicates a net outflow.

Gross Domestic Product (GDP) and Gross National Product (GNP)

Economists use several measures to quantify the total economic output of a nation. **Gross Domestic Product (GDP)** can be a complex calculation including consumer consumption, investment, governmental expenditures, and net exports and imports. However, the simplest definition of GDP is the total economic output that occurs within a nation's borders. **Gross National Product (GNP)** can be equally complex but is basically the same as GDP plus or minus economic output that occurs outside of a nation's border, income earned from foreign investments, and income earned by foreign residents inside the United States.

A corporation's activity from business within the United States would be included in GDP, but activity that the corporation conducts outside of the United States would not be included. For example, the value of a car manufacturer's output of cars created in a United States factory would be included in GDP, but the value of cars manufactured in Japan would not be included in GDP. GNP would include the value of cars manufactured in the United States as well as the cars manufactured elsewhere.

Exchange Rates

Exchange rates affect the securities market in one of two ways: directly by impacting the value of securities for foreign companies and indirectly when affecting the cost for domestic businesses to conduct business overseas. Exchange rates are affected by market interest rates in different countries, which, in turn, can attract or deter lenders.

This material is provided for exam preparation purposes only and does not indicate an endorsement of any specific scientific, political, or religious point of view. © TPB Publishing. You have been licensed one copy of this document for personal use only. Any other reproduction or redistribution is strictly prohibited. All rights reserved.

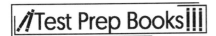

The **spot exchange rate** is the price to trade one currency directly for another at any given time, for delivery on the soonest viable value date. While the spot rate is often set by the foreign exchange market, some countries use mechanisms like a currency peg to influence or even actively set exchange rates.

The interbank market is where banks exchange the currencies of various countries. Their trading can be for customers or for the bank's own accounts. About half of all foreign currency transactions occur on the interbank market. Most developed countries have floating exchange rates. Investors often invest in currencies they believe will appreciate. Investors also use the foreign exchange market to protect themselves from fluctuations in the values of two currencies and to protect the return of their debt or equity investments.

They can do this in the **spot market** (where the exchange occurs immediately) or in the **forward market**, where the investor can lock in the exchange rate (the forward market allows an investor to buy or sell a currency at a specified exchange rate and at a specified time). There are market makers in foreign exchange markets just as there are in equities.

Governments and regulators often have controls in place that restrict the amount of trading that can be done in their currency (some countries could unfairly influence trade by buying or selling large amounts of another country's currency to make their own goods appear cheaper and that country's more expensive). Smaller countries with less economic stability will typically have more controls in place. Central banks often use the buying and selling of foreign currency as a monetary policy tool. A currency revaluation is when a government steps in and sets a currency's value even though that is not what the market dictates (an increase). A devaluation is the opposite.

Eurobonds are bonds that pay principal and interest in Eurodollars (i.e., U.S. dollars held in banks outside of the U.S.). These are not registered with the SEC, so there are typically lower costs and regulatory issues for the issuer. This means they can typically be sold with a lower interest rate than a comparable bond in the United States.

Counter currency refers to the currency that acts as the reference or second currency within a currency pair. Looking at an ISO currency code, the counter currency follows the base currency, separated by a slash. The U.S. dollar, the euro, and other major currencies usually act as the base currency in a given currency pair. Other ways to refer to the counter currency include the quote currency or the secondary currency.

Offerings

Roles of Participants

An investment bank is a corporation that advises companies when they begin to operate in capital markets. The basic activities of an investment bank include:

- Raising equity capital for a corporation. Sometimes this is an Initial Public Offering (IPO).

- Raising capital through debt issuance.

This material is provided for exam preparation purposes only and does not indicate an endorsement of any specific scientific, political, or religious point of view. © TPB Publishing. You have been licensed one copy of this document for personal use only. Any other reproduction or redistribution is strictly prohibited. All rights reserved.

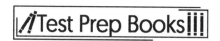
- Launching new financial products and instruments (derivatives, credit default swaps, new forms of securitization, etc.).

- Proprietary trading of the firm's own capital, including speculation, arbitrage, and other complex trading strategies.

Investment banks typically have a front office, middle office, and back office. The front office handles mergers and acquisitions, private equity, and research, which they sell as a product to investors to provide investment recommendations. The middle office handles compliance and capital flows. The back office confirms and settles trades.

Some critics believe investment banks have a conflict of interest, as they can use their investment opinions and research to acquire clients. They also have the means to manipulate markets. In recent years, some companies that are traditionally associated with investment banking have shifted their strategy to wealth management and broker-dealer activities. During the most recent financial crisis, investment banks shifted their structure to a more traditional commercial banking structure.

An underwriting syndicate is a group of investment banks that come together to underwrite an issuance of equity or debt. There is typically one investment bank that takes on the lead underwriter role and gets a larger portion of the underwriting spread (the difference between the amount the underwriter pays an issuing company and the amount the investment bank receives when those shares are offered). The purpose of syndicating is that it spreads the risk of not being able to sell an issue in its entirety across the syndicate banks. Typical underwriters include Goldman Sachs, Morgan Stanley, Citigroup, and Wells Fargo, among others.

When a municipality needs to raise capital for planned expenditures, it should hire a municipal advisor to assist in the offering of debt securities. Municipal advisors help the municipal entity to plan, sell, and close a debt offering by engaging in many activities to help ensure the municipality achieves its goals.

As a fiduciary, a municipal advisor assists in both the financial and legal aspects of a municipal offering. On the financial side, the municipal advisor will assist in generating cash flow projections, work with ratings agencies to obtain a favorable rating to increase the chances of better offering terms, and assist in the creation of a feasibility report, which analyzes the likelihood of the expenditures achieving the desired outcome.

On the legal side, the municipal advisor will work with law firms (if the advisor is not a law firm itself) to ensure that the language used in the offering documents accurately reflects the desired terms of the municipality. Some of the important terms of the offering to be negotiated are the interest rate, price of the debt securities, and the closing date of the offering. In addition, a municipal advisor will opine on whether or not the covenants of the offering are fair and reasonable to the municipality and the purchasers of the offering.

Types of Offerings

Public vs. Private Offering

In a public offering, all the SEC requirements must be fulfilled. The investment bankers and the investors agree on the offering price. Sales to 35 or more people are typically deemed to be public offerings. In a private placement, the securities are sold directly to the investor, typically a large institution like an insurance company. These types of deals are not required to be registered with the SEC. An advance

This material is provided for exam preparation purposes only and does not indicate an endorsement of any specific scientific, political, or religious point of view. © TPB Publishing. You have been licensed one copy of this document for personal use only. Any other reproduction or redistribution is strictly prohibited. All rights reserved.

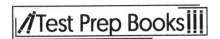

refunding occurs when new bonds are issued in place of callable bonds prior to the existing bonds' call date because the rate of interest is lower on the new bonds. The proceeds from the issue are invested in treasury bonds.

Initial Public Offering (IPO), Secondary Offering, and Follow-On Offering

An **initial public offering (IPO)** is an issuer's first attempt to raise capital from the general public to help grow their business. An IPO represents the general public's first opportunity to take an ownership interest in a growing company. IPOs often make the headlines as eager investors want the opportunity to share in the profits of company. IPOs are facilitated by an investment bank or a group of investment banks known as a syndicate.

Sometimes after an IPO, a second sale of the issuer's securities will be offered. This is referred to as a **secondary offering**. Secondary offerings can either be dilutive or non-dilutive. **Dilutive secondary offerings** reduce the value of the share price because additional new shares are now available in the market, but the company's value has not changed. In other words, there are now more owners of the same pie. Dilutive secondary offerings are also known as **follow-on offerings**.

Nondilutive secondary offerings do not reduce the value of the share price because no new shares are issued. The shares offered in a nondilutive secondary offering were previously registered and in existence at the same time as the IPO, but they were not available for sale to the public at the time of the IPO. In other words, because the number of shares does not change, and the company's value does not change, there is no decrease in the value of an individual share in a nondilutive secondary offering.

Methods of Distribution

An **underwriting commitment**—also called a **firm commitment**—is when the underwriter guarantees the purchase of all of the securities being offered in a sale (in case all of the shares can't be sold in an offering, though even when an offering is fully subscribed, investment banks will retain shares in their own portfolio). This type of agreement assures they will collect their underwriting fee right away. This puts the investment bank's own capital at risk if the entire offering can't be sold. Sometimes the investment bank only makes a "best efforts" commitment to sell all the securities. In this situation, they would try to sell all the shares but would not have to buy the unsold shares with their own capital.

Shelf Registrations and Distributions

Shelf registration allows a corporation to have shares registered and ready for issuance when market conditions become most favorable, which can help the company reduce the costs associated with multiple individual filings. Shelf registrations usually last for three years, during which the corporation can issue shares. Typically, companies must file a report on a quarterly basis. Shelf registration is available only to companies with established reputations with the SEC. This rule also allows for flexibility in issuing debt or equity, so the corporation can take advantage of the better form of financing (i.e., if interest rates are low, debt is preferable, if equity valuations are high, stock issuance would be preferable).

Shelf registrations allow the corporation to fulfill any regulation-related filings or procedures ahead of time and then market the shares quickly through broker-dealers. SEC forms S-3 and F-3 incorporate the filings after the shelf's effective date. A "takedown" is when an actual offering occurs and has been declared effective. In a continuous shelf offering, securities are offered within two days of their effective date. They will continue to be offered in the future as well. In a delayed offering, there is no present

This material is provided for exam preparation purposes only and does not indicate an endorsement of any specific scientific, political, or religious point of view. © TPB Publishing. You have been licensed one copy of this document for personal use only. Any other reproduction or redistribution is strictly prohibited. All rights reserved.

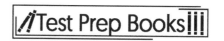

intention to offer shares, but those conditions can change. In a delayed primary offering of securities, the issuer will file a core or base prospectus. The official terms will be filed after the effective date.

Offering Documents and Delivery Requirements

An offering document must disclose all necessary information to potential investors. The document must contain all of the basic information about the company. This includes location, type of business, contact information, and any type of jurisdictional information. The document must disclose offering price, number of shares being issued, the form of the securities being offered, how escrow is handled, and how the proceeds will be used (to fund operations, to develop new products, to purchase new equipment, etc.). The offering document must also discuss management's experience, all risks involved with the investment, and the type of industry. The financial position of the company should be included as well.

A prospectus is similar to an offering document but is issued with mutual funds, stocks, and bonds. The prospectus is provided to potential investors by brokerages, underwriters, and investment bankers. The prospectus includes the financial status of the company, financial statements, information on executive compensation, pending litigation against the company, and profiles of the managers, the CEO, and the board of directors. The prospectus must be filed with the Securities and Exchange Commission. A preliminary prospectus is typically issued before a final prospectus, which may be amended. A mutual fund prospectus contains information on the fund's risks, investment strategy, performance, investment types, fund manager profiles, fees, and expenses.

A red herring prospectus is a preliminary prospectus. It is issued when a public offering of securities is made. It must be filed with the SEC. A red herring clearly states that the offering information is subject to change. Investments cannot be made based on information solely found in the red herring. Investors may only make an indication of interest. The red herring contains information on underwriter fees, purpose of the proceeds, a description of how securities will be marketed and offered, three years of financial statements, the underwriting agreement, a legal opinion, and copies of the articles of incorporation.

The final prospectus is the prospectus used as the legal offering document for an initial public offering. A final prospectus must be given to any potential investor that is offered the security or any actual investor of the security. The final prospectus must be delivered at or before the time of the sale of the initial public offering.

For municipal bonds, an official statement is the equivalent of a bond prospectus. The statement describes the official terms of the offering. The statement includes the interest rate, the manner of principal payments, the minimum denomination, the redemption terms, the sources of funds for payment, guarantees, the consequences of default, covenants, the trust agreement, and any legal matters. A preliminary statement is usually made available as well. Along with an official statement comes a notice of sale, which advertises the offering to the public.

Regulatory Filing Requirements

The Securities Act of 1933 requires the registration of securities before they are sold to the public, and it was the first major federal legislation to regulate the offer and sale of securities. It ensures the public will receive all necessary financial information in the offering prospectus for securities being sold. It confirms there is no fraud or misrepresentation by any of the parties involved (the syndicate or the

This material is provided for exam preparation purposes only and does not indicate an endorsement of any specific scientific, political, or religious point of view. © TPB Publishing. You have been licensed one copy of this document for personal use only. Any other reproduction or redistribution is strictly prohibited. All rights reserved.

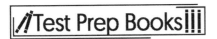
issuing corporation). Due diligence is required to ensure the prospectus contains complete and accurate information. Regardless of whether an offering is registered with the SEC, this law makes it illegal to commit fraud in conjunction with offering securities to the public. A defrauded investor can sue the issuer, the broker, or the underwriter if any of these parties was negligent in allowing fraud to be committed.

A registration statement typically includes a prospectus, a complex legal document that includes a proposed business plan of the enterprise, financial information, the company's history, its business objectives, its operations, the backgrounds of its board of directors and management, and any pending litigation against the company.

Once a corporation files a registration statement, there is a waiting or "quiet period." This is typically 20 days long, during which time only limited information may be released to the public so as not to influence the value of the stock offering. The first day after the waiting period is over is the effective date. This is the date when an offering that is registered with the SEC may commence. During the pre-filing period, the time between when a corporation agrees to offer shares and files their registration filing, the company is prohibited from making any oral or written offers to sell securities. This ensures all potential investors will get their information from the prospectus and will have equal access to information on the company and the filing.

An indication of interest is when an investor shows interest in shares that are still awaiting clearance by the SEC. These investors should receive a prospectus from the broker who will sell them the securities. This is not a commitment to buy securities. For large sale, new issuance (which is slightly different than a pre-IPO indication), the indication will contain:

- The security name
- Whether the participant wishes to buy or sell securities
- The number of shares the investor is considering buying
- An indication of the price they may be willing to pay for the securities

Indications of interest can happen on electronic trading platforms. These indications can happen in dark pools, so there is less of a chance investors will take advantage when large orders of interest are in the pipeline.

Blue sky laws are set by states to protect investors from fraud, and they require the registration of brokerage houses. Most of the laws are based on the Uniform Securities Act of 1956. Some states no longer have these types of laws and instead require that filings be registered through the National Association of Securities Dealer's Central Registration Depository system. The laws usually provide private causes of action (i.e., the right to sue) for private investors who have lost money due to securities fraud. Blue sky laws were originally enacted in Kansas in 1911.

This material is provided for exam preparation purposes only and does not indicate an endorsement of any specific scientific, political, or religious point of view. © TPB Publishing. You have been licensed one copy of this document for personal use only. Any other reproduction or redistribution is strictly prohibited. All rights reserved.

Glossary

Accredited Investors	Investors with sufficient net worth, annual income, and expertise to buy or sell private equity without protection from the SEC
Broker Loan Rate	The rate that banks charge brokers and dealers when lending money for a customer's margin accounts; It's also known as the call loan rate or the money rate.
Broker-Dealers	Financial institutions that affect securities transactions on behalf of individuals and entities or affect transactions for their own accounts
Cash Flow Statement	Reported with the income statement and represents cash flows from investing, operating, and financing activities
Cboe Global Markets (Cboe)	Self-regulatory organization which owns the Cboe Options Exchange
Clearing Brokers	Work for firms that ensure proper settlement of transactions so that investors are ensured that their transaction is completed properly
Counter Currency	Currency that acts as the reference or second currency within a currency pair
Depository Trust and Clearing Corporation (DTCC)	Serves as a custodian and clearing entity for a significant amount of all securities transactions across the globe
Dilutive Secondary Offerings (Follow-On Offerings)	Reduces the value of the share price because additional new shares are now available in the market, but the company's value has not changed; In other words, there are now more owners of the same share.
Discount Rate	The interest rate that the FRB charges to Federal Reserve Banks when the bank is issuing short-term loans
Eurobonds	Bonds that pay principal and interest in Eurodollars (i.e., U.S. dollars held in banks outside of the U.S.)
Federal Deposit Insurance Corporation (FDIC)	The FDIC audits and monitors member banks to ensure that they are adequately capitalized, that they are not taking excessive risk, that they have sufficient systems in place to prevent fraud, and that they follow bank regulations and guidelines. The FDIC currently insures a bank account up to $250,000.
Federal Funds Rate	The rate that the largest banks charge each other for overnight loans of $1 million or more. This is the most volatile interest rate, and short-term interest rates are linked to the federal funds rate.
Federal Reserve Board (FRB)	The FRB is a network of regional banks operating under the authority of the federal government. It's responsible for making impactful decisions that affect the stock market and the economy, including setting interest rates and increasing the money supply.
Financial Industry Regulatory Authority (FINRA)	It develops rules and regulations specifically for brokerage firms and their associates involved with securities trading and investments. It also has the authority to settle disputes between customers from the general public and banking firms; and all firms trading securities must be registered with it.

31

This material is provided for exam preparation purposes only and does not indicate an endorsement of any specific scientific, political, or religious point of view. © TPB Publishing. You have been licensed one copy of this document for personal use only. Any other reproduction or redistribution is strictly prohibited. All rights reserved.

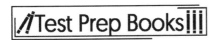

Fiscal Policy	Policy which is primarily concerned with government taxation and expenditures
Forward Market	Allows an investor to buy or sell a currency at a specified exchange rate and at a specified time
Fourth Market	An electronic network utilized specifically and only by institutions
Gross Domestic Product (GDP)	Complex calculation including consumer consumption, investment, governmental expenditures, and net exports and imports; total economic output that occurs within a nation's borders
Gross National Product (GNP)	GDP plus or minus output outside of a nation's border, income earned from foreign investments, and income earned by foreign residents inside the United States
Hedging	Process where traders take positions to reduce the risk of other positions
Income Statement	Shows the revenues and expenses of the company over a period of time and calculates a net profit or net income number (net of expenses, interest, taxes, etc.)
Initial Public Offering (IPO)	An issuer's first attempt to raise capital from the general public to help grow their business
Institutional Investors	Described as investors with the backing of immense amounts of capital
Interbank Market	Where banks exchange the currencies of various countries
Internal Revenue Service (IRS)	The Department of the Treasury uses the IRS to collect taxes.
Introducing Brokers	These are the future's market equivalent of a registered representative in the equities markets.
Investment Adviser	An individual or employee who is paid to provide investment advice, recommend the purchase or sale of securities, issue research reports, or otherwise analyze securities
Monetary Policy	Primarily concerned with how the money supply can be utilized to maximize economic growth
Municipal Advisors	Entities that specialize in the intricacies of financing operations of local governments, i.e., municipalities through bond offerings
Municipal Securities Rulemaking Board (MSRB)	Establishes rules that banks and securities firms must abide by when they engage in buying, selling, underwriting, or recommending municipal securities
Nondilutive Secondary Offerings	Do not reduce the value of the share price because no new shares are issued; The shares offered in a nondilutive secondary offering were previously registered and in existence at the same time as the IPO, but they were not available for sale to the public at the time of the IPO.

This material is provided for exam preparation purposes only and does not indicate an endorsement of any specific scientific, political, or religious point of view. © TPB Publishing. You have been licensed one copy of this document for personal use only. Any other reproduction or redistribution is strictly prohibited. All rights reserved.

North American Securities Administrators Association (NASAA)	An association devoted to investor protection and was created fifteen years before the SEC was created by Congress. It primarily creates "model" securities laws that broadly reach many potential securities regulation issues. It drafts these model acts that many states used as the foundation for the laws actually enacted by the state.
Open Market Activities	These are initiated and executed by the Federal Reserve to affect the money supply and economic growth. The Federal Reserve buys and sells United States Treasury securities from and to primary dealers. The operations are performed by the Federal Reserve Bank of New York.
Options Clearing Corporation (OCC)	The OCC guarantees that contracts on each side of an options contract are fulfilled, which primarily means that the seller or writer of a contract received a premium, and that the buyer of the contract received the underlying security from the seller of the option exercised.
Primary Market	Securities are created on the primary market.
Prime Brokers	Provide many different services to select clients who need more specialized, higher-level services
Prime Rate	The rate that banks charge low-risk customers (namely corporations) with excellent credit; This rate fluctuates based on the money supply set by the Federal Reserve Board.
Proprietary Traders	Market participants that engage in capital markets for a variety of reasons for their own account
Retail Investors	Described as individuals investing for their future through common security vehicles such as mutual funds, exchange-traded funds, and individual stocks and bond in standard brokerage accounts or retirement accounts such as IRAs and 401(k)'s
Secondary Market	Where previously issued stocks, bonds, and other financial instruments are available to buy and sell
Secondary Offering	After an IPO, a second sale of the issuer's securities will be offered. Secondary offerings can either be dilutive or non-dilutive.
Securities Exchange Act Of 1934 (The Exchange Act)	This act established and granted the SEC jurisdiction and authority to propose, draft, and enact laws in furtherance of its purpose.
Securities Investor Protection Corporation (SIPC)	The SIPC protects clients of brokers and dealers in case of financial failure of the broker.
Self-Regulatory Organizations (SROs)	Entities created to regulate industry segments within an organization itself and without reliance on an actual governmental authority
Spot Exchange Rate	The price to trade one currency directly for another at any given time, for delivery on the soonest viable value date. While often set by the foreign exchange market, some countries use mechanisms like a currency peg to influence or even actively set exchange rates.
Spot Market	Where the currency exchange occurs immediately
Third Market	Exchange-listed securities are actually traded in the over-the-counter (OTC) markets, which is usually where unlisted securities trade.

This material is provided for exam preparation purposes only and does not indicate an endorsement of any specific scientific, political, or religious point of view. © TPB Publishing. You have been licensed one copy of this document for personal use only. Any other reproduction or redistribution is strictly prohibited. All rights reserved.

Transfer Agent	Commercial bank that is a client of the corporation (or in some cases is the corporation itself) and that maintains records of all equity and bond holders
Underwriting Commitment	This, also called a firm commitment, is when the underwriter guarantees the purchase of all of the securities being offered in a sale.

This material is provided for exam preparation purposes only and does not indicate an endorsement of any specific scientific, political, or religious point of view. © TPB Publishing. You have been licensed one copy of this document for personal use only. Any other reproduction or redistribution is strictly prohibited. All rights reserved.

Practice Quiz

1. Broker-dealers must apply which of the following standards to all investments that they sell to clients?
   a. Fiduciary
   b. Growth
   c. Value
   d. Suitability

2. Which of the following information should be included with a mutual fund product?
   - I. What the prospectus contains
   - II. Where to find the prospectus
   - III. How to interpret the prospectus
   - IV. What to consider with regards to the mutual fund

   a. I, II, III, and IV
   b. I and II
   c. III and IV
   d. I, II, and IV

3. A mutual fund prospectus will contain information on which of the following?
   a. Fund risk and performance
   b. Analyst opinions
   c. Economic analysis
   d. Shareholder names

4. What are the basic functions of an investment bank?
   a. Raising capital for companies and regulating stock exchanges
   b. Issuing debt and equity for companies, as well as trading their own capital
   c. Trading the capital of its clients and advising the Federal Reserve
   d. Taking customer deposits and providing loans to customers

5. What are the components of the underwriting spread?
   a. Manager fees, the syndicate bid, and SEC fees
   b. Underwriter fees, the syndicate bid, and investment banking fees
   c. Manager fees, broker dealer fees, and stock exchange fees
   d. Manager, underwriter, and broker dealer fees

See answers on next page.

This material is provided for exam preparation purposes only and does not indicate an endorsement of any specific scientific, political, or religious point of view. © TPB Publishing. You have been licensed one copy of this document for personal use only. Any other reproduction or redistribution is strictly prohibited. All rights reserved.

Answer Explanations

1. D: Suitability is a standard that applies to all investment products sold to retail investors. The seller has an obligation to document how and why he or she feels the investment is suitable for the investor. The fiduciary standard is a much higher standard that only a few advisors and trustees will adopt. This standard requires the advisor to put the best interest of the client above their own and includes legal ramifications if he or she does not. The other two options are not standards but rather investment styles or strategies.

2. D: Most mutual fund products include a statement that advises the investor to evaluate investment objectives, risks, charges, and expenses for the product. Also included in the statement is what the prospectus contains and where to find the prospectus.

3. A: A mutual fund prospectus contains information on the risks of the fund and its historical performance against a benchmark and peer funds. The prospectus does not contain an analyst's opinions; these are found in research reports issued by investment banks. Economic analysis may be distributed by the fund but will not be found in its prospectus. There is no disclosure of investors or shareholders in the fund prospectus.

4. B: Investment banks raise capital and will often invest their own proprietary funds in capital markets. Investment banks are regulated by government agencies; they do not regulate on their own. They do not advise the Federal Reserve. Traditional commercial banks take deposits and provide loans to their customers.

5. D: Manager, underwriter, and broker dealer fees. A syndicate bid is not part of the fee structure, nor are SEC fees and stock exchange fees.

This material is provided for exam preparation purposes only and does not indicate an endorsement of any specific scientific, political, or religious point of view. © TPB Publishing. You have been licensed one copy of this document for personal use only. Any other reproduction or redistribution is strictly prohibited. All rights reserved.

Understanding Products and Their Risks

Products

Equity Securities

Common Stock

The primary risk that an investor must understand is that common stock only has a claim to the residual value of a company. This means the value of the common stock is what's left over after all credit facilities, short-term debt, long-term debt, loans, and other senior obligations of the company are paid off (which occurs if a company is liquidated).

The rights of common stock shareholders are specified in the company's charter and bylaws. Generally, these rights include:

- The right to inspect the financial records, systems, and bookkeeping of a corporation
- The right to evaluate the assets of a corporation
- The right to sue managers and officers of the corporation due to mismanagement
- The rights to transfer and sell their shares
- The right to recover the residual value of a company in the event of liquidation
- The right to receive an equal share of dividends (i.e., pro rata dividends)
- The right to vote on all issues affecting the corporation
- The right to purchase additional shares before the general public (see "preemptive right" below)

A preemptive right is the right granted to some shareholders to purchase new shares before the general public. This typically occurs after an initial public offering when a second round of shares is issued. The preemptive right ensures that the company's original investors maintain their ownership percentage of the company.

Most corporations allow one vote per share of stock owned when voting for or against management and the board of directors. This ensures that whoever controls more than 50% of the shares also maintains control of the board to represent their interests.

Limited liability means an owner is only liable for their initial investment. For example, if a company loses all of its equity value and still has debts due, the limited liability owners aren't required to repay the debt.

Preferred Stock

Cumulative preferred stock accumulates dividends in arrears. If a company doesn't have sufficient earnings to pay a dividend, common shareholders simply miss out. Once the company has the earnings to pay a dividend, all the dividends in arrears for preferred shareholders must be paid in full before any common stock dividends can be paid. Non-cumulative preferred stock is just like common stock. Missed dividends don't accrue and won't be paid even if there are earnings to do so.

Participating preferred stock is used when special measures are needed to attract new investors. These shares receive dividends and give stockholders the right to receive additional dividends along with

This material is provided for exam preparation purposes only and does not indicate an endorsement of any specific scientific, political, or religious point of view. © TPB Publishing. You have been licensed one copy of this document for personal use only. Any other reproduction or redistribution is strictly prohibited. All rights reserved.

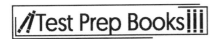

common stock shareholders. This is a common form of financing used by private equity and venture capital corporations. Non-participating preferred stock only pays stipulated dividends.

Convertible preferred stock grants the shareholder the right to convert their shares into a specific number of shares within a specified future time period. However, there are provisions that allow the issuer to force conversion of the shares. Convertible preferred stock is typically issued so the issuer can have more favorable terms than a traditional common stock issuance. These types of shares often carry a rating like traditional bonds.

Callable preferred stock shares give the issuer the right to call the shares back at a specified price over a specified time (as stated in the prospectus for the shares). This type of financing is advantageous to the issuing company if finance conditions become more favorable (i.e., interest rates are lower). The risk to the owner of the shares is that they will only be able to reinvest at a lower dividend or interest rate.

A sinking fund accrues a balance that's used to redeem bonds or preferred stock. This means the company must retire a specified amount of debt on an annual basis. This has advantages and disadvantages to the original bondholder. It does create liquidity for the bonds, but it also means funds will be invested at a lower interest rate.

Adjustable rate stock pays a dividend that's adjusted on a quarterly basis. The adjustment is typically tied to the change in Treasury rates or some other index rate. The price of these securities is typically more stable as it does not need to adjust to compensate investors for the rate of return they require given changes in interest rates.

Preferred stockholders typically receive priority treatment when it comes to the payment of dividends and the distribution of assets upon company liquidation. This means preferred stockholders must be paid dividends prior to common stockholders and have a better claim on company assets than do common stockholders in the event of dissolution. However, preferred stock ordinarily does not come with voting rights.

Rights and Warrants

A rights offering allows existing stockholders to buy newly issued shares at a discount before the general public can buy them. These transactions typically involve an investment bank having the right to buy any offered shares if the existing investors don't purchase all available shares in the rights offering.

Warrants are contracts attached to the ownership of a bond or preferred stock. They grant the holder the right to purchase additional stock over a specified time and at a set price (the "exercise price"). This creates an incentive for the warrant holder should the market price rise above the set price. Basically, warrants are a "sweetener" when debt is issued by a company. The company wants to issue debt at a lower interest rate than the market dictates (given the company's risk profile), so the warrant compensates the investor for buying the debt at the lower rate.

Warrants are tradeable securities and can be separated from the instrument to which they're attached. Typically, they're traded on over-the-counter markets. A warrant experiences "time decay" as it gets closer to its expiration date. Some examples of warrants include: basket warrants that mirror the performance of an industry; index warrants whose value is determined by the performance of an index; detachable warrants; and naked warrants. Warrants sometimes have an anti-dilution provision, which allows existing shareholders to purchase new shares on a pro rata basis. A convertible bond's value equals the bond's straight value plus the value of the warrant.

This material is provided for exam preparation purposes only and does not indicate an endorsement of any specific scientific, political, or religious point of view. © TPB Publishing. You have been licensed one copy of this document for personal use only. Any other reproduction or redistribution is strictly prohibited. All rights reserved.

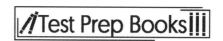

American Depository Receipts (ADRs)

American Depositary Receipts (ADRs) are securities that allow U.S citizens to purchase shares of foreign companies in the U.S. market without having to make the purchase on a foreign stock exchange. They are denominated in U.S. dollars and help reduce the administrative costs normally incurred with international transactions. It should be noted that ADRs do not eliminate currency or economic risks associated with investments in foreign companies.

Controls and Restrictions

The Securities Act Rule 144A was put in place to increase the liquidity in the restricted security market. The rule allows for easier trading of restricted securities by **qualified institutional buyers (QIBs)** (buyers with at least $100 million in assets). This rule induced foreign companies to sell restricted securities in the U.S. capital markets as well. It essentially provides a safe harbor from the registration requirements of the Securities Act of 1933. Since 1990, the National Association of Securities Dealers Automated Quotation (NASDAQ) offers a compliance review process that grants access to securities falling under this exemption. This rule should not be confused with Rule 144, which permits public (as opposed to private) unregistered sales.

Debt Instruments

Treasury Securities

The United States government issues a range of debt instruments including Treasury bills ("T-bills"), Treasury notes, and Treasury bonds. They also issue zero-coupon bonds (STRIPS) and **Treasury Inflation-Protected Securities (TIPS)**. They are backed by the full faith and credit of the U.S. government. Income from these securities is tax exempt at the state and local levels but is taxable at the federal level. Treasury bills mature in 1 year or less, Treasury notes mature in 1 - 10 years, and Treasury bonds mature 10 - 30 years from issuance.

Treasury bills are the primary instrument used by the **Federal Open Market Committee (FOMC)** to regulate the supply of money. TIPS have their principal amount adjusted for inflation as calculated by the **Consumer Price Index (CPI)**. These bonds compensate investors for the inflation that erodes the value of their investment (TIPS typically have a lower yield than comparable Treasury bonds or notes since they're compensated by the inflation adjustment to their bonds). The TIPS breakeven rate (i.e., the difference between the yield on TIPS and regular Treasury notes or bonds) is sometimes used to gauge the inflation that financial markets expect.

Treasury bills are issued in minimum denominations of $100 and continue in $100 increments. Treasury notes and bonds are quoted on the secondary market at the percentage of par in 1/32 point increments. Bond traders refer to each 1/32nd as a **tick**, and each percentage point or basis point as a **bip**. The **spread** is the difference between the yields of two different Treasury bonds (or any bonds). For example, if the 10-year bond is trading with a yield of 5.0%, and the 5-year bond is trading at 4.0%, the spread would be 1.0% (5.0% - 4.0% = 1.0%).

Traders typically look at spreads when deciding which Treasury bonds offer the most value. The advantages of investing in Treasury bonds is that they have essentially zero credit risk, so investors are guaranteed to get back all of the principal. With TIPS, investors are insulated from inflation risk. Treasuries do have a price risk, so if yields increase, the bonds decline in value. There's also reinvestment risk.

This material is provided for exam preparation purposes only and does not indicate an endorsement of any specific scientific, political, or religious point of view. © TPB Publishing. You have been licensed one copy of this document for personal use only. Any other reproduction or redistribution is strictly prohibited. All rights reserved.

After they have been sold at auction by the U.S. government, treasury bonds trade on the secondary market. Treasury markets are highly liquid due to significant trading by both institutional and retail investors in treasury bonds (they are actually the largest security market in the world).

Foreign governments also hold significant quantities of U.S. treasury bonds. Off the run treasuries are treasuries of a particular maturity that were issued before the most recent offering (where the most recent offering is called on the run treasuries). The New York Federal Reserve is the largest holder and trader of U.S. treasury bonds. To qualify as a primary dealer, a firm needs to be a broker-dealer, registered with the SEC, a member of FINRA, and have net regulatory capital of at least $50 million. A second option is for a firm to be a state or federally chartered bank or savings association and maintain at least $1 billion in Tier 1 capital (core capital held in reserves).

Agency

Agency bonds are issued by either a government agency or a government-sponsored enterprise (GSEs) such as Freddie Mac. Those issued by government agencies are low-risk because the federal government is backing them; whereas bonds issued by GSEs do not have such backing and carry credit risk. GSEs receive such a designation by being closely tied to the public interest.

An **asset-backed security (ABS)** is backed by the receivables a bank or servicer is owed on loans for everything from automobiles, credit cards, and mortgages to company inventory and student loans. These loans are originated by a bank or finance company and then packaged and sold to investors as ABSs. These securities typically have different tranches with varying levels of risk. The more senior tranches receive interest and principal first while the riskiest, equity-like tranches only receive the residual payment on the riskiest loans.

These securities are beneficial to banks and other lenders because they allow them to remove loans from their balance sheets and free up capital, even though it may reduce the incentive for them to make good loans (since most of the risk is passed onto the investor). A **collateralized mortgage obligation (CMO)** and a **collateralized debt obligation (CDO)** are riskier, asset-backed securities that have many levels of tranches. Some economists and experts believe these instruments were simply too complex to value and were a direct contributor to the financial crisis of 2007-2008.

Mortgage-backed securities (MBSs) are a type of asset-backed security (ABS). Generally, ABSs are securities that provide a rate of return based on the value of the underlying assets that comprise the security. MBSs are simply ABSs comprising mortgages that provide a rate of return based on the interest rate of the mortgages underlying the security.

The Government National Mortgage Association (GNMA or Ginnie Mae) is an entity that insures mortgage-backed securities (MBS) from approved lenders. Ginnie May provides security to investors by promising to pick up the payments and interest on an MBS if the issuer is not able to. New GNMAs are issued in $25,000 minimum denominations.

The Federal National Mortgage Association (FNMA or Fannie Mae) is a government-sponsored enterprise (GSE) that was created to provide stability to the housing market and allow low- to mid-income families greater access to mortgages. Fannie Mae achieves this by purchasing qualified mortgages from lenders, and either holding them or selling them in groups of mortgage-backed securities (MBS). This frees up enough capital for lenders to issue more mortgages.

This material is provided for exam preparation purposes only and does not indicate an endorsement of any specific scientific, political, or religious point of view. © TPB Publishing. You have been licensed one copy of this document for personal use only. Any other reproduction or redistribution is strictly prohibited. All rights reserved.

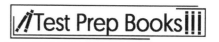

MBSs are created when financial institutions that originate loans desire to take the risk of holding the loans off of the financial institution's books. These financial institutions will sell pools of mortgages to other financial institutions with expertise in packaging the loans as a single security, in a process known as **securitization**. After packaging the loans into a security, the security can then be sold on the open market to market participants. Because the MBSs' rate of return is based on the interest rate of the underlying mortgages, MBSs are considered fixed-income securities.

Corporate Bonds

Corporate bonds are those issued by a corporation. Their basic features are:

- They are taxable securities.

- They have a set maturity (most corporate bonds pay the full principal at maturity, though some amortize like mortgage and asset-backed securities).

- They typically have a set par value of $1,000.

- They trade on major exchanges, but sometimes are traded over the counter.

A bond indenture is a formal agreement between the bond issuer and the investor. The key items in the bond indenture are:

- The form of the bond

- The total dollar amount of the particular bond issuance

- The property pledged behind the bond (though not all corporate bonds have property pledged)

- Any protective covenants. Covenants are acts that must be or cannot be performed by the issuer (e.g., working capital requirements, debt-equity ratio requirements, and restrictions on dividend payments)

- Redemption rights and call privileges

Corporate bonds accrue interest in the same manner as Treasury bonds except when a bond is "traded flat" (when the buyer doesn't have to pay the accrued interest to the seller). Usually this occurs when bonds are in default since there's no guarantee that the buyer will receive the entire interest payment that's due.

A callable bond or redeemable bond can be redeemed by the bond issuer before its stated maturity (i.e., the corporation has the right to call the bond away from the investor). Investors are usually compensated for this risk with a higher interest rate on a comparable bond, and a premium is paid to the investor when the call option is exercised. A bond is typically "called" when interest rates decline, and a company can find less expensive financing. A puttable bond grants the investor the right to "put" the bond back to the corporation that issued it and receive their principal.

This typically occurs in a rising interest rate environment where an investor realizes they can receive a higher interest rate for investing that same principal. Investors in puttable bonds typically accept bonds at a lower yield than they otherwise would have gotten for the optionality. Some bonds have both call and put options embedded. A make whole call allows the issuer to call the bond if such a call gives the

This material is provided for exam preparation purposes only and does not indicate an endorsement of any specific scientific, political, or religious point of view. © TPB Publishing. You have been licensed one copy of this document for personal use only. Any other reproduction or redistribution is strictly prohibited. All rights reserved.

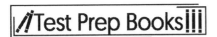
bondholder a lump sum equal to the present value of the coupons they'd have received if they'd held the bond until its scheduled maturity. This allows the issuer to reduce the amount of debt on its balance sheet.

Convertible bonds enable the bondholder to convert the bond into stock from the same company. These bonds sometimes have a variable interest rate (i.e., rather than a fixed coupon, the coupon rate fluctuates based on an index value). Variable rate bonds have more stable prices than fixed rate bonds. The conversion ratio determines the number of shares an investor receives upon the conversion of each bond. The ratio is the par value of the security divided by the conversion price, and there are conversion clauses that adjust the ratio to prevent shareholder dilution. With parity pricing, the price of the convertible bond is equal to the price of the underlying stock. When investors try to take advantage of pricing discrepancies between convertible bonds and the underlying stock, it is called **arbitrage**. Buying the undervalued asset and selling the overvalued asset until the prices align does, in theory, generate a profit for the arbitrageur. A forced conversion occurs when the issuer forces the bond holder to convert the bond to shares. This occurs when there's a significant decline in interest rates. The conversion ratio tells the investor how many shares they'll receive from converting each bond they own:

$$Conversion\ Ratio = \frac{Bond\ par\ value}{Conversion\ price}$$

Most bonds have an inverse relationship between their price and their yield. When the yield (i.e., interest rates) rises, prices fall. When interest rates fall, bond prices rise. Duration measures this relationship for small changes in prices and yields. **Convexity** (the second derivative of the price-yield relationship) is a more accurate measure of the relationship for larger changes in interest rates. For a bond with a duration of 4, each 1% rise in interest rates causes the bond to decline in value by 4% (or rise by 4% for each 1% decline in interest rates). The line marked duration in the graph below shows the price-yield relationship for Bond A and Bond B. Even when the bond price or yield moves, the relationship isn't reflected in the duration. This is where convexity is a better measure of the price-yield relationship.

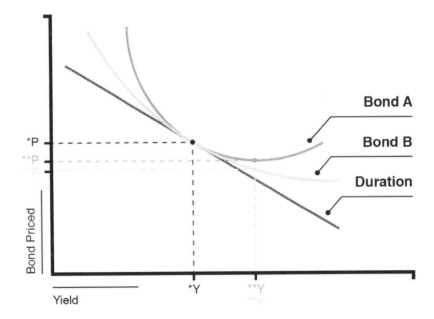

This material is provided for exam preparation purposes only and does not indicate an endorsement of any specific scientific, political, or religious point of view. © TPB Publishing. You have been licensed one copy of this document for personal use only. Any other reproduction or redistribution is strictly prohibited. All rights reserved.

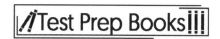

Municipal Securities

Municipal bonds are debt obligations issued by state or local governments. Municipal bonds are either general obligation (GO) bonds or revenue bonds. GO bonds are backed by the full faith and credit of the municipality and are paid with general revenue and borrowings. Revenue bonds are paid from the revenue tied to a specific project that the bonds have funded (e.g., tolls, stadiums, etc.).

Analyzing the debt of a **general obligation (GO)** municipal bond is different than analyzing a corporate bond. Some factors to consider include: the unemployment rate, demographic information, operational and management capabilities, the current debt profile, and the tax base. Investors can analyze the debt burden calculation to quantify a municipality's ability to pay debt. This is overall net debt divided by full valuation. Similar to a debt service coverage ratio, the ability of a municipality to make interest payments must be evaluated. Tax revenue must be evaluated on at least an annual basis to assure interest and principal can be paid. The demographics of the population must also be considered, as well as economic growth and activity of the municipality. The municipality's existing debt and when it will mature should also be considered.

Revenue bonds have different factors to evaluate. Though municipal bonds are typically backed by the ability to pay the debt with general taxpayer money, revenue bonds are backed by their ability to generate revenue from the project they fund. Feasibility studies are created by economists and government officials to determine whether a project is really needed (i.e., if a bridge should be built, if a road should be paved) and if it can generate sufficient revenue to fund itself. Legal and operational factors, as well as environmental factors, must also be considered.

Revenue bonds are tied to specific sources of revenue. Bondholders can't receive payment from the general taxpayer population for these bonds. Revenue can only come from the project pledged to repay the bonds and are from the actual operations of the financed project. If the project isn't profitable, a default may occur. Municipal bonds typically have strict bond covenants (negative and positive) to protect the issuer and the investor. Negative covenants prevent the issuer from certain actions (i.e., issuing additional debt, using funds from the finances project for something other than interest and principal payments), and positive covenants require certain actions by the issuer (i.e., having a sinking fund, requiring a set amount of cash reserves).

These bonds may also be subject to outside audits and financial reports. Investors can review credit ratings when assessing the credit risk of municipal bonds and be aware that credit ratings can change over time. Credit ratings are not a completely accurate source of investing advice or an indication that an investment is suitable. The **Electronic Municipal Market Access (EMMA)** website contains updated information regarding the issuer and municipal bond, as well as credit ratings information. It's also important to consider restrictions on the insurance of additional bonds and the flow of funds on a case-by-case basis.

Limited tax bonds are backed by the issuing entity but not by its full taxing power. Therefore, these bonds are riskier than bonds backed by the full taxing authority of a municipality. Tax anticipation notes are short-term obligations backed by expected taxes. These bonds even out cash flow and provide liquidity to balance out the irregularity of municipal and state income. Bond anticipation notes are issued in anticipation of the sale of long-term municipal bonds. Revenue anticipation notes are issued in anticipation of sales tax revenue. Tax-exempt commercial paper finances short-term liabilities. They provide the bond holder with some level of tax preference on their debt earnings (e.g., universities use this form of financing). Grant anticipation notes are backed by expected highway funding.

This material is provided for exam preparation purposes only and does not indicate an endorsement of any specific scientific, political, or religious point of view. © TPB Publishing. You have been licensed one copy of this document for personal use only. Any other reproduction or redistribution is strictly prohibited. All rights reserved.

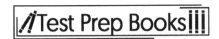

A special tax bond is paid through an **excise tax**, which is a tax on specific goods such as gasoline, tobacco, and alcohol. These usually aren't backed by the taxing power of the municipality. A special assessment bond is repaid from the taxes of those who benefit from that specific good. For example, if a bond finances a new road, anyone who buys a home or starts a business on that road pays a special tax levy to pay for the bond that funded the road. The interest is tax free for the residential bond holders. A moral obligation bond is backed by the moral obligation of a state government.

Pre-funded municipal bonds have funds set aside to pay them off at their call date. An advance refunding occurs 90 days before the call date. A double-barreled municipal bond has its interest and principal guaranteed by a larger municipal entity. With these bonds, if the revenue from the financed project isn't sufficient, the municipality still backs the payment of the bonds. **Certificates of participation (COPs)** are where investors purchase a share of lease revenues rather than securing them with the actual revenues. These bonds are dependent on the legislative appropriations process.

Auction rate securities have long maturities so their rate is regularly reset through Dutch auction. A **Dutch auction** is where the price is lowered until it matches a bid. Municipal bonds and Treasury bonds are sold through Dutch auction.

In a competitive municipal bond sale, bonds are advertised. The advertisement includes the terms of the sale and the particular issue. The bonds are sold to the bidder with the lowest interest rate and therefore the highest price. In a **negotiated sale**, the bonds are structured to meet the demands of both the investors and the issuer. An underwriter is selected to buy the bonds being sold. This type of sale will have the underwriter seek indications of interest. Negotiated sales occur when the issuer has poor credit, the issue is large, the terms of the deal are exotic, the company does not have a strong earnings history, or when the market is volatile.

Variable rate demand notes (VRDNs) are bonds issued by local municipalities to private investors. These bonds are sold to obtain funds for public projects. A VRDN has two significant advantages to investors. First, the loan's interest rate fluctuates based on the market value. This means that there is less interest rate risk associated for the investor. The second reason these loans appeal to private investors is they carry a put option that allows the investor to sell back the loan to the issuer at any time (usually with a 1 weeks' notice). This allows the investor to maintain a lot of liquidity in their investment. VRDNs can also be back by reputable banks providing an extra layer of security for the investor.

Other Debt Instruments

Commercial paper is used by corporations, and sometimes municipalities, to fund operations on a short-term basis. Maturities typically range from overnight (often called the Repo market) to 270 days. The advantage to issuing commercial paper is that it doesn't require the cost of SEC registration if it matures within 270 days of being issued. Commercial paper is typically found in a money market fund. There is also Asset Backed commercial paper where corporations can fund inventory such as dealer floors for automobiles. This is also where mortgages might be warehoused before they can be packaged into Mortgage Backed Securities. Commercial paper doesn't pay a coupon but is simply issued at a discount that reflects current interest rates (usually LIBOR plus some type of spread given the risk of the issuer). There are restrictions, similar to bond covenants, around what the funds from commercial paper issuance may be used for. This usually means only using that capital for funding inventories but can't be used on fixed assets.

Brokered **certificates of deposit (CDs)** are bought in bulk by the brokerage firm and resold to its customers. These CDs typically pay a premium (usually 1%) as compared to CDs issued by traditional

This material is provided for exam preparation purposes only and does not indicate an endorsement of any specific scientific, political, or religious point of view. © TPB Publishing. You have been licensed one copy of this document for personal use only. Any other reproduction or redistribution is strictly prohibited. All rights reserved.

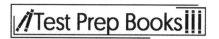
banks. They are tradeable instruments whereas regular CDs are not (which can result in a loss to the investor), and they do not require an investor to pay a commission upon purchase.

Eurodollar bonds pay principal and interest in Eurodollars (i.e., U.S. dollars held in banks outside of the U.S.). These bonds are not registered with the SEC, so there are typically lower costs and fewer regulatory issues. This means they can be sold with a lower interest rate than a comparable bond in the U.S.

Variable rate preferred shares are a preferred stock where the dividend varies with a specified index. This is typically the Treasury rate, and the dividend fluctuates based on a formula (i.e., the Treasury bill rate plus 1%).

The **banker's acceptance** is a negotiable piece of paper that functions like a post-dated check, although the bank rather than an account holder guarantees the payment. Banker's acceptances are used by companies as a relatively safe form of payment for large transactions. Bankers' acceptances can be found in money market funds. These are instruments issued by a company that are guaranteed by a commercial bank. They trade at a discount on the secondary market and are often used in international secondary markets.

Money market funds are <u>not insured</u> by the FDIC (Federal Deposit Insurance Corporation). Therefore, the SEC mandates that the prospectus states that the federal government doesn't guarantee the money, and there's no guarantee that the funds will maintain a net asset value of a dollar. In addition, money market funds must be mainly invested only in short-term securities with the average maturity not exceeding 90 days. No securities in the portfolio can have a maturity of more than 13 months.

Customers are prohibited from selling securities before the shares are paid for in full. Attempting to sell securities before full payment is made may put the account on a 90-day trading restriction.

Yield

There are a number of ways to calculate the yield on a Treasury bond. The Treasury coupon is the initial dollar rate paid on a bond. A bond that has a par value of $1,000 may have a stated coupon rate of 10%, which means the bond would pay $100 per year in interest. Treasury bonds typically pay interest on a semi-annual basis, so the bond would pay $50 every six months until its maturity. The coupon rate and the dollar interest are constant throughout the life of a regular Treasury bond so even if the bond's value declines to $900 (due to rising interest rates), the coupon rate stays at 10% and the bond's holder still receives $100 in annual interest. The current yield is the interest on the bond divided by the price. In the case above where the bond's value is $900, the bond's current yield would be 11.1%. If the bond's value increases to $1,000, the current yield and coupon would be equal at 10% each.

Ratings and Rating Agencies

The bonds of most major companies are rated by the major rating agencies, including Fitch, Standard & Poor's, and Moody's. Please note that these agencies are only rating the credit worthiness of the issuer and that particular bond issue. They're not making any buy or sell recommendations on the bonds. Also note that the rating agency is being paid a fee to rate them by that particular company. The agencies rate everything from corporate bonds and privately issued mortgage-backed securities to commercial paper, CMOs, and CDOs. Some critics feel these ratings don't accurately reflect the risk of the instruments that rated them highly before the financial crisis of 2007-2008.

This material is provided for exam preparation purposes only and does not indicate an endorsement of any specific scientific, political, or religious point of view. © TPB Publishing. You have been licensed one copy of this document for personal use only. Any other reproduction or redistribution is strictly prohibited. All rights reserved.

Ratings agencies assign a rating to companies that are issued debt. There are three major rating agencies: Fitch, S&P, and Moody's. The ratings are intended to reflect the issuer's ability to make interest and principal payments on debt. Ratings agencies also rate government, municipal, and structured debt products. The ratings that the agencies publish are assumed to be independent because the agencies are not money managers or investment banks. This means there is no conflict of interest or incentive for them to assign securities a particular rating.

The table below shows the current ratings assigned by two of the major agencies and their meanings:

Moody's	S&P	Meaning
Investment Grade Bonds		
Aaa	AAA	Bonds of the highest quality that offer the lowest degree of investment risk. Issuers are considered to be extremely stable and dependable.
Aa1, Aa2, Aa3	AA+, AA, AA-	Bonds are of high quality by all standards but carry a slightly greater degree of long-term investment risk.
A1, A2, A3	A+, A, A-	Bonds with many positive investment qualities.
Baa1, Baa2, Baa3	BBB+, BBB, BBB-	Bonds of medium grade quality. Security currently appears sufficient but may be unreliable over the long-term.
Non-Investment Grade Bonds (Junk Bonds)		
Ba1, Ba2, Ba3	BB+, BB, BB-	Bonds with speculative fundamentals. The security of future payments is only moderate.
B1, B2, B3	B+, B, B-	Bonds that are not considered to be attractive investments. Little assurance of long-term payments.
Caa1, Caa2, Caa3	CCC+, CCC, CCC-	Bonds of poor quality. Issuers may be in default or are at risk of being in default.
CA	CC	Bonds of highly speculative features. Often in default.
C	C	Lowest rated class of bonds.
--	D	In default.

Options

Types of Options

For investors seeking to add active investments to their portfolios, options serve as a unique tool to help reduce the risk of the investment. Given the potential of fluctuating stock prices, options can provide the investor a choice to buy or sell. Furthermore, options can also help investors increase their returns.

Options can be categorized into two forms: American and European. Both types of options have different parameters for how they are exercised. Primarily exclusive to the United States, American options are exercised or closed at any time prior to the date of expiration. Unlike American options, European options stipulate a shorter duration of time in which the option can be exercised. This window of opportunity is usually just prior to or on the expiration date.

An option that is sold on a registered exchange is called a **listed option**. Listed options include securities such as market indexes, common stocks, and exchange-traded options. These options have predetermined exercise prices and expiration dates. However, an options contract can be adjusted in special circumstances, such as when the underlying company experiences some type of reorganization.

This material is provided for exam preparation purposes only and does not indicate an endorsement of any specific scientific, political, or religious point of view. © TPB Publishing. You have been licensed one copy of this document for personal use only. Any other reproduction or redistribution is strictly prohibited. All rights reserved.

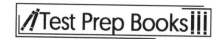

Puts and Calls

Put and call options are types of derivative instruments whose value is dependent on a specific security, index, commodity, currency, or investment. A call option will increase in value when the price of the security to which it is tied increases in value. The amount of correlation (i.e., the amount the call option increases in value with the underlying asset) varies but can be as much as just a fraction of correlation to being completely correlated with the asset's value.

A put option will increase in value when the underlying asset declines in value (or declines in value when the asset increases in value). These are assets that are a product of financial engineering and can be used for either hedging (when the investor owns the underlying asset and the derivative) or speculation (when the investor owns only the derivative instrument and not the actual underlying asset). Puts and calls have specific strike prices. The **strike price** is the price at which the option can be exercised by the investor. The exercise date is the time by which the option can be exercised, if it does, in fact, exceed the strike price.

For example, a stock that has a $20 price may have a call option with a strike price of $25 that expires in one month. If the stock price moves to $30 in two weeks, the investor can exercise the option and the stock will be "called" away from the seller (or "writer") of the contract at the strike price of $25. If the stock doesn't exceed the $25 stock price within that month, the option will expire as worthless.

An **option class** is all options tied to a particular stock or index. An **option series** is a subset of an option class that has the same strike price and expiration date.

Equity vs. Index

Every listed option has the following characteristics: class, style, type, expiration date, symbol, strike price, multiplier, and contract size. The class identifies whether the option is a call or put option. The style of the option refers to whether the option is American or European. The type of the option identifies whether the option is an equity index or exchange-traded security. The symbol varies according to the company. The strike price varies as it is a specified price measured per share. Strike prices will be discussed in more detail later.

Another characteristic is the multiplier. Usually, the multiplier initially starts at 100. The multiplier is used to determine the amount of the underlying asset attached to some options contracts. This amount is called the **contract size**. Initially, the contract size is 100, meaning when one contract option is exercised, 100 shares will be bought or sold. As mentioned, when a company experiences a reorganization, some of these characteristics may experience an adjustment. These changes may affect some of the characteristics, such as the strike price, symbol, or even a multiplier. However, the expiration date typically remains unchanged. There are many reasons for adjustments to options. Some of these causes may include stock dividends, stock splits, or mergers.

Premium

An option premium is the price that an investor is willing to pay for the opportunity to buy an asset at a specified price within a specified time period. Some investors consider the equity of a company a call option, since the stockholder reserves the right to call the residual income away from a company. The premium is comprised of an intrinsic value and a time value. The **intrinsic value** is the value of the option were it to be exercised immediately. If the option is out-of-the-money, that value will be zero; if the option is in-the-money, its intrinsic value is the difference between its price and the exercise price.

This material is provided for exam preparation purposes only and does not indicate an endorsement of any specific scientific, political, or religious point of view. © TPB Publishing. You have been licensed one copy of this document for personal use only. Any other reproduction or redistribution is strictly prohibited. All rights reserved.

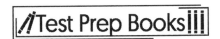

The second part of the value is its time value. Although an option is out-of-the-money, it still has some value because there is the possibility it will exceed the exercise price before the expiration date. An option that is in-the-money will have a premium value greater than its intrinsic value because there is the potential for the price to move even further past the strike price before expiration. As an equation, this means *Option Premium = Time Value + Intrinsic Value*. For a call option, this means *Value = Stock Price - Exercise Price*, and for a put option, the equation is *Value = Exercise Price – Stock Price*.

Along with the strike price, asset price, and time to expiration, the volatility of the underlying asset will affect the premium of the option. The more volatile the asset, the more likely its price will exceed the strike price of the option contract. Quantitative analysts use various techniques and models to value options and calculate their premiums. The Black-Scholes model incorporates the asset value, the strike price, and the asset's volatility (among other variables) to calculate an option premium.

Put-call parity is a more simplified model that traders and investors can use to determine if puts and calls are under- or overvalued than their relationship to each other. Put-call parity states that the call value less the put value should be equal to the difference between the forward value of the asset less the strike price of the contract discounted at the risk-free rate. When these relationships don't hold, investors can buy or sell options (or even the underlying asset) to take advantage of any mispricing.

Underlying or Cash Settlement

Just like equities, there are published volumes on the number of options contracts traded on exchanges. Options traders usually evaluate options volume relative to the volume of the underlying security. When there is a spike in the volume of options and the underlying stock, it is a sign of a trend. Along with volume is open interest, the total number of open options contracts. With equities, there is a fixed number of shares. However, new options contracts can be created at any time as long as there's a buyer and seller.

When options expire or have an offsetting contract opened, the open interest will decline. When investors open new positions, the open interest will rise. Of course, one side of the transaction may be opening a transaction while the other is closing a position, which would leave the total open interest number unaffected. Open interest is primarily used to evaluate the amount of liquidity in an options market to assure there is active trading. In options trading, a position limit is the maximum number of contracts an investor can hold on an underlying security.

The Chicago Board Options Exchange usually establishes these limits based on the amount of liquidity in a stock and the number of shares outstanding. Limits prevent excess leverage in the market and promote price stability. Some experts believe that the excessive financial engineering in the collateralized debt obligations (CDO) and structured product markets helped create the financial crisis in 2008. This was the result of having too many derivatives being traded on a small number of underlying securities. An **exercise limit** is the maximum a person can exercise on one particular options class within a set timeframe. This prevents one investor from artificially influencing the prices of options.

Options and derivatives must be adjusted when the underlying asset pays interest or dividends. When a bond makes an interest payment or a stock pays a dividend, it will affect the price of the asset and the value of the option. In the case of stocks, the stock price will fall by the amount of the dividend. The value of the option will increase as the option holder may receive the dividend or interest payment, depending on the date the option expires and if it is exercised. When a company pays a dividend on a consistent quarterly basis, the stock price should decline by the amount of the dividend on the ex-dividend date. Options reflect this information in the form of higher premiums for calls and lower

This material is provided for exam preparation purposes only and does not indicate an endorsement of any specific scientific, political, or religious point of view. © TPB Publishing. You have been licensed one copy of this document for personal use only. Any other reproduction or redistribution is strictly prohibited. All rights reserved.

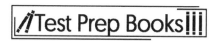

premiums for puts when the dividend is high (which reduces the probability that a stock's price will exceed the strike price of the contract).

The same applies to options on indices. Option traders and investors simply must account for stock dividends when valuing an option contract. If a company stops paying a dividend, the seller of the option may not have received enough of a premium for the risk he or she is taking. There is also the fact that the stock price will fall if the company fails to pay a dividend, since this may mean future financial difficulties for that company. Option investors must also account for the fact that if they own a stock at the time of the dividend payment, they receive the full dividend. This may give an investor the incentive to exercise an option early if the underlying asset will be paying a dividend. The investor needs to determine if the profit to be received from the exercise of the option, plus the amount of the dividend to be received, outweighs the potential upside of waiting for further price appreciation in the underlying asset.

In-the-Money, Out-of-the-Money
In options trading, the difference between in-the-money and out-of-the-money is a matter of the position of the strike price relative to the market value of the underlying stock.

In-the-Money (ITM)
An **in-the-money (ITM)** option contract has intrinsic value. Call options are in-the-money when the underlying asset's current price is higher than the agreed-upon price (the strike price). Under the option contract, the buyer could exercise their discretion to buy the underlying asset at a price below its current value; this defines the intrinsic value of the call.

Out-of-the-Money (OTM)
When an option contract is **out-of-the-money (OTM)**, then it lacks an intrinsic value. Call options are out-of-the-money when the underlying asset's current price is lower than the agreed-upon price. The call option's buyer would not exercise their discretion to purchase the underlying asset because doing so would force them to pay more than the asset's current market value.

Covered vs. Uncovered Strategies
Options strategies vary from the basic to the more complex. When investors own stocks and want to earn extra income, they may write call or put options on their shares by writing covered calls and puts.

Protective Put
Options can be used to hedge an investor's position. Essentially, the protective put can be used to protect the investor's unrealized gains. If the investor fears the market might decrease temporarily, they can buy put options to protect their portfolio investments. If the market instead rises, they will still see the appreciation in securities they held onto, but the rate of return will be reduced by the premiums they paid to buy the protective puts. Investors can even take advantage of markets that are trading sideways by simultaneously selling put and call options and collecting premiums as profit. Investors with large portfolios can hedge the risk of the entire portfolio using index options, assuming their portfolio is similar enough in structure to the index the options are tied to. International investors can also protect themselves from foreign currency value fluctuations in their international investments with options and derivatives.

This material is provided for exam preparation purposes only and does not indicate an endorsement of any specific scientific, political, or religious point of view. © TPB Publishing. You have been licensed one copy of this document for personal use only. Any other reproduction or redistribution is strictly prohibited. All rights reserved.

Covered Call and Put Writing

When a party enters into an option contract and owns the underlying asset, the party is considered "covered." If the investor feels their stock will rise in value, put options can be written. This will increase the return on the investment by the amount of the premium the put buyer has paid. Investors can use the same strategy if they believe the value of a stock they own might rise, but not enough to exceed the strike price, in which case the security will be called away. Writing options is a risky strategy because their security can be called away. However, this is less risky than uncovered or "naked" option writing in which the writer will have to purchase the security on the open market, since this can lead to unlimited losses for the writer of the contract.

Yield-based options are valued using the difference between the exercise price and the value of the yield on the underlying debt instrument. A call position will increase when interest rates rise (which actually decreases the value of the underlying security).

American and European Style Exercise

When an option is in-the-money, it can be exercised, but the investor needs to decide when to exercise it. The assignment is when the investor makes the decision to exercise and notifies the broker. When the assignment occurs, the broker notifies the Options Clearing Corporation (OCC). The OCC then randomly selects another party at the exchange that has the opposite side of the position (a writer of the contract if the broker's client is the buyer). There are various opinions about the optimum time to exercise an American-style option. If an investor is long a call option that is in-the-money, some experts believe it is best to wait until the expiration date and only exercise the option if it is still in-the-money.

In theory, this protects the investor from downside risk if the stock falls below the strike price. However, the investor could simply exercise the option and immediately sell the stock and receive the profit of the difference between the asset's price and the strike price. European options differ from American options in that after-hours trading does affect their settlement price. This means that a European option might actually be exercised out-of-the-money when the investor thought the position was a profitable in-the-money position.

Settlement Date, Exercise, and Assignment

Just like buying a stock or bond, an investor needs to open the transaction (and close it when wishing to sell the position, assuming it has not expired). A **buy to open contract** is when an investor buys a call option on a stock or index. A **sell to open contract** is when the investor sells the right to the buyer to call the stock from (or put the stock to) the investor. For this, the seller receives a premium for bearing the risk of the transaction. The inverse of each transaction would be a buy or sell to close, where investors would take the opposite of their opening positions. When investors close their positions, they will either earn a profit if they have bought calls and the stock rises above the strike price, or they have bought put options and the stock price declines below the strike price.

The sellers or writers of the contracts profit when the options expire as worthless, with the profit being the premium they received upon entering into the contract. A loss will be the premium paid by the buyers of the options if the options expire worthless. The loss for the writers of the contract will be the difference between the securities price and the exercise price on the option contract under most scenarios. With European options, the closing transaction will only take place on the expiration date, assuming the option is not worthless (and is in-the-money or has exceeded the strike price of the contract). Option contracts can be closed simply by trading the actual contract to another party, which can be done through some brokers and exchanges.

This material is provided for exam preparation purposes only and does not indicate an endorsement of any specific scientific, political, or religious point of view. © TPB Publishing. You have been licensed one copy of this document for personal use only. Any other reproduction or redistribution is strictly prohibited. All rights reserved.

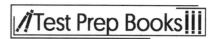
Settlement dates vary depending on the type of security. While stocks and exchange-traded funds settle three market days (a day public sales are held) after the trade date, options are settled only one market day after the trade date.

The **trade date** is the date when the buyer exercised the right to buy the underlying shares. Or, in a put contract, the trade date is when the buyer exercises the right to sell underlying shares. When the buyer has decided to exercise their right, the buyer must notify the writer of the option contract. This notification is called an exercise notice. The exercise notice is the broker's notification of the intended transaction. The broker then forwards the exercise notice to the seller. The forwarding process is completed through the OCC.

After buyers have executed their options, sellers or options writers are obligated to fulfill their terms of the contract and deliver the agreed-upon terms. This is known as the **assignment**. When the assignment is executed on a call option, the seller or writer is obligated to sell the specified quantity of the underlying security at the strike price. When the assignment is executed on a put option, the options writer is obligated to purchase the predetermined quantity of the underlying security at the strike price. To ensure compliance of these transactions, the OCC oversees the fair practices concerning the distribution of assignments.

Varying Strategies

A **spread strategy** is when an investor buys the same number of call and put options with varying maturities and strike prices. These strategies can be broken down further into horizontal, vertical, and diagonal spreads. In a **vertical spread strategy**, all of the options on the single security expire in the same month but have varying strike prices. In **horizontal spreads**, the expirations vary, but the strike prices are all the same. **Diagonal spreads** have varying expiration dates and strike prices. In each of these strategies, there is limited risk (the total loss is simply the sum of the premiums paid by the investor).

The **butterfly spread** is an even more advanced strategy. In a basic butterfly, an investor buys a call option at a certain strike price, writes two calls at a higher strike price, and buys a second call at an even higher strike price. This allows the investor to fund the two long positions with the premium earned from writing the two calls. There is the risk that if the stock has a significant price increase—and if the investor does not own the underlying shares, the investor will have to go onto the open market and buy the shares to cover the second position written. In a modified butterfly, the strategy becomes more complex, since calls and puts are both used. A modified butterfly has only one breakeven price. Conversely, a regular butterfly has multiple breakeven points that can potentially be hit throughout the life of the trade. Below are various diagrams of some options strategies.

This material is provided for exam preparation purposes only and does not indicate an endorsement of any specific scientific, political, or religious point of view. © TPB Publishing. You have been licensed one copy of this document for personal use only. Any other reproduction or redistribution is strictly prohibited. All rights reserved.

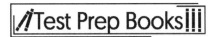
The graphic below is a long straddle showing strike prices at $35 for the put option and at $45 for the call option:

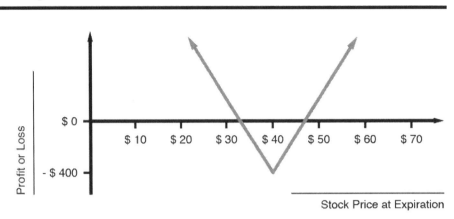

Below is the profit and loss for a bear put spread:

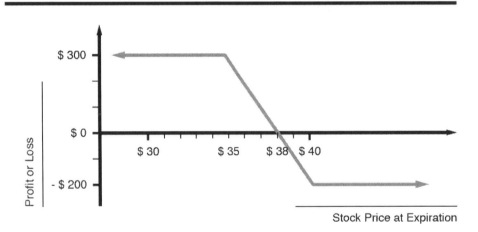

This material is provided for exam preparation purposes only and does not indicate an endorsement of any specific scientific, political, or religious point of view. © TPB Publishing. You have been licensed one copy of this document for personal use only. Any other reproduction or redistribution is strictly prohibited. All rights reserved.

Below is a collar:

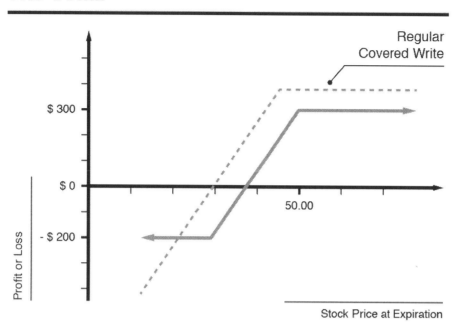

Below is a long butterfly:

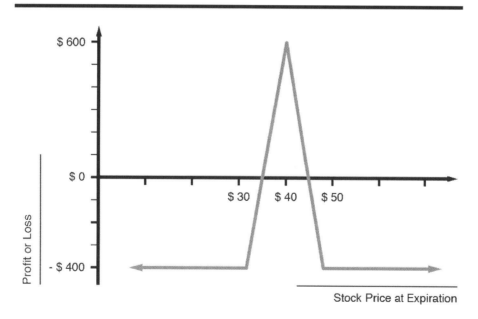

This material is provided for exam preparation purposes only and does not indicate an endorsement of any specific scientific, political, or religious point of view. © TPB Publishing. You have been licensed one copy of this document for personal use only. Any other reproduction or redistribution is strictly prohibited. All rights reserved.

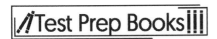

Special Disclosures

Brokerage firms and investment banks typically provide documents for consumers that cover anything from account details, explanation of risk, legal disclaimers, or brokerage fees. These documents, or **special disclosures**, are encouraged by FINRA to increase transparency between firms and customers. One type of special disclosure is an options disclosure document.

The Options Clearing Corporation (OCC)

The **Options Clearing Corporation (OCC)** is an equity derivatives clearinghouse that provides its services to 14 different exchanges. The OCC guarantees that contracts on each side of an options contract are fulfilled, which primarily means that the seller or writer of a contract received a premium, and that the buyer of the contract received the underlying security from the seller of the option exercised. The OCC holds about $120 billion in collateral each day and is regulated by both the Securities and Exchange Commission and the Commodity Futures Trading Commission. The OCC has its own board of directors and generates revenue on the fees it receives from settling options transactions. The OCC is rated by all three major bond rating agencies. The OCC settled options traded on exchanges only until 2011, when it began to settle over-the-counter options trades. The OCC has made changes to its settlement process in recent years. In 2013, expirations moved from Saturdays to Fridays. The OCC has both weekly and monthly expirations that can expire on a consistent and repeated process and is now aligned with global option market settlement schedules.

The OCC issues the **options disclosure document (ODD)** which is a publication meant to provide guidance for options traders. It is formally called *Characteristics & Risks of Standardized Options* and is especially useful for first time options traders.

Long-Term Options (LEAPS)

Long-term equity anticipation securities (LEAPS) are simply options with expiration dates significantly further out than a typical option. Traditional options have maturities on a monthly basis going out 12 months. More liquid stocks may have more frequent options expirations, while companies traded more thinly may only have expirations every three months or so. LEAPS have maturities that go as far as two years or more. All LEAPS expire in January and are mostly traded on specific stocks that have significant trading volume. The expiration is always on the third Friday of January. Investors must pay a higher premium than on normal equity options, since they have significantly more time for the stock to exceed the listed strike price. In theory, an investor could simply roll into new options contracts as the regular contracts expire, but this does expose the investor to strike prices being adjusted as the security value moves in either direction.

Margin is required when purchasing LEAPS. 75 percent of the option's current value is required when there are more than nine months to the expiration of the contract. When selling or writing LEAPS (this is the party that agrees to deliver the underlying security at the exercise price), 100 percent of the contract value is required to be put down. LEAPS are taxed at the long-term capital gains rate of 20 percent. Just like regular options, LEAPS can be used for speculation or hedging, while strategies like straddles and butterflies can be used to take advantage of any anticipated movement in the price of a stock. LEAPS can be used in an IRA under certain circumstances.

This material is provided for exam preparation purposes only and does not indicate an endorsement of any specific scientific, political, or religious point of view. © TPB Publishing. You have been licensed one copy of this document for personal use only. Any other reproduction or redistribution is strictly prohibited. All rights reserved.

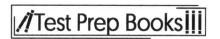

Packaged Products

Investment Companies

Investment companies are business entities that invest pooled capital from investors into a variety of financial securities. This type of company is also referred to as a fund company or a fund sponsor. Offering investors diversification and professional management, mutual funds are very attractive to a wide range of investors. Through pooling funds, investors enjoy both safety and high-growth opportunities. Mutual funds are utilized by individual investors, individual retirement accounts, 401(k) accounts, and 403(b) accounts. Mutual funds are typically divided into three classifications: open-end funds, closed-end funds, and exchange-traded funds.

Types of Investment Companies

Closed-end funds differ from open-end funds in that shares are publicly traded, and capital is raised through an initial public offering of the fund's shares. Open-end funds are what is traditionally considered a mutual fund. Most closed-end funds focus on a specific industry or sector. Closed-end funds have a finite number of shares issued at the fund establishment. Usually, after the IPO, the number of shares is constant and new shares cannot be issued. Where open-end funds usually have an NAV directly tied to their assets that is calculated on a daily basis, closed-end funds often trade at a discount or premium to their actual NAV. This usually depends on how well or poorly the assets of the fund are being managed.

An **exchange-traded fund (ETF)** is a basket of securities that is traded in exchanges and usually passively managed, like an index fund. ETFs can be made up of all of the stocks in an index, bonds, commodities, or currencies. ETFs typically trade at their NAV. ETFs have grown in popularity due to their low-cost structure relative to mutual funds, which are managed against an index. ETFs are usually offered through broker dealers, who distribute shares through creation units, but some ETFs are available through mutual-fund companies or can even be purchased online. ETFs are liquid investments.

Just like open-end funds, closed-end funds can be small cap or large cap, and they can be growth or value oriented. They can focus on a certain sector, or they can be managed to beat an index like the S&P 500 or the New York Stock Exchange. Closed-end funds themselves do not pay taxes. Their taxation is the responsibility of the investor and shareholder. To maintain their tax-free status, closed-end funds must pass on to investors 90% of their income from dividends and interest payments. They also must pass on at least 98% of capitalized gains. Distributions must be linked back to their initial source.

All funds are required to provide a prospectus that provides complete disclosure on issues related to the fund.

Unit investment trusts (UITs) are different from traditional funds, closed-end funds, and exchange-traded funds. They are fixed portfolios that are established for a specific duration of time. UITs are redeemable securities that the issuer will buy back at the NAV. Shares are issued with an IPO. UITs can be made up of bonds or stocks or both. Investors can make a decision based on the UIT's strategy, the sectors it invests in, its credit quality, or its weighted duration (if rates rise, a UIT with a shorter duration will perform better than one with a long duration). UITs can be redeemed by having the originator repurchase the shares, assuming the issuer has enough cash and is liquid enough to purchase shares of the UIT.

UITs invest across all asset classes. Some trusts specifically employ a buy-and-hold strategy and have a stated termination date on which the fund will sell all holdings and pay out to all shareholders. Strategy

This material is provided for exam preparation purposes only and does not indicate an endorsement of any specific scientific, political, or religious point of view. © TPB Publishing. You have been licensed one copy of this document for personal use only. Any other reproduction or redistribution is strictly prohibited. All rights reserved.

trusts have a specific strategy, typically long or contrarian, based on the historical data the fund uses to select securities and on their outlook. Sector trusts invest in companies in one specific industry that are typically newer, less established companies.

A UIT's expenses and costs are listed in its prospectus. Fees include annual operating expenses, creation and inception fees, deferred sales charges, and initial sales charges. There are also administration fees. The initial sales charge is paid upon the purchase of the UIT. The deferred sales charge is paid monthly. The creation fee is paid from trust assets and covers the costs of developing a strategy, marketing the trust, and purchasing the securities.

Sales charges are made up of three components: the initial sales charge, the deferred sales charge, and the creation and development fee. The initial sales charge is usually a percentage of the dollar amount of the investment, 1.0% in most cases. The deferred sales charges are deducted in increments on a quarterly or monthly basis during the offering period. Finally, the creation and development fee are costs allocated to establish and build the fund. The UIT needs to create an objective, develop a strategy, pay marketing fees, pay administrative fees, pay salaries, and pay broker and trading fees to start the trust. These fees are charged at the end of the offering period.

Unit holders are subject to taxation on dividends, interest, and capital gains. UITs can be found in IRAs and receive the same tax benefits, so taxes on distributions are deferred until distributions are taken from the account. When shares are traded, the investor is responsible for reporting any gain or loss with their annual tax filing.

Variable life insurance is a permanent life insurance with the added characteristic of reflecting the performance of a subinvestment. While this feature allows the policyholder the opportunity for higher returns, it also carries a greater risk, which is assumed by the policyholder. Variable life insurance does provide a minimum death benefit and maintains a fixed premium. Additionally, the policyholder can realize a greater death benefit when earnings on the subinvestment are performing well.

Variable life-insurance policies can also have unique modifications to a policy, such as an accidental death benefit or a cost-of-living protection. These examples of modifications are called "riders." **Riders** are modifications to a policy presented as an attachment to the actual policy.

While life insurance covers the death of the insured, their loss of income, contributions to the family, and perhaps even death, it does not offer a provision for usage during life. This is where annuities have responded to the need for additional income while living.

Annuities are contracts most often issued by life-insurance companies. They continue to provide an income as long as the annuity owner is alive. Annuities make either a fixed payment, like a coupon payment on a corporate or Treasury bond, or variable payments, based on the performance of an index of basket of securities. Because their payment is based on an index, a variable annuity is a riskier investment than a fixed annuity. An annuity with a minimum guarantee means payments are guaranteed for a specified number of years regardless of when the annuity holder passes away. Payments with minimum guarantees are typically smaller than with a regular annuity because they are less risky. If the annuity holder dies before the guarantee expires, the payments are made to an estate or beneficiary.

This material is provided for exam preparation purposes only and does not indicate an endorsement of any specific scientific, political, or religious point of view. © TPB Publishing. You have been licensed one copy of this document for personal use only. Any other reproduction or redistribution is strictly prohibited. All rights reserved.

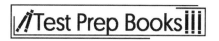

Annuity riders are options added to a typical annuity agreement. A cost-of-living-adjustment rider assures annuity payments will rise along with an inflation index. Lump-sum riders assure the full principal is paid if it has not been paid over the life of the annuity.

Mutual-Fund Characteristics

Mutual funds vary in their characteristics. Open-end funds report a **net asset value (NAV).** This is the total value of assets owned by the company less its liabilities. It is often reported on a per share basis to communicate to investors how much their investment has changed in value. This is the value at which the shares for open-end funds are bought and sold. Close-end funds are quite different. Their value is determined by supply and demand, combined with investor's expectations and the value of the counterpart investments in the portfolio.

Cost is another varying characteristic of mutual funds. Before investing in a mutual fund, the cost of the fund should be compared with other investments to ensure the financial benefits are greater than the required costs. In terms of cost, mutual funds are usually classified into two categories: load funds and no-load funds. A **load fund** requires investors pay a commission fee for every purchase. Load charges, also known as front-end charges, can quickly reduce gains. The average load charge is usually between 3% and 5% but can be greater than 8%. This cost supports the fund's sales team.

Here is an example of a load charge:

An investor decides to invest $100,000. The fund charges a sales load of 4.25%. The amount of the sales load is:

$$\$100,000 \times 0.0425 = \$4,250$$

The sales load is subtracted from the initial investment of $100,000. Therefore, the available investment is actually $95,750.

Unlike a load fund, no-load funds do not charge any commissions. No-load funds do not have a sales force. Therefore, investors choosing this option will purchase shares directly from the investment company. Load and no-load funds offer the same investment opportunities and the same potential for equivalent returns.

As an alternative to the basic load or no-load funds, some mutual funds charge a contingent deferred sales load, also known as a back-end fee. This charge is deferred until a withdrawal is made from the fund. This deferred fee can range from 1% to 5%.

Here is an example of a contingent deferred sales load:

An investor decides to withdraw $10,000. The contingent deferred sales load charge is 4%. This fee is deducted from the withdrawal. The amount of the fee is $10,000 \times .04 = \$400$. Thus, the amount the investor will receive is $10,000 - \$400 = \$9,600$.

Funds also vary in the way they distribute capital gains. Most funds simply reinvest dividends in the same fund by purchasing more shares. Some simply distribute payments to shareholders to reinvest on their own. Funds also vary in their fee structures. Some funds charge up-front fees, and some have redemption fees when investors want to leave a fund. Most funds charge a management fee on a quarterly basis. The management fee is usually a percentage based on the fund's asset value, typically not more than 1.5%.

This material is provided for exam preparation purposes only and does not indicate an endorsement of any specific scientific, political, or religious point of view. © TPB Publishing. You have been licensed one copy of this document for personal use only. Any other reproduction or redistribution is strictly prohibited. All rights reserved.

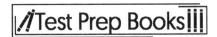

Additional fees may include a distribution fee, also known as a **12b-1 fee**. It is an ongoing annual fee that is capped by the SEC at 1% of the assets' value. Investors should be sure to evaluate the net return of their investment to ensure fees being charged are commensurate with a fund's performance.

Mutual-Fund Sales Practices

There are certain practices for selling securities and shares of mutual funds. In selling mutual funds to investors, there are several sales techniques that can be employed; such as dollar-cost averaging, computing the sales charge, or breakpoints.

A systematic investment technique is achieved through dollar-cost averaging. With this technique, investors systematically purchase a set or fixed amount of a specified investment. This technique does not make adjustments for varying share prices. Rather, it incorporates the anticipated fluctuations and pursues returns based on the average of the share prices with consistent purchases over time.

Computing the sales charge is another sales technique. In this technique, a percentage of the public offering price (POP) is computed. The calculation for the sales charge is determined by subtracting the net asset value from the POP and dividing the determined difference by the POP.

For example: Assume a mutual fund has a POP of 25.08 and a net asset value of 23.06.

$$Sales\ charge = \frac{Public\ offering\ price - net\ asset\ value}{Public\ offering\ price}$$

$$Sales\ charge = \frac{25.08 - 23.06}{25.08}$$

$$Sales\ charge = \frac{2.02}{25.08} = 0.081\ or\ 8.1\%$$

In this example, the sales charge for the assumed mutual fund would be 8.1%.

In addition to dollar-cost averaging and computing the sales charge, breakpoints can be utilized to attract large investors. Breakpoints are discounts granted on the up-front fees on funds when investors purchase a certain dollar amount or amount of shares of a fund. The discount usually applies to Class A shares of a fund but, via a Letter of Intent or through **Rights of Accumulation (ROA)**, an investor can receive the same discount. Rights of Accumulation basically allows an investor to aggregate shares (401k funds, pensions, related party shares) to receive the discount.

Late trading is the illegal selling of shares after the NAV has been calculated for shares of a fund. When there is bad news about securities in the fund, this practice gives the late trader the opportunity to dump shares before the market has moved, and the value is reflected by the NAV.

Investment Fees

Investors need to account for fees, commissions, and costs when calculating the return on their investment. Investors should focus on the net return when evaluating the potential profitability of a trade. The breakeven rate is the rate at which the investor receives a return of capital plus enough of a profit to recoup only transaction fees. The term applies to regular stock and bond trades, and also to options transactions for which a premium is paid that must be accounted for when calculating a breakeven rate.

This material is provided for exam preparation purposes only and does not indicate an endorsement of any specific scientific, political, or religious point of view. © TPB Publishing. You have been licensed one copy of this document for personal use only. Any other reproduction or redistribution is strictly prohibited. All rights reserved.

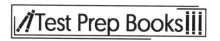

Rights of accumulation can be used to keep costs down and lower the breakeven rate for mutual fund investors. This simply assures that funds account for all of an investor's transactions in the aggregate, when processing transaction discounts that require a minimum transaction size.

A Letter of Intent outlines the agreement of two parties who are entering into a transaction before it becomes finalized. This letter is required for mergers and acquisitions, joint ventures, private equity partnerships, and real estate lease agreements. They are typically not binding agreements.

The markup represents the difference between the lowest current offering price for an investment and the higher price that a dealer will actually charge an investor. Markups occur when dealers trade with firm capital, not customer accounts. Dealers earn their compensation this way, rather than in the form of a fee. The dealer is assuming significant risk in this type of transaction because the price of the security may go up or down while the dealer has the security in inventory.

Commissions are the fees paid by investors to their broker each time they buy or sell securities. Commissions are commensurate with the dollar amount of the size of each trade. Some brokers use fee-based structures where investors simply pay a quarterly fee. This reduces the incentive for brokers to churn their client's accounts.

Some mutual funds include a sales charge, or a **load**, which is a commission fee for the service of the broker or adviser selling the fund to an investor. There are firms that offer no-load funds, which are essentially mutual funds without a sales charge. Loads can be front-end (paid when you buy), back-end (paid when you sell, also called "deferred"), or level (known as 12b-1 fees).

A net transaction occurs when a broker receives a customer order and executes the trade with another broker. This must occur with the customer's consent for complete transparency and to ensure the customer receives the best execution and pricing.

Most mutual funds offer a range of share classes, as well as individual issuers of shares of stock. Different share class holders have different rights. For individual shares of stock, this typically means common shares that have voting rights versus preferred shareholders who do not have voting rights. Mutual funds usually list share types alphabetically, A, B, C, D, or I (for institutional).

A non-discretionary fee-based account is an account where the investor still has total control and directs the broker as to what accounts they can trade. The broker does not earn commission but receives a quarterly fee, based on the account's value.

A surrender fee is the fee that the holder of an insurance policy must pay upon cancellation of the policy.

Municipal Fund Securities

Municipal fund securities are similar to mutual funds and could be classified as investment companies if not for section 2(b) of the Investment Company Act of 1940 which excludes securities issued by government entities. Examples of municipal fund securities include 529 savings plans, local government investment pools (LGIPs), and ABLE accounts.

529 Plans
The **529 savings plan** is probably the most well-known savings plan. These plans provide tax advantages and can be used to match financial aid and education grants. 529 plans can be either prepaid or savings

This material is provided for exam preparation purposes only and does not indicate an endorsement of any specific scientific, political, or religious point of view. © TPB Publishing. You have been licensed one copy of this document for personal use only. Any other reproduction or redistribution is strictly prohibited. All rights reserved.

plans. A benefit of the prepaid plan is that it shields the investor from the effects of inflation, but it does have stricter requirements on what it covers. These plans can be either **direct-sold** from the state itself or **adviser-sold** by investment advisers. Savings plans succeed based on how the market and the underlying securities in the plan perform. They are similar to IRAs, and contributions to the plans can't exceed the actual cost of the education they fund.

These plans offer the flexibility to change the asset allocation, usually based on the risk the beneficiary can take given their age. Withdrawals can be made with the payment of a tax penalty. A 529 plan cannot be used to pay a student loan. Plans can be transferred and rolled over into another family member's plan. In 2011, computers became qualified expenses under 529 plans. 529 plans offer tax deductions at the state (but not federal) level. The donor maintains complete control, not the beneficiary, and can even make withdrawals from the fund. 529 assets can be reclaimed by the donor if not used in their entirety. While planning for college education, it is important to consider the potential impacts of anticipating the 529 plan to complement financial aid, as the funds in a 529 plan may reduce the eligibility for financial aid and potential tax credits. Per the Tax Cuts and Jobs Act, 529 plans can now be used to pay up to $10,000 a year towards K-12 tuition expenses.

Local Government Investment Pools (LGIPs)

A **local government investment pool (LGIP)** is a pool of government owned funds invested to provide a rate of return just like any other investment. While a LGIP may consist of the funds of one governmental entity, sometimes several governments will combine their investment funds into one investment pool. For example, City A, which doesn't have much investment capital, might seek to combine their fund with Cities B, C, D, E, and so on, such that collectively, the amount of their investment funds can provide the benefits that usually accompany larger amounts of investment funds. Some of the most common benefits include sharing in reduced expenses for investment values above a certain amount, the ability to attract a competent money manager, and the ability to invest in more than one investment in cases where minimum investment amounts are not available for a single government entity.

ABLE Accounts

ABLE accounts are accounts specifically designed for individuals with a qualifying disability. The underlying rationale for ABLE accounts is supported by public policy that people with certain disabilities should have assistance in living not provided by ordinary investment and savings accounts. Like other accounts with a designated purpose, ABLE accounts are characterized by special ownership, contribution and withdrawal, and tax treatment. In an ABLE account, the beneficiary can be the owner (the disabled individual). Contributions can be made to the account by anyone with after-tax dollars (similar to a Roth IRA) but are limited to $15,000 annually. Each ABLE account owner may own only one ABLE account. Distributions to the owner of the ABLE account will not be taxed so long as the proceeds from the distribution are used for expenses commonly associated with living with a disability. Common examples include specialized housing, transportation, education, and support needed to live life with a disability.

Direct Participation Programs

A direct participation program enables an investor to participate in a business venture's cash flow and taxation benefits.

These vehicles primarily invest in real estate, energy, futures and options, and equipment leasing. They are structured as limited partnerships or limited liability companies that allow profits to flow through to the investor on a pretax basis. There are no taxes at the corporate level with this type of investment.

This material is provided for exam preparation purposes only and does not indicate an endorsement of any specific scientific, political, or religious point of view. © TPB Publishing. You have been licensed one copy of this document for personal use only. Any other reproduction or redistribution is strictly prohibited. All rights reserved.

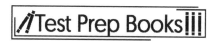

DPPs are usually not publicly traded instruments, so their value is not market driven and simply derived from the profits and cash flow they produce. Limited partnerships mean the partners have limited liability and no management authority. This means they are not responsible for any debts and have no liability if any legal action is taken against the company. The limited partners have a defined return they will receive outlined in the prospectus or partnership agreement.

DPPs issue investment opportunities in "units" as opposed to the "shares" that many stock market investors are accustomed to seeing.

DPPs are usually organized as S Corporations (referring to their status as described in Chapter S of the Internal Revenue Code) or limited partnerships. Units are sold to investors and the profit and losses from the DPP investment passes through to the investors from the DPP entity level. So, each year, the investor is allocated their share of the gains and losses from the DPP investment. The investor then reports those gains or losses on their individual tax returns.

Units of DPPs are not listed on a stock exchange for trading like stocks. Because the units are not listed, this creates a situation where DPP investors do not have an easy way to liquidate their investment if they decide that the DPP is no longer a good investment. This can cause serious problems for investors who want their investment capital returned.

While a DPP investor can seek a buyer for their units, the process of finding a buyer for the units can be exhaustive and in conflict with the investor's original goal of making an investment without expending an unreasonable amount of time. As such, DPPs are generally not considered a liquid investment, or an investment that can be converted to cash or cash equivalents without substantial effort.

Types of DPPS

There are risks that come with DPP investments. They rely upon the general manager to manage the investment, and these investments often consist of blind pools. This can potentially be compromising, as the investor may not have the transparency to evaluate the risks of the investment directly. DPPs are thinly traded, so there is significant liquidity risk. Real estate DPPs invest in raw land, the construction of new buildings (usually commercial properties), existing properties, and low-income and government-assisted housing. Land investments are mostly speculative investments to be sold at a later time. The land is not developed or rented, so it is a non-income-producing investment. These are highly risky investments as property values can go up or down, and there is no real strategy that can be changed to improve profitability.

Limited partnerships in real estate can be facilitated by products like non-traded REITs and tenants in common (TIC) partnerships. Tenancy in common is when two or more people share ownership of property. Each owner can choose to leave their share to a beneficiary of their choosing.

Some DPPs buy existing properties, lease, and manage them much the same as a real estate investment trust would, but they are more likely to invest in more risky properties that don't have significant tenants or produce income yet. One of the more conservative DPP investments is in low-income properties. DPPs that invest in these properties are income-producing investments (through the rent their tenants pay), the investors receive tax credits that other DPPs are not eligible for, and they are backed by the US government. Equipment DPPs purchase equipment and lease it out to other companies. These DPPs have good cash flow and have the advantage of being able to write off the depreciation of the equipment they own.

This material is provided for exam preparation purposes only and does not indicate an endorsement of any specific scientific, political, or religious point of view. © TPB Publishing. You have been licensed one copy of this document for personal use only. Any other reproduction or redistribution is strictly prohibited. All rights reserved.

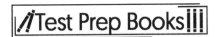

There are four types of oil and gas DPPs: exploratory, developmental, income, and combination. Exploratory DPPs fund the search of unproven oil reserves. These are risky investments, as there is potential that only small reserves will be found, or even none at all, which can result in the complete loss of investment. They do have the potential for significant returns if productive wells of oil and gas are found. Developmental DPPs drill close to where wells are known to have produced. Income-producing DPPs purchase wells that are developed and producing. Combination DPPs are diverse in that they invest in both producing and nonproducing wells.

DPPs require potential limited partners to complete a subscription agreement. The general partner uses the criteria from this form to determine whether or not an investor is suitable to become a limited partner. The agreement is similar to what an investment advisor needs to consider when evaluating an investor's willingness and ability to take risk, so they can select the right investment for them. The agreement will include their net worth, income, a clear explanation of the risks of the partnership, and a power of attorney agreement that allows the general partner to make all investment decisions.

The more common DPPs include nontraded REITs, equipment leases, and energy companies. Like more traditional investments, due diligence and analysis should be completed by the potential investor. The investor needs to consider overall market conditions and whether or not there is a market for what the DPP will be investing in (DPPs often invest in new industries or niche markets). Financial statements (if available) should be analyzed, as well as where potential revenue growth will come from. Experience of the general partner should be considered as well.

Real Estate Investment Trusts (REITs)

Real estate investment trusts (REITs) are companies that own, manage, or finance income-producing (usually commercial) real estate.

REITs typically go through several rounds of financing as they purchase properties. Most REITs obtain some form of seed capital through initial investors, then issue shares through an IPO, and then obtain revolving lines of credit of bank loans to finance their operations. Shares are initially issued and typically cannot be traded until a specific time. Some REITs have a dividend reinvestment program (DRIP) that allows existing investors to purchase more shares at a discount, whereas new investors will be required to pay full price for shares. Shares of new REITs are often traded over the counter until they become available on exchanges.

This material is provided for exam preparation purposes only and does not indicate an endorsement of any specific scientific, political, or religious point of view. © TPB Publishing. You have been licensed one copy of this document for personal use only. Any other reproduction or redistribution is strictly prohibited. All rights reserved.

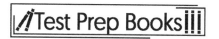

Some REITs calculate an NAV, which is normally calculated by valuing all of the properties or equity a REIT has in its portfolio—though some NAVs are calculated using the cash flow that comes from their properties. The NAV does not always equal the price of a REIT. If the price is higher than the NAV, it may reflect the investor's anticipation that management will create value as they acquire properties and improve cash flow and profitability. In other words, $100 million in property represented by 10 million outstanding shares may have an NAV of $10 per share ($100 million $\div$ $10 million = $10), but investors may be willing to pay $13 per share if they feel the managers of the REIT can enhance the property's value through better management. The image below is a basic depiction as to how investors buy shares. Capital is used to buy properties, income is generated, and then profits are distributed to investors as dividends.

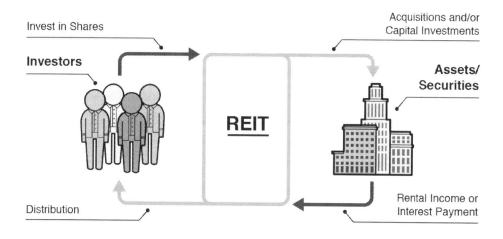

Real Estate Investment Trust (REIT) Types

REITs can be both public and private. Publicly traded REITs that are listed and traded on a securities exchange are known as listed REITs. Like other exchange listed securities, listed REITs provide much more liquidity because they can be bought and sold daily at the exchange. REITs can also be considered public REITs, but not be traded on an exchange.

Because public, nontraded REITs are not readily marketable on an exchange, an investor holding a public, nontraded REIT might have a more difficult time exiting their holding because there is no immediate secondary market. However, both publicly traded listed REITs and public, nonlisted REITs are required to by registered with the Securities and Exchange Commission.

On the other hand, private REITs are REITs that do not have to be registered with the Securities and Exchange Commission and are not listed on a securities exchange. Because private REITs are not listed on a securities exchange, investors must be aware of the additional liquidity risk that private REITs carry.

REITs can vary by industry and strategy. Some are focused on one property type, such as office properties, hospitals, condominiums, or hotels. They can also be diversified. An equity REIT is a company that actually owns a property. These REITs also manage the property and find tenants. After expenses and management fees, the REIT pays out profits in the form of dividends to investors; to qualify as a REIT, they are required to pay out 90% of their income. Equity REITs also turn a profit by selling properties they own after they have appreciated.

This material is provided for exam preparation purposes only and does not indicate an endorsement of any specific scientific, political, or religious point of view. © TPB Publishing. You have been licensed one copy of this document for personal use only. Any other reproduction or redistribution is strictly prohibited. All rights reserved.

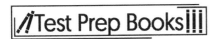

Mortgage REITs invest in mortgage-backed securities, as well as commercial mortgage-backed securities, the financing behind properties. They are also required to distribute 90% of their income to qualify as a REIT. A hybrid REIT owns both actual properties and mortgage debt. REITs are often considered an alternative to investing in bonds because they consistently pay out income, as opposed to some stocks that pay no dividends. They also have appreciation potential, which fixed-income securities do not.

REITs are often good investments due to their tax treatment. REITs follow the same taxation rules as UITs. This means REITs are taxed at the corporate level first, and then the investor is taxed by the IRS. REIT rental income is tax deductible, as this is a REIT's main income stream. All expenses related to rental income are tax deductible. Income that is currently earned is not taxed to the REIT under most circumstances. Basically, REITs are tax exempt as long as they pay out 90% of their income but taxed on any income retained on their balance sheet. The investor is taxed at the ordinary rate on received dividends. REITs may pay qualified dividends, which are taxed at the long-term capital-gains rate.

Hedge Funds

The Investment Company Act of 1940 applies to companies that invest or trade in securities, as well as those that issue securities. The act seeks to protect the public interest in investing by eliminating conflicts of interest.

There are thousands of hedge funds in the investment universe. As such, there are many different types of requirements that an investor may discover when investigating whether or not to invest with a particular hedge fund. First, an investor may notice a substantially higher minimum investment required to invest in a hedge fund. Hedge funds require a higher minimum investment because they usually have much fewer investors than a mutual fund. Having fewer investors makes it easier for the hedge fund to stay within the parameters required to avoid registration with the Securities and Exchange Commission.

Hedge funds can become exempt from the act under Sections 3c1 and 3c7. Under 3c1 the fund can't be owned by more than one hundred beneficial shareholders. Under 3c7 the fund must be owned by qualified purchasers, usually investors with high net worth and high incomes, and less than five hundred investors. Privately-placed funds require a private placement memorandum. A "blank check" hedge fund is a fund that has no stated objective or investments yet. These funds invest in highly speculative investments in their seed-capital stage.

Hedge funds usually pay the manager a fixed annual percentage, around 1% to 2%, and then a performance-based fee, which is sometimes as much as 20% of the return on the assets managed by the fund. Institutions typically hold anywhere from 1% to 2% in hedge funds or some form of alternative investment. In 2013, hedge fund assets were estimated to be valued at $2.1 trillion collectively. Some hedge funds fall under the regulation of the US Commodity Futures Trading Commission. The Volcker Rule, which limits speculative investment made by banks, encompasses hedge funds (many large investment banks fund hedge funds).

Some hedge funds have lock-up periods. This means investors can't withdraw their initial investment for a specified period of time. Funds that invest in more-liquid assets like stocks and bonds will have shorter lock-up periods. After the lock-up period, investors still must follow a set redemption schedule. Hedge funds can vary in the strategies they employ. Where most regular mutual funds are long only, hedge funds can employ a long-short strategy where they can profit off of the value of companies going down using derivatives and options for selling shares short. A market-neutral fund will minimize its exposure to the stock market, a strategy that will be profitable when the market experiences downturns. Some

This material is provided for exam preparation purposes only and does not indicate an endorsement of any specific scientific, political, or religious point of view. © TPB Publishing. You have been licensed one copy of this document for personal use only. Any other reproduction or redistribution is strictly prohibited. All rights reserved.

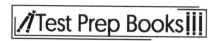

funds attempt to profit off of larger global events like changes in currency values. Arbitrage funds attempt to profit off of the mispricing of securities. Distressed funds invest in the debt of companies that are on the verge of bankruptcy and buy their bonds at large discounts.

Like hedge funds, private equity investments can have higher initial minimum investment requirements and will likely be illiquid. Private equity investments are usually long-term investments in a privately-held company where the group purchasing the equity has long-term plans for investment or for improving the company so that it can eventually be involved in a public offering. Because those timeframes are uncertain and dependent on market conditions, private equity investments are generally reserved for investors with significant capital to invest over the long term.

Because the fund manager is compensated from the profits earned on the fund due to hedge fund structure, the fund manager is taxed as return on investment as opposed to at the ordinary income-tax rate. Partners in the fund are taxed as they earn the income, rather than when they actually receive profits (so the taxes are effectively deferred). Hedge funds are taxed at the long-term capital gains rate of 20% due to the longer investment horizon. There is controversy over whether or not this is a sufficient rate, as it is basically half of the marginal income-tax rate, and most fund managers make the majority of their money from the long-term gains of their funds.

Exchange-traded Products (ETPs)

Exchange-traded Funds (ETFs)

Exchange-traded funds (ETFs) are shares of mutual funds that trade on exchanges, like actual shares of stock. These typically trade in 50,000 share blocks. The advantages of ETFs over mutual funds are that they can be traded at any time during the trading day, bought on margin, sold short, and they have low expense ratios.

ETF shareholders receive a percent of profits that come from dividends and interest. They will receive the residual value of the securities owned by the fund if a fund is liquidated. Shares of ETFs are highly liquid and easily traded in a similar way to equities. Some ETFs utilize gearing or leverage through the use of derivative securities. There are also inverse ETFs, so investors can profit from a basket of stocks in that ETF going down. ETFs provide diversification to investors, and their expense ratios are usually lower than a mutual fund. The SEC defines an ETF as a company that:

- Issues shares in exchange for the deposit of basket assets

- Identifies itself as an ETF in any sales literature

- Issues shares that are approved for listing on an exchange

- Discloses its daily net asset value publicly, as well as any premium or discount from the actual basket of underlying securities

- Is an index fund

Some ETFs use derivatives to enhance the return on the index they are modeled after or to protect their value when the market declines. ETFs can consist of large cap, small cap, growth, or value companies. They can replicate entire indices of just one sector of the market—i.e., energy, industrials, consumer staples, or technology. Some ETFs are actively managed, but this means the manager must disclose all holdings to investors. Inverse ETFs are designed to produce the inverse of an index. For example, the ETF

65

This material is provided for exam preparation purposes only and does not indicate an endorsement of any specific scientific, political, or religious point of view. © TPB Publishing. You have been licensed one copy of this document for personal use only. Any other reproduction or redistribution is strictly prohibited. All rights reserved.

may be the inverse of the S&P 500, so when the S&P returns 5%, the ETF should see a decline of 5% in value. Basically, this is a product investors can use as a hedge if they anticipate a market downturn. ETFs are also permitted in Roth IRA accounts where short selling is not permitted, so investors who anticipate a bear market might invest in an inverse ETF.

ETFs are also tax-efficient vehicles with low transaction costs. Shareholders receive an annual report, similar to that provided to shareholders by management of individual companies at the year's end. When there is strong demand for an ETF, such as if it is a new and successful product or a stable bond fund during an equity market downturn, the share price may rise above the actual NAV. This creates a small arbitrage opportunity some larger investors try to take advantage of, usually by selling ETF shares short and buying the underlying securities until the prices align, and the NAV accurately reflects the value of the underlying securities.

Exchange-traded Notes (ETNs)

Exchange-traded notes (ETNs) are notes of indebtedness that are traded on a securities exchange like stocks and exchange-traded funds (ETFs). ETNs have some similarities to investing in pure debt securities, but there are some major differences that investors must be aware of before making an investment decision. Generally, ETNs are unsecured, unsubordinated notes issued by a bank.

Unlike a typical debt instrument that issues coupon payments and returns the principal amount of the debt instrument at maturity, ETNs simply return an amount that tracks an underlying index. ETN investors do not ever actually own the assets underlying the benchmark. Instead, investors receive the value of the index at the time of maturity.

ETNs can be traded throughout the day on a securities exchange and are generally more liquid than most debt instruments. However, because ETN investors do not receive coupon payments during the life of the ETN, they must wait longer for a return of their capital unless they choose to sell the note on the open market on a securities exchange. Although ETN investors do not actually own any assets underlying the note, they do face a risk particular to ETNs. If the bank that issues the ETN should fail, then investors holding the ETN would be forced to participate in the bankruptcy liquidation protocol. In other words, ETN investors are subject to the credit risk of the bank issuing the ETN.

Investment Risks

Risk Types

It is important to understand the types of risks associated with investments. **Call risk** is the risk that an investment can be called away. The term mostly applies to callable bonds, but applies to call options as well. When an investor buys a callable bond, they are typically compensated with a higher yield than that of a comparable bond. If interest rates fall, the issuer may call the bond, forcing the investor to invest in a bond at a lower rate than that for the comparable non-callable bond.

Capital risk is the risk that the investor may lose all or part of their initial investment. Equity investors need to understand that there is the potential for the price of their shares to go to zero, should the company be unprofitable or go bankrupt. Bonds have capital risk as well, particularly high yield bonds. Treasury bonds are assumed to have no capital risk, as they are fully backed by the government.

Credit risk is the risk that the borrower won't be able to make payments on their debt. Ratings agencies evaluate this type of risk. A company with sufficient earnings and cash in their balance sheet will have

This material is provided for exam preparation purposes only and does not indicate an endorsement of any specific scientific, political, or religious point of view. © TPB Publishing. You have been licensed one copy of this document for personal use only. Any other reproduction or redistribution is strictly prohibited. All rights reserved.

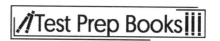

less credit risk because they have the funds to service their debt. A start-up company or a company that is unable to generate cash flow has a higher probability of not being able to make interest payments or even return the original principal invested.

Currency risk is the risk of an investment declining in value due to fluctuations in the value of a currency. An investor in the United States may invest in shares of a company that is traded in Euros. If, over the course of the year, the shares increase in value by 10% but the value of the Euro relative to the U.S. Dollar declines by 5%, when those shares are sold and converted back to dollars, the return will be reduced to 5%. This is the risk investors incur when investing internationally.

Inflationary risk is similar to currency risk in that it erodes the value of an investment. If investors choose to hold cash, the value of their cash will be eroded by the amount of inflation. Therefore, if an investor holds $1,000 in cash over a year and inflation is 4%, the value of the cash becomes $960 in inflation-adjusted dollars. Essentially, this means that the original $1,000 value of cash can only buy $960 worth of goods when adjusted for inflation. Bond investors are particularly concerned with inflation risk, as bonds pay a fixed interest rate and do not usually have the potential to appreciate in value. Bond prices can rise, but investors will still only receive the principal invested when the bond matures.

Interest rate risk is the risk that an asset's value—usually a bond or some other type of fixed income security—will decline with an increase in interest rates. The longer the maturity, the greater the interest rate risk because there is more time for interest rates to rise and fall over the life of the investment. Interest rate risk is measured on bonds by calculating the security's duration. This is a measure of the relationship between the amount that an investment's interest rate change will fluctuate and the value of that security.

Liquidity risk is the risk that an asset will not be able to be sold quickly enough, so that the time it takes to execute a sale affects the value of the security. Liquidity risk is minimal for securities that trade on larger and more established exchanges. Thinly-traded securities and assets like real estate have liquidity risk. Liquidity risk is measured by the bid ask spread on a security.

Market risk or **systematic risk** is the risk that various factors that affect the financial market as a whole will impact an investment's value. It is the risk that can't be avoided with diversification and is measured by Beta—the correlation between a security's value and that of the overall market. For example, recession, interest rate spikes, financial crisis and other global events often affect entire financial markets rather than just parts of it.

Non-systematic risk is risk that can be alleviated by having a diversified portfolio. This type of risk, also called specific risk, affects a specific industry or company. Individual companies can face lawsuits, they can develop new products that are unsuccessful, or a company's service may become obsolete due to newer technologies.

Political risk is the risk that decisions made by politicians or government will affect the way business can be conducted. This includes environmental regulations, FDA approval, and decisions made by financial regulators. Political risk also occurs when international countries become unstable and affect a country's financial markets.

Prepayment risk is the risk most often associated with mortgage-backed securities but is applicable to other asset classes. Prepayment risk is the risk that the borrower will repay the loan before it is

This material is provided for exam preparation purposes only and does not indicate an endorsement of any specific scientific, political, or religious point of view. © TPB Publishing. You have been licensed one copy of this document for personal use only. Any other reproduction or redistribution is strictly prohibited. All rights reserved.

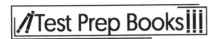

anticipated to be repaid. This usually occurs when interest rates fall, and the borrower can receive more favorable terms on a new loan. The issuer will not receive the interest payments they would have, had the prepayment not occurred and will, in all likelihood, have to make new loans with that capital at a lower interest rate.

Reinvestment risk is the risk that capital will be reinvested at the lower interest rate. Reinvestment risk comes with call risk as well. If an investor owns a callable bond and it is called, the investor will likely have to invest in a riskier security to receive the same interest rate.

Timing risk is the risk incurred when an investor attempts to buy and sell securities at the most profitable point. Any market participant who invests incurs some form of timing risk. Investors who move into cash risk missing out on any upward movement in the market. Investors who don't want to sell securities incur the risk that the market may move down, causing their portfolio decline, whereas if they had moved into cash, their portfolio would not have lost value.

Mitigating Risk

Investing in financial markets can have huge rewards over the long term, but the long term also carries significant risks that investors must incorporate into their investment decisions. The most important action an investor can take to mitigate risk in financial markets is to spread out the risk of any individual investment by not putting all of their eggs in one basket. The technical term used for this process is **diversification**.

Businesses face risks every day. There are endless events that can cause a business and the securities tied to that business to decrease in value. Competition, regulation, politics, interest rates, changes in management, and the like can all have potential negative effects on the value of a security. The risks can be even broader, affecting entire industries. Investors must protect themselves from those risks.

To mitigate those potential risks, investors should invest in more than one company or one industry and in more than one asset class. For example, an investor should avoid investing solely in technology companies, health care companies, financial companies, retail companies, consumer staple companies, and the like. Investors should also invest in more than one asset class. The most notable asset classes are equities, fixed-income securities, real estate, and alternative investments.

An investor's choice of a mix of asset classes will depend on many factors including annual income, net worth, and their age. For example, a common diversification metric is for a portfolio to have seventy percent invested in equities and thirty percent in fixed-income securities like bonds. However, a wealthy, younger investor might invest in a more aggressive portfolio with eighty percent in equities and twenty percent in fixed-income securities. The reasoning supporting this sample allocation is that the younger investor has more time to make up any losses that might occur in a more aggressive portfolio.

On the other hand, an investor already in the retirement stage of the lifecycle might have eighty percent in fixed-income securities and only twenty percent in equities. The reasoning supporting this sample allocation is that the retired investor does not have as much time as the younger investor to make up any losses that might occur in a more aggressive portfolio.

Notwithstanding savvy financial planning, a portfolio can evolve and no longer represent an investor's desired mix of securities. Equity securities might rise or fall significantly due to market conditions. If equity prices rise substantially, an investor might find that the equity portion of their mix now represents more than the planned percentage.

This material is provided for exam preparation purposes only and does not indicate an endorsement of any specific scientific, political, or religious point of view. © TPB Publishing. You have been licensed one copy of this document for personal use only. Any other reproduction or redistribution is strictly prohibited. All rights reserved.

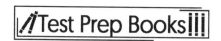

For example, assume an investor has a target portfolio allocation of seventy percent equities and thirty percent fixed-income securities in a portfolio worth $100,000 at the time of initial investment and planning. Suppose that the broader equities market doubles in value over ten years, and the fixed-income securities in the portfolio have the same value as their value at the time of initial investment. The new value of the portfolio would be $170,000, and $140,000 of that new value would be attributable to the equity portion of the portfolio, which would now represent just over eighty-two percent of the portfolio.

Because the investor's portfolio had a target portfolio allocation of seventy percent in equities, and it now has an actual allocation of eighty-two percent in equities, the investor needs to adjust the investor's equities exposure. To do so, the investor should sell twelve percent of the equities in the portfolio and invest the proceeds into fixed-income securities to reach the initial target portfolio allocation of seventy percent equities and thirty percent fixed-income securities. This process is referred to as **portfolio rebalancing**.

In addition to portfolio rebalancing, an investor experiencing a lopsided portfolio could hedge against the investor's position. There are many ways to hedge a portfolio, but some of the most basic hedging strategies involve the use of derivatives. When Wall Street professionals discuss derivatives, they are usually referring to futures and options contracts.

Futures contracts generally comprise financial futures contracts and commodities futures contracts. Financial futures contracts are traded on all three major indexes: the Dow Jones Industrial Average, the S&P 500, and the Nasdaq. Financial futures contracts can be used by investors in many ways. For example, if an investor has a large equity exposure in their portfolio, is worried that the market may be going down, but doesn't want to sell their equity positions (possibly to avoid incurring capital gains taxes), the investor might hedge their position by selling a financial futures contract on an index. By selling the contract, the investor will profit on the contract if the market goes down even though their equity portfolio will lose value. The profit on the contract serves to offset the losses on the investor's equity portfolio.

This material is provided for exam preparation purposes only and does not indicate an endorsement of any specific scientific, political, or religious point of view. © TPB Publishing. You have been licensed one copy of this document for personal use only. Any other reproduction or redistribution is strictly prohibited. All rights reserved.

Glossary

12b-1 Fee	Ongoing annual fee that is capped by the SEC at 1% of the assets' value
529 Savings Plan	Provide tax advantages and can be used to match financial aid and education grants; can be either prepaid or savings plans
ABLE Accounts	Accounts specifically designed for individuals with a qualifying disability; The underlying rationale for ABLE accounts is supported by public policy that people with certain disabilities should have assistance in living not provided by ordinary investment and savings accounts.
American Depositary Receipts (ADRs)	Securities that allow U.S citizens to purchase shares of foreign companies in the U.S market without having to make the purchase on a foreign stock exchange
Arbitrage	When investors try to take advantage of pricing discrepancies between convertible bonds and the underlying stock
Asset-Backed Security (ABS)	Securities are backed by the receivables a bank or servicer is owed on loans for everything from automobiles, credit cards, and mortgages to company inventory and student loans.
Assignment	After buyers have executed their options, sellers or options writers are obligated to fulfill their terms of the contract and deliver the agreed-upon terms.
Banker's Acceptance	Negotiable piece of paper that functions like a post-dated check, although the bank rather than an account holder guarantees the payment
Bond Indenture	A formal agreement between the bond issuer and the investor
Butterfly Spread	This is when an investor buys a call option at a certain strike price, writes two calls at a higher strike price, and buys a second call at an even higher strike price. This allows the investor to fund the two long positions with the premium earned from writing the two calls.
Buy To Open Contract	When an investor buys a call option on a stock or index
Call Risk	This is the risk that an investment can be called away.
Callable Bond (Redeemable Bond)	Can be redeemed by the bond issuer before its stated maturity (i.e., the corporation has the right to call the bond away from the investor). A bond is typically "called" when interest rates decline, and a company can find less expensive financing.
Callable Preferred Stock	These shares give the issuer the right to call the shares back at a specified price over a specified time (as stated in the prospectus for the shares).
Capital Risk	The risk that the investor may lose all or part of their initial investment
Certificates Of Deposit (CD)	These are bought in bulk by the brokerage firm and resold to its customers. These CDs typically pay a premium (usually 1%) as compared to CDs issued by traditional banks. They are tradeable instruments whereas regular CDs are not (which can result

This material is provided for exam preparation purposes only and does not indicate an endorsement of any specific scientific, political, or religious point of view. © TPB Publishing. You have been licensed one copy of this document for personal use only. Any other reproduction or redistribution is strictly prohibited. All rights reserved.

	in a loss to the investor), and they do not require an investor to pay a commission upon purchase.
Certificates Of Participation (COPs)	This is where investors purchase a share of lease revenues rather than securing them with the actual revenues. These bonds are dependent on the legislative appropriations process.
Collateralized Mortgage (Debt) Obligation (CMO or CDO)	Riskier, asset-backed securities that have many levels of tranches
Commercial Paper	Used by corporations, and sometimes municipalities, to fund operations on a short-term basis
Common Stock	Purchasing shares of common stock gives the purchaser a percentage of ownership in a company as well as specific "rights" (e.g., voting, preemptive rights, dividends).
Contract Size	The amount of the underlying asset attached to some options contracts
Convertible Bonds	These enable the bondholder to convert the bond into stock from the same company.
Convertible Preferred Stock	Grants the shareholder the right to convert their shares into a specific number of shares within a specified future time period
Convexity	This is the second derivative of the price-yield relationship and is a more accurate measure of the relationship for larger changes in interest rates.
Corporate Bonds	Debt securities issued by a corporation
Credit Risk	The risk that the borrower won't be able to make payments on their debt
Currency Risk	The risk of an investment declining in value due to fluctuations in the value of a currency
Cumulative Preferred Stock	Dividends accumulate until paid. Unpaid dividends are called "dividends in arrears".
Diagonal Spreads	Have varying expiration dates and strike prices.
Direct Participation Program (DPP)	Enables an investor to participate in a business venture's cash flow and taxation benefits; Examples are real estate, energy, futures/options, and equipment leasing.
Diversification	When an investor wants mitigate risk in financial markets by spreading out ownership of an individual investment to multiple investments
Dutch Auction	Where the price is lowered until it matches a bid; Municipal bonds and Treasury bonds are sold through this type of auction.

This material is provided for exam preparation purposes only and does not indicate an endorsement of any specific scientific, political, or religious point of view. © TPB Publishing. You have been licensed one copy of this document for personal use only. Any other reproduction or redistribution is strictly prohibited. All rights reserved.

Electronic Municipal Market Access (EMMA)	Their website contains updated information regarding the issuer and municipal bond, as well as credit ratings information.
Exchange-Traded Funds (ETFs)	Basket of securities that is traded in exchanges and usually passively managed, like an index fund or like actual shares of stock
Exchange-Traded Notes (ETNs)	Notes of indebtedness that are traded on a securities exchange like stocks and exchange-traded funds (ETFs)
Excise Tax	A tax on specific goods such as gasoline, tobacco, and alcohol
Federal National Mortgage Association (FNMA or Fannie Mae)	A government-sponsored enterprise (GSE) that was created to provide stability to the housing market and allow low- to mid-income families greater access to mortgages. Fannie Mae achieves this by purchasing qualified mortgages from lenders, and either holding them or selling them in groups of mortgage-backed securities (MBS). This frees up enough capital for lenders to issue more mortgages.
Federal Open Market Committee (FOMC)	Responsible for open market operations - the purchase and sale of securities in the open market by a central bank
General Obligation (GO) Bond	This is a municipal bond that is not backed by assets but by the credit and taxing ability of the issuing jurisdiction.
Government National Mortgage Association (GNMA or Ginnie Mae)	An entity that insures mortgage-backed securities (MBS) from approved lenders. Ginnie May provides security to investors by promising to pick up the payments and interest on an MBS if the issuer is not able to.
Government Sponsored Entities (GSEs)	These are private corporations that are granted government charters because their activities are deemed important to public policy.
Hedge Fund	Requires a higher minimum investment because it usually has fewer investors than a mutual fund.
Horizontal Spreads	Expirations vary, but the strike prices are all the same
Inflationary Risk	Similar to currency risk in that it erodes the value of an investment
Interest Rate Risk	This is the risk that an asset's value—usually a bond or some other type of fixed income security—will decline with an increase in interest rates.
In-The-Money (ITM)	Call options are in-the-money when the underlying asset's current price is higher than the agreed-upon price.
Limited Tax Bonds	These bonds are backed by the issuing entity but not by its full taxing power. Therefore, these bonds are riskier than bonds backed by the full taxing authority of a municipality.
Liquidity Risk	This is the risk that an asset will not be able to be sold quickly enough, so that the time it takes to execute a sale affects the value of the security.
Listed Option	Option that is sold on a registered exchange

This material is provided for exam preparation purposes only and does not indicate an endorsement of any specific scientific, political, or religious point of view. © TPB Publishing. You have been licensed one copy of this document for personal use only. Any other reproduction or redistribution is strictly prohibited. All rights reserved.

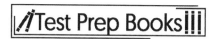
Load	Commission fee for the service of the broker or adviser selling the fund to an investor
Load Fund	Requires investors pay a commission fee for every purchase
Local Government Investment Pool (LGIP)	Pool of government owned funds invested to provide a rate of return just like any other investment
Long-Term Equity Anticipation Securities (LEAPS)	Options with expiration dates significantly further out than a typical option
Market Risk (Systematic Risk)	This is the risk that various factors that affect the financial market as a whole will impact an investment's value. It is the risk that can't be avoided with diversification and is measured by Beta—the correlation between a security's value and that of the overall market.
Money Market Funds	These funds are uninsured by FDIC and invested in short-term securities with average maturity of ≤ 90 days. All securities must have a maturity of less than 13 months.
Mortgage-Backed Securities (MBS)	A type of asset-backed security (ABS); MBSs are simply ABSs comprising mortgages that provide a rate of return based on the interest rate of the mortgages underlying the security. These are created when financial institutions that originate loans desire to take the risk of holding the loans off of the financial institution's books.
Municipal Bonds	These bonds are debt obligations issued by state or local governments. They are either general obligation (GO) or revenue bonds.
Municipal fund securities	These are similar to mutual funds. Examples of municipal fund securities include 529 savings plans, local government investment pools (LGIPs), and able accounts.
Negotiated Sale	The bonds are structured to meet the demands of both the investors and the issuer.
Net Asset Value (NAV)	The total value of assets owned by the company less its liabilities
Non-cumulative Preferred Stock	Unpaid dividends do not accumulate, so investors may not receive dividends, including in the event of liquidation.
Non-Systematic Risk	Risk that can be alleviated by having a diversified portfolio
Option Class	All options tied to a particular stock or index
Option Premium	Price that an investor is willing to pay for the opportunity to buy an asset at a specified price within a specified time period
Option Series	Subset of an option class that has the same strike price and expiration date
Options Disclosure Document (ODD)	A publication meant to provide guidance for options traders

This material is provided for exam preparation purposes only and does not indicate an endorsement of any specific scientific, political, or religious point of view. © TPB Publishing. You have been licensed one copy of this document for personal use only. Any other reproduction or redistribution is strictly prohibited. All rights reserved.

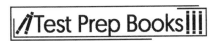
Out-Of-The-Money (OTM)	Call options are out-of-the-money when the underlying asset's current price is lower than the agreed-upon price.
Participating Preferred Stock	Used when special measures are needed to attract new investors. These shares receive dividends and give stockholders the right to receive additional dividends along with common stock shareholders. This is a common form of financing used by private equity and venture capital corporations.
Political Risk	The risk that decisions made by politicians or government will affect the way business can be conducted
Portfolio Rebalancing	When an investor adjusts their investments to better meet a targeted portfolio percentage
Preemptive Right	The right granted to some shareholders to purchase new shares before the general public
Preferred Stock	Like common stock, but usually lacks voting rights and are first in line during liquidation and dividends
Pre-Funded Municipal Bonds	These bonds have funds set aside to pay them off at their call date.
Prepayment Risk	This is the risk most often associated with mortgage-backed securities but is applicable to other asset classes. Prepayment risk is the risk that the borrower will repay the loan before it is anticipated to be repaid.
Put And Call Options	Types of derivative instruments whose value is dependent on a specific security, index, commodity, currency, or investment. A call option will increase in value when the price of the security to which it is tied increases in value. A put option will increase in value when the underlying asset declines in value.
Qualified Institutional Buyers (QIBs)	Buyers with at least $100 million in assets
Real Estate Investment Trusts (REITs)	Companies that own, manage, or finance income-producing (usually commercial) real estate
Reinvestment Risk	The risk that capital will be reinvested at the lower interest rate
Revenue Bonds	These are bonds which are backed by their ability to generate revenue from the project they fund.
Riders	Modifications to a policy presented as an attachment to the actual policy
Rights of Accumulation (ROA)	Allows an investor to aggregate shares (401k funds, pensions, related party shares) to receive the discount
Rights Offering	Allows existing stockholders to buy newly issued shares at a discount before the general public can buy them
Securitization	When financial institutions sell pools of mortgages to other financial institutions with expertise in packaging the loans as a single security

74

This material is provided for exam preparation purposes only and does not indicate an endorsement of any specific scientific, political, or religious point of view. © TPB Publishing. You have been licensed one copy of this document for personal use only. Any other reproduction or redistribution is strictly prohibited. All rights reserved.

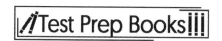

Sell To Open Contract	When the investor sells the right to the buyer to call the stock from (or put the stock to) the investor
Special Disclosures	These are essentially documents provided for consumers by brokerage firms and investment banks that cover anything from account details, explanation of risks, legal disclaimers, or brokerage fees. These are encouraged by FINRA to increase transparency between firms and customers.
Spread Strategy	When an investor buys the same number of call and put options with varying maturities and strike price
Timing Risk	This is the risk incurred when an investor attempts to buy and sell securities at the most profitable point.
Trade Date	Date when the buyer exercised the right to buy the underlying shares
Unit Investment Trusts (UITs)	Different from traditional funds, closed-end funds, and exchange-traded funds; . They are fixed portfolios that are established for a specific duration of time. UITs are redeemable securities that the issuer will buy back at the NAV. Shares are issued with an IPO. UITs can be made up of bonds or stocks or both.
Variable life insurance	Permanent life insurance with the added characteristic of reflecting the performance of a subinvestment
Variable-Rate Demand Note (VRDN)	A variable-rate demand note (VRDN) is a debt instrument that has a variable interest rate, which changes with respect to a certain benchmark. VRDNs can also be redeemed by the holder at any point, and the issuer must return the principal and any accrued interest to the holder at that time.
Vertical Spread Strategy	All of the options on the single security expire in the same month but have varying strike prices.
Warrants	These are contracts attached to the ownership of a bond or preferred stock, and they are tradeable securities which can be separated from the instrument to which they're attached.

This material is provided for exam preparation purposes only and does not indicate an endorsement of any specific scientific, political, or religious point of view. © TPB Publishing. You have been licensed one copy of this document for personal use only. Any other reproduction or redistribution is strictly prohibited. All rights reserved.

Practice Quiz

1. Which of the following is important to NOT include in an advertisement concerning a collateralized mortgage obligation (CMO)?
   a. The yield
   b. A government guarantee
   c. Information about the risks of the investment
   d. The tranches already in existence and the specific tranche that is being solicited in the advertisement

2. What is the ODD?
   a. Option Deposit Designation
   b. Options Disclosure Document
   c. Opportunity Disclosure Declaration
   d. Options Declaration Document

3. When can a municipal security advertisement contain information related to an outdated yield or price?
   a. When the date is provided as to when the yield or price was accurate
   b. When the outdated information was not knowingly included
   c. When it is not included in the official statement
   d. When the security acknowledges certain risks

4. If a security has the characteristics of a money market fund, language must be included that explains that the security is not insured or guaranteed by what agency?
   a. FINRA
   b. SEC
   c. FDIC
   d. Cboe

5. Disclosures related to performance data must include which of the following?
   a. Past performance is indicative of future performance
   b. Sales Ratio
   c. Fees
   d. Operating Cycle

See answers on next page.

This material is provided for exam preparation purposes only and does not indicate an endorsement of any specific scientific, political, or religious point of view. © TPB Publishing. You have been licensed one copy of this document for personal use only. Any other reproduction or redistribution is strictly prohibited. All rights reserved.

Answer Explanations

1. B: CMO advertisements are explicitly forbidden from implying, or otherwise mentioning, that the government guarantees the security in any way. The rest of the options are elements that must be provided in a CMO advertisement to assist the investor with making an educated decision about whether to invest.

2. B: The ODD is the Options Disclosure Document which must be received by investors before any other communication can take place.

3. A: An advertisement may include information related to a yield or price that is outdated or has changed if the advertisement also contains the date when the yield or price was accurate.

4. C: If a security has the characteristics of a money market fund, language must be included that explains that the security is not insured or guaranteed by the FDIC like a checking account at a chartered bank would be. The SEC, FINRA, and Cboe are not relevant to this situation.

5. C: Performance data must include disclosures related to fees, sales loads, and total operating expense ratio. There also must be a disclosure to explain that past performance does not always represent future performance.

This material is provided for exam preparation purposes only and does not indicate an endorsement of any specific scientific, political, or religious point of view. © TPB Publishing. You have been licensed one copy of this document for personal use only. Any other reproduction or redistribution is strictly prohibited. All rights reserved.

Trading, Customers Accounts, Prohibited Activities

Trading, Settlement, and Corporate Actions

Orders and Strategies

Types of Orders

A **market order** is simply an order that is executed at whatever the market price is. In a **limit order**, the investor has more control, and the order is not executed if the market price does not fall within the limit range. A **stop order** means the trade is only executed when the price surpasses a certain point. A **day order** expires if criteria is not reached for a trade to occur during that day. A **good-til-canceled (GTC)** order means the order is in place until executed, unless the investor cancels the order.

Certain types of orders are also strategies in options trading. When option traders buy or sell to open, they are essentially opening a position on a stock, bond, or index. A buy-to-close or sell-to-close order closes a trade that has been opened, and the investor will incur a loss or gain from their trade. This basically eliminates the exposure he or she had when the trade was opened. In a spread strategy with options—not to be confused with the bid-ask spread—an investor enters into multiple options transactions, with different strike prices and expiration dates.

This enables the trade to be more diverse than compared to one trade that has a single-strike price and exercise date. A **straddle** is an options trading technique that involves an investor simultaneously buying a put and a call of the same underlying stock with the same strike price and expiration date. An investor who expects significant volatility in the price of a security will set up this type of strategy. It is only when the security has significant ups and downs that an investor will profit from this type of transaction.

When an investor or trader is considering a financial market transaction, the investor or trader will have several options when placing an order. If the investor or trader allows someone to place the order on their behalf without first giving consent to the order, the investor or trader has granted discretionary authority to someone else to place the order. Discretionary authority is usually granted prior to the order by a discretionary agreement for transactions. If the investor or trader must first give consent before someone else places the order on their behalf, the investor or trader has granted nondiscretionary authority to someone else.

An additional distinction can be made regarding the order. If the investor or trader is contacted by a professional affecting a transaction to induce the investor or trader to initiate a transaction, the order is considered a **solicited order**. On the other hand, if the investor or trader contacts the professional affecting the transaction to initiate a transaction, the order is considered a **non-solicited order**.

Bid-Ask

Most securities are traded with a bid and ask system. The **bid** refers to the price that buyers are willing to pay for a bond or a share of stock, and the **ask** refers to the seller's asking price. The difference between the two amounts is known as the **bid-ask spread,** or simply as the **spread**. If the ask is $25 and the bid $24, then the spread is $1.

The bid and the ask are constantly changing as buyers and sellers enter and exit the market. If the market is made up of one buyer and one seller with an ask of $25 and a bid of $24, either no trade will occur, or the two parties will move their amounts up or down until the two are equal. This means the

This material is provided for exam preparation purposes only and does not indicate an endorsement of any specific scientific, political, or religious point of view. © TPB Publishing. You have been licensed one copy of this document for personal use only. Any other reproduction or redistribution is strictly prohibited. All rights reserved.

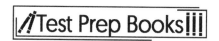

parties agree on the price of the security, and the trade will be executed. On electronic exchanges, thousands of these trades are executed instantly. A firm quote guarantees the bid or the ask up to the amount quoted. This is different from a nominal or subject quote, where neither the amount nor the quantity of the trade is set. These types of quotes are made to test the market for a security's value. A not held quote is used for a trade that an investor wants executed on a best efforts basis, which allows the broker or trader to buy or sell without a limit.

Trade Capacity

A NASDAQ market maker executes both principal trades (which are for its own account) and agency trades (trades for its customers). These market makers aren't in the exchange, as they are for the New York Stock Exchange (NYSE). They are required to quote both sides of a trade (bid and ask). A bid wanted announcement occurs when a seller wants to entertain bids on securities. In this transaction, the response does not need to be specified, as the price may be negotiated. On the other side, an offer wanted can occur. The SEC order handling rules state market makers must display customer limit orders that are priced better than the market maker's quote or add to the size associated with the market maker's quote when the market maker is at the best price.

Strategies

FINRA Rule 4320 outlines the requirements for short sales. The rule specifically addresses failure to deliver situations. This is when the broker or dealer on the sell side of the contract—the short seller—has not delivered the securities to the buyer. If this occurs, the seller will not receive payment if the trade is profitable. This is the credit risk associated with this type of transaction. Most firms do due diligence to prevent this type of situation from arising, but because of the risk inherent in short-selling, these situations do arise. The rule states any failure to deliver position outstanding for more than 35 days requires the participant to close the position by purchasing a similar security. The rule also applies if only a portion of a trade fails to deliver, simply to the balance of what has not been delivered.

Typically, short sales must be order marked so that it is clear that the investor is not actually in possession of the underlying security in the transaction, that the shares are actually borrowed either out of a broker or customer account, and that margin has been posted. In short sales, allocation occurs when a broker approves a short sell to be executed.

Regulation SHO took effect in 2004 and requires the documentation of what has transpired for the allocation to occur. According to this rule, the actual securities do not have to be borrowed and in possession of a trustee. As long as a security is easily attainable—usually a liquid security that is actively traded on a market on a daily basis—the allocation requirement is considered to be fulfilled. If a security cannot be borrowed, this would be considered a naked short.

Although the idea of a short sale is pretty straightforward—an investor wants to profit from the decline in a security's value—there are more dynamic strategies that can be undertaken. An investor may simply notice that a stock is highly overvalued. Perhaps the price/earnings (P/E) ratio is significantly higher than similar stocks, or perhaps an investor believes a company's growth estimates are not realistic. If an investor does not own the stock and wishes to profit from a short sale, this is speculation. Speculation is different from investing in that there is more inherent risk in the trade than in a traditional long position. An investor that believes the security may be overvalued can hedge their position through a short sale. This may be less costly than selling the shares outright. It also allows investors to protect themselves from a price decline if they feel it is short-term or temporary and still retains shares as a long-term investment.

This material is provided for exam preparation purposes only and does not indicate an endorsement of any specific scientific, political, or religious point of view. © TPB Publishing. You have been licensed one copy of this document for personal use only. Any other reproduction or redistribution is strictly prohibited. All rights reserved.

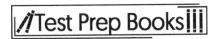

Investors may or may not have complete hedge in place. A fully hedged position would mean that a gain or loss on the shares the investor owns is directly offset by their short position. A hedge ratio is usually calculated so that the investor can quantify the exposure from both positions. Another strategy with short sales is arbitrage. An investor may utilize this strategy if he or she feels different markets are pricing the same security differently. The strategy here is to take advantage of the mispricing by buying the security on one market—at a lower price—and then selling the security on the other market at a higher price. The image below shows the potential payoff of a put option versus short selling the stock.

Another strategy involves covered or naked calls and puts. As mentioned, uncovered or "naked" call or put writing exposes the investor to an extreme amount of risk. Experienced, risk-tolerant investors approach this strategy with caution. The term "naked" refers to the absence of an underlying instrument "backing" the options contract. Clearly, risk is imminent. However, this can prove to be rather profitable for the writer. Profitability can happen when the buyer is unable to exercise the option due to a lack of money.

Bearish and Bullish

An investor or trader's orders and strategies will depend on whether the investor perceives that the security will increase or decrease in value. If an investor or trader perceives that the security will increase in value, they are considered **bullish**. A bullish investor or trader will initiate a purchase transaction, which is known as going "long" the security. Similarly, the investor or trader may purchase a call option, which will increase in value if the underlying security increases in value. A bullish investor or trader might also sell a put option, which allows the investor or trader to keep the option premium if the underlying security increases in value.

On the other hand, if an investor or trader perceives that the security will decrease in value, they are considered **bearish**. A bearish investor or trader will initiate a short sale transaction, which is known as going "short" the security. An investor or trader that is short borrows the security from a brokerage firm, sells the security on the open market at a perceived high price, and hopes to purchase the security on the open market at a later date for less than the original short sale price, return the borrowed shares to the brokerage, and keep the difference in the value of the shares. A bearish investor or trader might also buy a put option, which will increase in value if the underlying security decreases in value. A bearish investor or trader might also sell a call option, which allows the investor or trader to keep the option premium if the security decreases in value.

This material is provided for exam preparation purposes only and does not indicate an endorsement of any specific scientific, political, or religious point of view. © TPB Publishing. You have been licensed one copy of this document for personal use only. Any other reproduction or redistribution is strictly prohibited. All rights reserved.

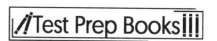

Investment Returns

Components of Return

Some stocks reward investors for holding their shares by paying dividends. Dividends are paid out of a company's earnings. Any earnings not paid out as dividends are reported on the balance sheet as retained earnings. There are different theories around the importance of dividends. The "bird in hand" theory is that it is better for the investor to have the dividend and decide how to reinvest it, rather than have the company retain that cash and invest it back in the company's operations. Companies typically try to pay a consistent percentage of the stock price as a dividend, as opposed to a percentage of earnings. Companies want to pay a consistent dividend. It is often a sign that a company is struggling if it historically paid a consistent dividend but is now no longer able to do so.

Similar to stocks, bonds pay interest in the form of a coupon. While not all stocks pay dividends, nearly all bonds pay interest, although some bonds (called **zeros**) pay no interest and simply pay a set discounted amount of principal at maturity. Most bonds pay a fixed dollar rate based on the coupon. This payment is usually made semiannually. The actual interest fluctuates to reflect current market rates due to changes in the bond's value, but the actual coupon dollar amount is the same throughout the life of the bond. Some bonds pay a floating rate of interest based on some index or benchmark. These bonds pay a different dollar amount with each adjustment.

The interest on bonds is taxable, except for municipal bonds, which pay interest that is tax free. Almost all bonds are not taxable at the federal level, and typically when an investor buys bonds issued by the state they live in, they are exempt at the state and local level as well. Investors usually calculate a tax equivalent yield to determine if the net yield they will receive on a taxable bond is higher or lower than a municipal bond of equal risk.

A **capital gain** is the profit received when assets like stocks, bonds, or real estate are sold. There is a gain if the asset is sold at a higher price than when it was purchased. Interest and dividends are not considered capital gains because they are not returns associated with the sale of an asset. Capital gains in assets held for more than a year are taxed at a long-term capital gains rate, which is lower than the short-term capital gains rate. This encourages investors to invest for the long term rather than just investing for short term profits. There are certain exemptions from capital gains where applicable, usually to increase entrepreneurship and investments in new and growing industries.

Return of capital is when an investor receives all or a portion of their original principal invested. They are not taxed as capital gains. Return of capital occurs on mortgage-backed securities when the investors pay the required portion of principal as dictated by an amortization schedule. Investors and brokers must track investments in a cost basis, so that it is clear what portion of an investment should be taxed at a capital gain and what is simply the return of capital. The calculation is even more difficult when an investment is a partnership. This is usually tracked through each partner's capital account.

Dividends

Dividends are the portion of a company's earnings paid out to stockholders. Typically, dividends are paid on a quarterly basis and determined by the company's board of directors. Some companies increase their dividends at the same rate as the growth of earnings. Investors often value securities based on how consistently they pay dividends and maintain stability in the company's retained earnings. Though dividends are typically paid in cash, some companies pay dividends in the form of stock shares (often at a discount to the stock's market value). This is referred to as a **Dividend Reinvestment Plan (DRIP)**.

This material is provided for exam preparation purposes only and does not indicate an endorsement of any specific scientific, political, or religious point of view. © TPB Publishing. You have been licensed one copy of this document for personal use only. Any other reproduction or redistribution is strictly prohibited. All rights reserved.

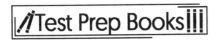
Dividends are calculated using the dividend yield formula, which involves dividing the annual dividend by the current stock price.

As noted, dividends can be in the form of cash or stock. Some companies have a dividend requirement, which means the company has to achieve a certain dollar level of earnings or earnings per share to pay a dividend (usually for preferred share classes). The **dividend payout ratio** is the percentage of earnings paid out as a dividend. More mature companies typically have higher payout ratios since they have less room for growth and investment. Younger companies usually have a lower ratio since they have more investment opportunity and the chance for a greater rate of return.

Dividend Payment Dates

When a corporation decides to pay a dividend to its common stockholders, there are a few key dates for an investor to follow closely. First, the **record date** is the date that a stockholder must own the stock in order to receive the dividend. This means that the stock must have settled and be owned by the stockholder on the record date. Second, the **ex-dividend date** is the first day the stock trades without the dividend, which means the amount of the dividend is subtracted from the stock price. Third, the **payable date** is the date when the dividend will actually be paid by the corporation.

Concepts of Measurement

Investments are only as good as the returns they provide investors. In order to fully understand an investment's return, investors need to have a basic understanding of how returns are measured. The most important measure of return is the percent return. Percent's are often subdivided and referred to in terms of 'basis points'. A basis point is $1/100^{th}$ of a percent. For example, one basis point is .01%, 10 basis points is .10%, 50 basis points is .50%, and 100 basis points is equal to 1.00%.

In addition, investments often have two different ways to return an investor's profits. The first is income. For stocks, this is usually in the form of a dividend. For fixed-income securities, this is usually in the form of a coupon payment.

The second is capital appreciation. For stocks, this is the value that represents the difference between the initial investment and the current market value of the investment. For fixed-income securities, this is the value that represents the difference the amount paid and the maturity value. In order to accurately measure an investment's return, both the return from the income component and capital appreciation component should be included. The combination of these components of return is referred to as the total return of the investment.

The **yield to maturity (YTM)** is a complex concept. This is the yield an investor can expect to earn if they hold the bond until it matures. This is the discount rate at which the present value of all interest payments equals the price of the bond. It assumes that all interest received is reinvested at the YTM (hence, there are various assumptions that go into calculating a bond's YTM). **Yield to call (YTC)** is the total return that a bond investor can receive if he holds a bond until its call date. Not every bond is callable. The **yield to worst (YTW)** is the yield assuming the worst-case scenario for the bond, whether it matures or is called first. The **discount yield** is the yield on a Treasury bond sold at a discount (annualized).

Cost Basis Requirements

Typical cost basis per share is determined by the purchase price per share plus any fees per share. The basis per share on convertible securities exchanged for common shares of stock usually are valued at the same basis as the convertible security. Cost basis per share on equity that is inherited is based on

This material is provided for exam preparation purposes only and does not indicate an endorsement of any specific scientific, political, or religious point of view. © TPB Publishing. You have been licensed one copy of this document for personal use only. Any other reproduction or redistribution is strictly prohibited. All rights reserved.

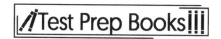

the market value on the date of death of the original owner. The cost basis for gifted securities depends on whether it is sold for a gain or a loss. With the former, the basis is equal to the gift giver's basis. If securities are sold for a loss, then the basis is the lesser of the original owner's basis or the market value on the date the gift was received. Average cost basis calculations take into account the total cost of an investment including purchases, dividends that are reinvested, returns of capital, and capital gains.

When selling shares, there are different methods to determine cost basis of the particular shares that are sold. Identified shares are those bought at a particular date for a particular price. Marking shares in this way allows the investor to possibly lower their tax liability. The FIFO (first in, first out) method assumes that the shares sold were the oldest shares, or those purchased the earliest. The LIFO (last in, first out) method in turn prices the shares sold at the price of the most recently purchased shares. The final way to determine cost basis is based on the use of identified shares to state specifically which shares are being sold and determining basis on the original purchase price of those specific shares.

Benchmarks and Indices

The basis of modern portfolio theory is that investors are compensated for the risk they take (i.e., the volatility of their investment or portfolio) with higher returns. The chart below is a graphical representation of the capital asset pricing model (CAPM). The vertical axis represents the return an investor can expect to earn given the amount of volatility (risk) they're willing to accept (the horizontal axis). To apply asset classes to the chart, to the left under "Risk" would be the safest asset class. Short-term treasury bonds, highly-rated money market funds, and other safe, short-term securities would be expected to earn the risk-free rate. If an investor wants to earn a higher return, they should move further out on the efficient frontier, but this requires the willingness to take on more volatility. Securities such as equities, options, and commodities will be on the far end of the curve.

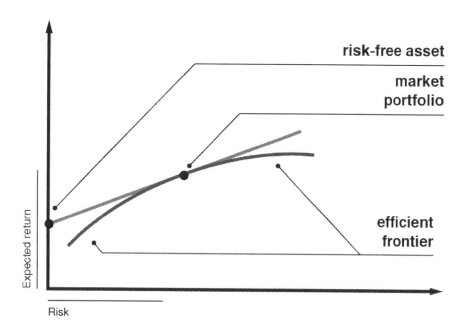

Most customers invest hoping to outperform some type of broad market index. The S&P 500 and NASDAQ are examples of indices that many fund managers will benchmark themselves against. Fund managers want to achieve excess return (also known as Alpha) so that their customers know they're

This material is provided for exam preparation purposes only and does not indicate an endorsement of any specific scientific, political, or religious point of view. © TPB Publishing. You have been licensed one copy of this document for personal use only. Any other reproduction or redistribution is strictly prohibited. All rights reserved.

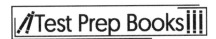

earning a greater return than if they simply invested in the index itself. For example, if the S&P 500 returns 5% in 2016 and a fund manager whose benchmark in the S&P 500 returns 8%, they've generated an Alpha of 3%. However, investors often look at the return on a net basis.

If the index returns 5% and the fund returns 5.5%, but the fund fees are 1.5% per year (meaning the net return of the fund is 4%), then the investor would have been better off buying the index. Beta is another concept that's the foundation of the CAPM. Beta is the relationship or correlation between a stock and the broader market index. A stock with a Beta of 2 means that, when the market rises by 5%, the stock rises 10% (theoretically, though, the relationship between a stock and its index changes over time). A stock with a Beta of 0 will be uncorrelated with the broader market, and a stock with a negative Beta will be inversely correlated with the market.

Trade Settlement

Settlement Time Frames

A securities transaction is not complete and ownership is not transferred until the securities transaction settles. The procedure and time for settlement depend on the security involved in the transaction. When a transaction settles is vitally important in terms of ownership and what the former owner and new owner may now do with their capital. For example, an investor will not receive a dividend from a common stock unless the securities transaction has settled by the record date. In addition, a seller of a security will not have access to the proceeds of a securities transaction until the transaction settles.

The securities industry uses a "T+" system to describe when a particular securities transaction settles. "T" represents the transaction date, which is the date the transaction is placed. For example, if an investor sells a stock on Monday, "T" is Monday. Stocks settle "T+2," which, in this example, would mean the stock settles on Wednesday because Wednesday is two days after Monday. Options contracts settle "T+1" and other securities have different settlement dates. An investor needs to be aware of when the investor's transaction settles.

Physical vs. Book Entry

When an investor purchases a security, the investor needs to obtain proof of ownership of the security, just like a person who purchases a home needs the deed to the home for proof of ownership. In the securities industry, the two most common forms of evidencing ownership are physical ownership of the certificates representing the security and ownership of the security as represented by a book entry system, which is typically an electronic system that simply tracks who the current owner of a security is at any given time.

With advances in technology, the physical type of evidencing ownership has faded away, although some securities' ownership is still recognized by an individual actually possessing a certificate, which includes the details of the security, type, terms, and other relevant information needed to evidence ownership. The need to move away from this physical type of ownership was driven by the need to settle a securities transaction in a timely manner. For example, owners of securities whose ownership was represented by a physical certificate would not be as competitive in the market with securities whose ownership could be evidenced electronically.

The need for speed in settlement led to the book entry system of evidencing ownership in a security. Because investors no longer had to physically produce the certificate of ownership, securities could be transferred more effectively. Notwithstanding the efficiencies of book entry systems, securities must still endure a settlement process, which can vary in number of days depending on the type of security.

84

This material is provided for exam preparation purposes only and does not indicate an endorsement of any specific scientific, political, or religious point of view. © TPB Publishing. You have been licensed one copy of this document for personal use only. Any other reproduction or redistribution is strictly prohibited. All rights reserved.

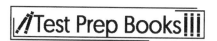

Corporate Actions

Types of Corporate Actions

The value of a security can be substantially affected by decisions made at the corporate level by a board of directors. A board of directors may vote to initiate a stock split. Stock splits are often executed to reduce the per-share price of a company's stock. This has the effect of making a share of a security more affordable and therefore more marketable to retail investors. For example, a company whose stock is trading at $1,000 per share with 1,000,000 shares outstanding could initiate a 10-for-1 stock split. The result of such a split reduces the price per share to $100 but increases the number of shares outstanding to 10,000,000. The enterprise value of the company does not change as the result of a stock split.

A board of directors may vote to initiate a reverse stock split. Reverse stock splits are executed to increase the per-share price of a company's stock. This has the effect of making a share of a security more expensive and therefore appear to be of higher quality than lower priced shares. For example, a company whose stock is trading at $10/share with 1,000,000 shares outstanding could initiate a 1-for-10 stock split. The result of such a split would be to increase the price per share to $100/share but decrease the number of shares outstanding to 100,000. The enterprise value of the company does not change as the result of a reverse stock split.

A board of directors may vote to initiate a stock buyback. Stock buybacks are often executed to reduce the amount of public ownership of a company and reduce the supply of the stock on the open market, causing the remaining supply available to the public to increase in value. Because the enterprise value of the company does not change as the result of a stock buyback, the remaining owners of the stock will own a larger portion of the company than they did immediately before the stock buyback was executed.

A board of directors may vote to initiate a **tender offer**, which is one type of a stock buyback. In a tender offer, the company proposes to buy a certain number of shares at a certain price from existing shareholders. If enough investors agree to the tender offer, the company will purchase their shares according to the terms of the tender offer, which reduces the number of shares outstanding.

A board of directors may vote to initiate an exchange offer. **Exchange offers** occur when a company has several different asset classes of securities or when a company is the parent company to subsidiary companies under the direction of the parent company. An exchange offer can comprise many different types of exchanges such as stocks for different classes of stocks, stock in one company for stock in a commonly controlled company, or stock for different types of securities like bonds.

A board of directors may vote to initiate a rights offering. A **rights offering** gives existing shareholders the right to purchase additional shares of additional securities offered by the company. A rights offering is often executed so that existing shareholders have the option to buy the securities to ensure that their current ownership is not diluted by the issuance of new shares. Rights offerings often come in the form of a "right of first refusal," which gives existing shareholders the first chance to buy additional securities before they are offered to the open market.

A board of directors may vote to initiate a merger or an acquisition. A **merger** is simply when one company combines with another company to form one new company. Mergers are executed for a variety of different reasons including business synergies, to be more competitive, and long-term growth.

A board of directors may vote to acquire another company. An **acquisition** is simply when one company buys another company usually with money or an exchange of securities of the entities involved.

This material is provided for exam preparation purposes only and does not indicate an endorsement of any specific scientific, political, or religious point of view. © TPB Publishing. You have been licensed one copy of this document for personal use only. Any other reproduction or redistribution is strictly prohibited. All rights reserved.

Stock Splits

A stock split occurs when a company increases the number of outstanding shares. This should not affect the shareholders' dollar amount of equity or the market value at the time of the split. It simply means that the share price will decline relative to the number of new shares issued. For example, a company has 100 outstanding shares and the price per share is $1.00. If the company issues 100 new shares, the price would drop to $0.50 per share. If an investor previously owned 10 shares (totaling $10 in value), he or she would now own 20 shares (still totaling $10, but at $0.50 per share x 20 shares = $10). Stock splits (also known as "stock consolidation") make shares more affordable to a broader investor base. In a reverse stock split, the opposite occurs. If the same company does a reverse split, there would be 50 outstanding shares at $2 per share.

Adjustments to Securities

To meet investor demands and to meet the requirements of the capital structure desired by the Board of Directors, corporations will often engage in activities that require the value and amount of securities to be adjusted. For example, corporations may initiate a stock split, which increases the amount of shares outstanding but decreases the value of each share. A corporation may initiate a reverse stock split, which decreases the amount of shares outstanding but increases the value of each share. A corporation may announce a stock buyback program, which reduces the amount of shares outstanding. A corporation may announce a tender offer, which reduces the amount of shares outstanding if the tender offer is accepted by existing shareholders. A corporation may announce a rights offering, which increases the amount of shares outstanding. A corporation may announce a cash dividend will be paid to existing shareholders, which decreases (in theory) the value of each share outstanding, but does not increase or decrease the amount of share outstanding. In addition, a corporation may announce a stock dividend, which increases the amount of shares outstanding, but does not decrease the value of each share outstanding.

Delivery of Notices

When customers have shares or interests in a corporation, it's the broker's responsibility to notify their customers about all corporate actions that might affect the value of their stocks. This includes activities such as: splitting stock, issuing new stock, establishing shareholder voting, and repurchasing stock. The broker can furnish a corporation's annual report and other reports, as well as provide copies of all notices of corporate action at any time. It's the broker's responsibility to communicate major changes in a timely manner, which they can do via regular mail or email correspondence, depending on the nature of the information.

Proxy Voting

Proxy voting occurs when someone delegates their voting power to another party. Sometimes "proxies" are used to create a voting bloc to give a group that has common interests more influence when voting. In a proxy fight, another company may try to persuade the shareholders of the company they want to acquire to sign over their proxy rights because they think management has not performed well.

This material is provided for exam preparation purposes only and does not indicate an endorsement of any specific scientific, political, or religious point of view. © TPB Publishing. You have been licensed one copy of this document for personal use only. Any other reproduction or redistribution is strictly prohibited. All rights reserved.

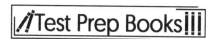
Customer Accounts and Compliance Considerations

Account Types

To best serve financial customers, brokers can set up different account types:

- **Cash Account:** A standard brokerage account in which the customer makes cash deposits for trading purposes. Under Regulation T, a cash deposit must be made within two days of purchasing a security. Funds cannot be borrowed from the broker using this type of account.

- **Margin Account:** An account created when a broker lends money to a customer and uses cash and securities as collateral for the loan. The margin covers some or all of the credit risk for a transaction.

- **Options Trading :** A higher risk type of trading, with more regulations, where the customer is allowed to hold options. Brokerages require that option traders use a margin account.

- **Retirement Account:** Is a tax-advantaged brokerage account that can be either a cash or margin account. Examples include: IRA, Roth IRA, SEP IRA, and SIMPLE IRA.

- **Day Trading :** This is a designation rather than a type of account. Brokers will label a customer as a "pattern day trader" if they execute four or more day trades within five business days. The "patter day trader" designation only applies to margin accounts. Different SEC rules apply to both cash and margin accounts that are used to day trade.

Some customers need special services such as operational support, cash management, and securities lending. In these cases, the broker sets up a prime brokerage account, which is used mostly by hedge funds as a clearing facility and to net transactions. These brokers profit from the "spreads" earned on each transaction with these funds.

Other account types and procedures include:

- **Delivery Versus Payment (DVP):** A settlement procedure where the buyer's payment for securities is due at the time of delivery. Other names include cash on deliver, delivery against payment (DAP), and delivery against cash (DAC). The purpose of this transaction is to mitigate settlement risk since both sides of the transaction are executed simultaneously.

- **Receive Versus Payment (RVP):** A settlement procedure where the buyer's payment for securities is due at the time of receipt. It's also called receive against payment (RAP).

- **Advisory Account:** An account for customers working with a financial advisor (to be better informed about investment decisions) but still wanting to retain all rights to authorize purchases. The fee structure for these accounts is asset based, not commission based. This eliminates the broker's incentive to turn a portfolio over or "churn" an account to receive the highest fees.

- **Fee-Based Account:** An account where the financial advisor receives a commission based on a percentage of the customer's assets.

This material is provided for exam preparation purposes only and does not indicate an endorsement of any specific scientific, political, or religious point of view. © TPB Publishing. You have been licensed one copy of this document for personal use only. Any other reproduction or redistribution is strictly prohibited. All rights reserved.

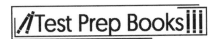

- **Discretionary Account:** Also known as a "managed account," this is created when brokers are given the authority to manage transactions without the customer's consent. This account requires both parties to sign a discretionary disclosure document. Typically, the customer sets up specific parameters (asset class, transaction type, security type, etc.) around what can be traded.

- **Education Accounts:** There are two main types of educational savings account. The IRS refers to these accounts as **Qualified Tuition Programs (QTP)**. The most well-known is the 529 College Savings Account. These accounts can pay for approved college expenses. Each state has their own 529 Plans with different rules on taxation and contribution limits. Another type of education account is called a **Coverdell Education Savings Account**. These accounts also have certain tax advantages and can pay for elementary through college education. The contribution limit for a Coverdell ESA is $2,000 per child. Parents can contribute to both a 529 Plan and a Coverdell ESA for the same child in the same tax year if it is less than the annual gift tax exclusion amount ($15,000).

Customer Account Registrations

Brokers are able to register several types of accounts (including joint accounts and business accounts) to assign control to appropriate parties. These accounts can include stocks, bonds, options, mutual funds, exchange traded funds, and IPOs. The broker may work with individuals and businesses to provide brokerage services and must obtain specific information to set up the accounts.

Individual and Joint Accounts

Individual accounts are opened in the name of one person. Business accounts are designed specifically for sole proprietors, business partnerships, and corporations. In a sole proprietorship, there's no distinction between the owner and the business.

A Joint tenants with rights of survivorship (JTWROS) account is where authorized individuals have equal authority over the account and retain control even when one of the joint tenants dies.

A joint tenants in common (JTIC) account is an account where authorized individuals do not retain control over the account if the joint tenant dies but may receive a portion of the assets as outlined in the deceased's will.

Only married couples can maintain a community property brokerage account, which is a type of JTWROS account. Each person has equal rights to the income and appreciation of assets in the account. Marital accounts are set up to ensure that marital or community property and trust accounts are managed by a trustee.

Transfer on death (TOD) account is when an accountholder identifies which assets will be transferred to various parties upon their death without the probate process.

An estate account is held in the name of the estate of someone who's deceased and is managed by a representative.

Corporate/Institutional and Partnership Accounts

In a corporation, a group of people or managers are authorized to act as a single entity. An institutional account is set up in the name of an institution such as banks or mutual funds. In a partnership, two or

This material is provided for exam preparation purposes only and does not indicate an endorsement of any specific scientific, political, or religious point of view. © TPB Publishing. You have been licensed one copy of this document for personal use only. Any other reproduction or redistribution is strictly prohibited. All rights reserved.

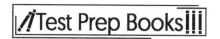

more individuals form a joint venture. Nonprofits and unincorporated businesses are accounts designed specifically for organizations comprised of volunteers.

Trust and Custodial Accounts

Trust accounts are set up by one party in order to benefit another party. Revocable trusts allow for alterations, changes, and even cancellation depending on the grantor. An irrevocable trust is not allowed to be amended or cancelled without the beneficiary's approval. A custodial account is a trust account managed on behalf of a minor (under 18 to 21 years of age depending on the state). These can be **Uniform Gifts to Minors Act (UGMA)** or **Uniform Transfers to Minors Act (UTMA)** accounts. UGMAs often fall under the UTMA category since they allow the transfer of all asset types, including real estate, art collections, securities, cash, and intangible assets.

Retirement Accounts

An **individual retirement account (IRA)** is an investment vehicle provided by most employers and corporations that provide investments with significant tax advantages. Most IRAs are managed by global investment managers and mutual funds. Investments from traditional stocks and bonds, to hedge funds to private equity, to alternative investments can be found in an IRA. In a traditional IRA, all contributions are invested before any taxes are applied. If funds are not withdrawn until retirement (or under some special circumstances), they will be taxed at the ordinary income rate. However, funds can incur taxes if withdrawn prematurely. A **Roth IRA** is a variation of a traditional IRA, but the tax break occurs when the money is withdrawn, not invested. The IRS has a set schedule with restrictions on the total dollar amount that can be invested in an annual basis.

A **Simplified Employee Pension IRA (SEP IRA)** is an investment instrument used by small businesses to provide tax-free investing for their owners and employees. These funds are taxed at the ordinary rate when withdrawn if the beneficiary has reached the age of 59 1/2. Employees can contribute up to 25 percent of their wages into the SEP IRA. A **SIMPLE IRA** is similar to a 401(k) or 403(b) plan many employers offer. They can be funded with pretax dollars but are still subject to social security, Medicare, and unemployment taxes. Early withdrawals are taxed at 25 percent.

In 2015, the IRS introduced new rules on the rolling over of an IRA. This occurs when the beneficiary takes actual possession of the plan assets. Under the new rules, only one IRA can be rolled (per beneficiary) per 12-month period. There is no limit to how many times an IRA can be moved from trustee to trustee, and rollovers from traditional to Roth IRAs are unlimited. Rollovers must be completed within 60 days to avoid incurring taxes.

There are various strategies and different tools that investors should be aware of when investing in an IRA. IRS tax Form 5329 should be filed for any contributions over the restricted amount for a given year. Without this document being completed, penalties can be assessed years later when withdrawals are made. Investors should always take advantage of the trustee-to-trustee rollover when possible, since more than one direct rollover in a year will be penalized at a 6 percent rate.

There are strategies for spousal beneficiaries as well. If a spouse is under 59 1/2 years old, one strategy is to set up an inherited IRA. Setting up the account this way makes it exempt from the 10 percent penalty for early withdrawal. A spousal rollover is the better choice if the spouse is over 59 1/2, since these funds can be rolled over after that age anyway.

For Roth IRAs, funds cannot be withdrawn for five years, or a tax penalty generally must be paid. The amount of the penalty depends on when the withdrawal is made, whether the amount was simply from

This material is provided for exam preparation purposes only and does not indicate an endorsement of any specific scientific, political, or religious point of view. © TPB Publishing. You have been licensed one copy of this document for personal use only. Any other reproduction or redistribution is strictly prohibited. All rights reserved.

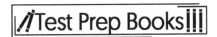

contributions or from earnings on contributions, and what the purpose of the funds withdrawn is for. Funds can usually be used to make a down payment on a first home or to pay for education without a penalty.

IRAs often have required minimum distributions, typically on an annual basis. These distributions begin on April 1 after the beneficiary has reached 70 1/2 years of age. This is called a lifetime distribution. They are not required for a Roth IRA. There is a 50 percent penalty on the dollar amount that was required to be withdrawn (in addition to taxes and fees paid on funds that are withdrawn). The rules are designed to distribute the funds over the life expectancy of the beneficiary, as well as to incent the beneficiary to leave the funds as an inheritance. Required withdrawals are ineligible for being rolled over into another IRA.

IRAs allow a wide range of investments. Real estate, stocks, bonds, annuities, and mutual funds are all permissible investments in an IRA. There are some prohibited investments. For instance, life insurance can't be used in an IRA, nor can derivatives with undefined or unlimited risks be used. This includes uncovered writing of options contracts and other speculation using derivatives of options. Antiques and any other collectible items can't be used in an IRA. Real estate is a permissible investment, but only if the beneficiary doesn't receive income directly from the property (so Real Estate Investment Trusts, or REITs, and other shares of real estate are permissible).

An employee-sponsored retirement plan provides employees of a company with a low-cost and tax-efficient way of saving earnings on a regular basis. Plans usually take the form of a 401(k) or an IRA. Non-profit employers provide 403(b) plans. All of these plans have mostly replaced employee pension plans that were often inflexible and only allowed employees to purchase company stock—not invest in a diverse pool of assets. The Employment Retirement Security Income Act sets minimum standards for pension plans. The rule requires full disclosure of financial statements and status of the plan to investors and beneficiaries.

The act also sets standards for plan administrators and fund managers. ERISA is enforced by the Department of Labor, the Internal Revenue Service, and the Pension Benefit Guarantee Corporation. ERISA requires employers to vest benefits after a specific number of years. There are also certain funding requirements that must be met. The Pension Benefit Guarantee Corporation ensures beneficiaries who have paid into a plan will receive benefits even if their company's plan is terminated. There are two types of pension plans: defined benefit and defined contribution. Defined benefit plans provide retirees benefits based on years of service, salary, and other variables. Defined contribution plans provide benefits based on how the portfolio of investments performs.

A 401(k) is a tax-qualified defined contribution plan. Under these plans, most employers match contributions at some level and at a pre-tax rate, meaning funds are contributed before income taxes. This gives the beneficiary the incentive to contribute to the account. In 2022, the maximum amount an individual could contribute is $20,500 per year. Nonprofits have 403(b) plans, and the government has 457(b) plans that are similar to how a 401(k) is structured. Required minimum distributions are required for 401(k)'s (unless it's a Roth 401(k) account). Under certain circumstances, a 401(k) can be "forced out," which means that if a fund is not above a minimum amount, typically $1,000, the account can be closed.

In a profit-sharing plan, the employer decides how much is paid into a plan and when those payments are made. The amount each employee receives is based on salary and tenure with the company. The amount employees receive also depends on the company's financial performance, typically as measured

This material is provided for exam preparation purposes only and does not indicate an endorsement of any specific scientific, political, or religious point of view. © TPB Publishing. You have been licensed one copy of this document for personal use only. Any other reproduction or redistribution is strictly prohibited. All rights reserved.

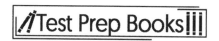

by its net income and profit margin. This aligns the incentives of both employees and management of the company. A money purchase plan is a similar type of defined contribution plan. However, the amounts paid into the plan are fixed. Regardless of how profitable a company is, the same amount must be contributed each year. At the end of an employee's employment, the amount he or she is entitled can then be rolled into an annuity.

Some companies have employee stock options or stock purchase plans. Employees can sometimes purchase stock at a discount through these plans. These plans also align the incentives and management. In public companies, management often receives stock options that are only profitable if certain benchmarks are met or if the stock price of the company reaches a certain level, much like how a call option works. In a deferred compensation plan, an employee's income is simply paid out at a later date. Pension plans, retirement plans, and stock options can be in the form of deferred compensation. These plans can be both qualifying and non-qualifying. Under a non-qualifying plan, companies choose who can get the deferred benefits. They are generally more flexible than qualified plans. These plans are called "golden handcuffs" because the benefits are used to encourage employees to remain employed with their current employer.

Some characteristics of non-qualifying plans include:

- The employer chooses the vesting schedule and rate.
- Contractors can be included.
- Under non-qualified rules, contributions are not tax-deductible.
- Earnings are taxed as earned (not when they are actually paid).

Anti-Money Laundering (AML)

The deliberate concealment of illegally obtained funds is defined as **money laundering**. In 1970, the United States Congress enacted the Bank Secrecy Act in part to prevent the act of money laundering, which is generally known as the process of turning money made from illegal activities and not legally justifiable into money that appears to have been made from legal activities and thus is legally justifiable. Although the Bank Secrecy Act was enacted almost fifty years ago, the terrorist attacks in the United States on September 11, 2001 increased lawmaker scrutiny of these illegal activities because the attacks were funded in part by money made from illegal activities. In response, the United States Congress passed the USA Patriot Act to increase and strengthen the regulatory regime governing illegal activities that could potentially affect the long-term safety of the nation.

Although money laundering is often romanticized and complex in popular culture, the process of money laundering is definable in certain steps. The first step in a money laundering scheme is called **placement.** In the placement stage, the illegal money is placed into a bank or other financial institution by using standard depositing methods. The second step in a money laundering scheme is called **layering**. In the layering stage, the illegal money is transferred numerous times between numerous accounts in an attempt to disguise where the money originally came from. Another way layering is practiced is by **structuring** the money, or by making small deposits of money over time into accounts. When this occurs, suspicion is usually not aroused, because the deposits are not large.

The layering stage is what is often portrayed in television shows and movies where criminal enterprises are seeking to legitimize the funds for future use. Once the funds are layered, the funds are then integrated into other accounts with money that was obtained legally in a final attempt to cover the true

This material is provided for exam preparation purposes only and does not indicate an endorsement of any specific scientific, political, or religious point of view. © TPB Publishing. You have been licensed one copy of this document for personal use only. Any other reproduction or redistribution is strictly prohibited. All rights reserved.

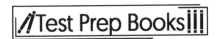

source of funds, which then enables money launderers to use the funds for whatever purpose they choose.

Because the amount of funds from illegal activities is vast, the securities industry is a prime candidate to be abused for attempts to launder money. In response, the securities industry has taken critical steps to ensure that the capital markets are used for legitimate purposes. The primary tool used by regulators to identify and reject money laundering attempts is found in the Investment Advisers Act of 1940, which requires that investment advisers develop and maintain written supervisory procedures that are reasonably designed to prevent violations of the securities laws, including the prevention of anti-money laundering procedures.

In the United States, the government has implemented regulations and procedures for anti-laundering compliance to ensure all parties involved with financial transactions are operating under a strict set of rules. These include:

- **Suspicious Activity Reports (SARS):** These must be delivered to the **Financial Crimes Enforcement Network (FinCEN)** at the U.S. Department of Treasury to report suspicious transactions and individuals. Brokers who identify customers involved in suspicious activity must contact the U.S. Department of Treasury immediately.

- **The Bank Secrecy Act (BSA):** Also known as the Currency and Foreign Transactions Reporting Act, this is a protective measure to detect money laundering activities. Under the act, financial institutions must maintain accurate records of all cash purchases of negotiable instruments, file all purchases over $10,000, and report suspicious activity that might indicate money laundering, tax evasion, or other criminal activity. BSA regulations require financial institutions to submit five types of reports: Currency Transaction Report (FinCEN Form 112); Report of International Transportation of Currency or Monetary Instruments (FinCEN Form 105); Report of Foreign Bank and Financial Accounts (FinCen Form 114); Suspicious Activity Report (SAR); and Designation of Exempt Person (FinCEN Form 110).

- **Currency Transaction Reports (CTRs):** All currency transactions exceeding $10,000 must be filed with the federal government by all U.S. financial institutions in the form of a CTR. Banks typically file these reports electronically for any deposit, withdrawal, exchange, payment, or transfer of more than $10,000 by or through the bank. Multiple currency transactions exceeding $10,000 in a single business day are managed as a single transaction.

- **The Office of Foreign Asset Control (OFAC):** This organization is affiliated with the U.S. Treasury Department and is responsible for tracking terrorist activity and uncovering financial activities associated with financing them. The OFAC also maintains a list of Specially Designated Nationals (SDNs) who are prohibited from doing business with U.S. citizens and institutions.

92

This material is provided for exam preparation purposes only and does not indicate an endorsement of any specific scientific, political, or religious point of view. © TPB Publishing. You have been licensed one copy of this document for personal use only. Any other reproduction or redistribution is strictly prohibited. All rights reserved.

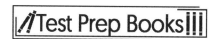

Books/Records and Privacy Requirements

Retention Requirements

Brokers are responsible for maintaining accurate books and records for all financial customer transactions and accounts. Under MSRB Rule G-8, brokers must maintain the following:

- **Records of Original Entry:** An itemized daily record of purchases and sales of municipal securities, receipts showing transactions, and receipts of cash disbursements. It should also include debits and credits associated with municipal securities transactions and any other cash receipts and disbursements.

- **Account Records:** Records that reflect purchases and sales of municipal securities, receipts and deliveries of municipal securities, and receipts and disbursements of cash. They also include debits and credits associated with the account.

- **Securities Records:** These show all positions of municipal securities separately.

- **Subsidiary Records:** Records that reflect municipal securities in transfer, municipal securities to be validated, municipal securities borrowed or loaned, and any municipal securities transactions that weren't completed on the settlement date.

- **Put Options and Repurchase Agreements:** These are records of all written or oral options to sell municipal securities (put options) and any repurchase agreements made.

- **Records for Agency Transactions:** A memorandum of each agency order that includes instructions for the purchase or sale of securities, terms and conditions of the sale, and any other information related to the transaction.

- **Records for Transactions as Principal:** This is a memorandum of all municipal transaction securities for a given account. It includes details such as the price and date of execution, the customer's order, and any and all account designations.

- **Records of Primary Offerings:** Records of the description and aggregate par value of securities, terms and conditions, and all orders received for the purchase of securities by any selling group.

Brokers must also maintain copies of confirmations, periodic statements, and notices sent to customers regarding their account or account status throughout the term of their contract or relationship. Broker-dealers are also responsible for keeping a record of all complaints received from both customers and those acting on their behalf.

Confirmations and Account Statements

Cboe Rule 9.11 covers options trade confirmations. The rule specifies that the customer must receive confirmation that includes what the underlying security is, the expiration date of the contract, the exercise price, the quantity, the premium being paid or being received for writing the options contract, the broker's fee and commission, the trade date, the settlement date, and whether or not the trade was for a customer's account or with the firm's own capital.

Cboe Rule 9.12 outlines what should be on a customer's statement. The statement must show the customer the value of all open positions, the margin he or she has posted, and funds due to the

This material is provided for exam preparation purposes only and does not indicate an endorsement of any specific scientific, political, or religious point of view. © TPB Publishing. You have been licensed one copy of this document for personal use only. Any other reproduction or redistribution is strictly prohibited. All rights reserved.

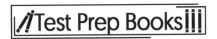

customer or owed by the customer. The statement should be able to tell the customer exactly what their financial position is with that particular account.

FINRA 2232 addresses customer confirmations. 2232 simply states that customers must be notified when they have purchased an equity security that is a callable security. Most equity shares are not callable, so it should be clear to an investor when shares can be called away by the issuer if certain conditions are met.

MSRB G-15 governs municipal bond trade confirmations. These guidelines require the customer to be notified of all parties involved with a trade and how the broker acted on their behalf. The principal, the agent, and any third parties must be included when notifying the customer. More traditional bond metrics must be included as well. The par value, the maturity date, the selling price, and the yield must all be included. The yield must be the lower of the call or maturity date—sometimes referred to as yield to worst.

Rule 10b-10 under the Securities & Exchange Act of 1934 covers disclosures for MBS and ABS securities. Under this rule, the date and time of the transaction must be communicated. This rule specifies that the capacity of the agent or principal must also be included. It must also clarify to the customer that the yield on the asset will be affected by the payments and prepayments on the underlying assets and loans, and it must state if the security is unrated.

Customer Mail

Brokers must have a system in place to maintain customer account records with a high degree of confidentiality. Sensitive information that's stored in paper files or digitally must be kept in a secure place and only be accessible by certain parties. When brokers enter into an agreement with a customer, they assume this liability and must take steps to protect all information. This includes protecting customer contact information, details about accounts, statements, disclosures, and any other information related to transactions and the relationship.

In addition to maintaining accounts with a high degree of confidentiality, it's the broker's responsibility to review customer account details regularly and ensure customers are well-informed about all changes and updates. Communicating this information to the customer by certified mail or private email may be necessary.

Account maintenance tasks can include:

- Assessing a customer's changing assets
- Assessing a customer's investment objectives
- Updating a change of address
- Holding customer mail and sending notifications
- Sending notifications to inform customers of risks associated with new or existing accounts

Business Continuity Plans

Business continuity and disaster recovery plans (BC/DR) take place when the broker-dealer or firm takes actions to resume the firm's operations after a significant event disrupts activities. A BC/DR plan must be drafted as a written document for approval by a principal and include a list of preventive measures the firm will take in the event of a future disaster. These might include having a backup location for employees to work from, ensuring data is backed up regularly, and setting up a system where customers can have secure access to their accounts.

This material is provided for exam preparation purposes only and does not indicate an endorsement of any specific scientific, political, or religious point of view. © TPB Publishing. You have been licensed one copy of this document for personal use only. Any other reproduction or redistribution is strictly prohibited. All rights reserved.

Customer Protection

The broker is responsible for protecting the customer's assets and must take appropriate steps to safeguard all physical assets the customer owns and furnishes to them. This includes checks, cash deposits, and cash equivalents.

When taking customer assets into their possession, the broker must set up a safe or a locked drawer and store them appropriately. They must also take necessary security measures (e.g., changing lock combinations, changing locks, periodically changing access codes) to reduce the risk of theft. Anyone with access to a safe, lockbox, or another security device must be authorized by the broker. The broker assumes the liability associated with possessing a customer's assets when they enter into the customer agreement.

Privacy Requirements

Broker-dealers must follow specific privacy regulations (set forth by the SEC in Regulation S-P) to protect customers from identity theft, fraud, and unauthorized access to privileged information. Financial institutions are prohibited from disclosing nonpublic, customer information to third parties unaffiliated with the customer unless the customer has agreed, in writing, to share this information. Institutions must also provide a current notice of privacy policies and practices that outlines how they protect their customers' information.

Under this act, the SEC has the authority to establish appropriate standards for financial institutions to protect customer information. Brokers and dealers are subject to these rules and requirements of the Gramm-Leach-Bliley Act.

They must also take steps to protect confidential information, such as proprietary, personal customer, and transaction data. Encrypting email interactions, using password-protected laptops and software programs, and using appropriate measures to safeguard information are a few ways to increase information security.

Communications with the Public

Communications and Telemarketing

All public communication must be approved by a supervisory member of the firm before it is distributed or filed with FINRA, whichever is first.

Accurate records of all public communications must be kept, including the date and content of the communication. The records must be in a FINRA-approved format.

Certain public communications must be filed with FINRA at least 10 business days prior to their use or publication. This includes information related to certain investment company products, such as exchange traded funds or mutual funds, communications about security features, and certain bonds that feature a volatility statistic.

All communication must follow certain general guidelines, such as using clear and accurate information, avoiding misleading investors, and being sure to include differences between products when those products are compared in sales literature or other communication.

Any products that claim to be or are exempt from certain taxes, such as state or federal taxes, must state explicitly from which taxes the product is and is not exempt from.

This material is provided for exam preparation purposes only and does not indicate an endorsement of any specific scientific, political, or religious point of view. © TPB Publishing. You have been licensed one copy of this document for personal use only. Any other reproduction or redistribution is strictly prohibited. All rights reserved.

Research reports are not to be approved or checked before publication by any member of the firm's investment banking department to avoid conflicts of interest.

No salesperson or employee of a FINRA member firm may make an outbound telephone call to any residence before 8 a.m. or after 9 p.m., unless a prior business relationship has been established with that person.

They also may not call any individuals who have stated they do not want to receive outbound telephone calls from that specific number or are on the National Do-Not-Call List (National DNC). To be exempt from the National DNC restriction, there must be a business relationship, a personal relationship, or prior written consent.

Telemarketing salespeople and their firms must have established practices for maintaining a do-not-call list, training employees about the regulations of this list, and a process for adding individuals to the list.

Telemarketing salespeople of FINRA member firms must not conceal identification information, such as the number they are calling from, in any way. Firms must get permission before leaving most automated messages.

Suitability Requirements

FINRA Rule 2111 addresses determining the suitability of an investment for a customer. The rule states that the advisor must take reasonable steps to do due diligence when deciding the best investments for their customer. Advisors are required to collect information on: the customer's age; what comprises their total investment portfolio (e.g., 401(k), pension fund, mutual fund, etc.); their net income and any debt; their tax bracket; their retirement goals; and how liquid their investments need to be. For example, customers who are closer to retirement need income, so bonds are a more suitable investment. For customers who manage their own businesses, more liquid investments such as money market funds may be needed to pay their employees. Another example would be investors who plan to leave investments to their children and may want an allocation in equities with the potential for price appreciation. The rule also discusses how recommended strategies should be implemented around customer profiles.

FINRA Rule 2360 covers options. The section on due diligence is the most relevant for suitability considerations. The advisor is required to obtain the customer's: objectives, employment status, income, net worth, liquidity, age, marital status, educational needs (of the account owner or their dependents), and experience with investments. Even when used carefully and properly, options are inherently risky instruments. They have more volatility than most investments, and there are such risks (e.g., credit and counterparty risk) that even if an investment is profitable it may not be paid off. Investors with high risk tolerance (those who are willing to allow their investments to decline more in anticipation that they will rebound) are typically best suited for options trading, even when it's for hedging or insurance purposes on a balanced portfolio in which they're invested.

The rule is very specific about where the customer information is retained and how it's verified (customers must be specifically approved to execute options trades on an exchange). An account agreement must be signed by the customer before any trading in their account can commence, and the customer must fully understand the rules in the agreement. This rule also has specific guidelines for trading uncovered short options contracts. For these transactions, the investor bears the risk of buying the security in the open market. For example, if the investor is selling call options on a stock with an exercise price of $10, and the price of the security goes to $100 for each share in the contract, the

This material is provided for exam preparation purposes only and does not indicate an endorsement of any specific scientific, political, or religious point of view. © TPB Publishing. You have been licensed one copy of this document for personal use only. Any other reproduction or redistribution is strictly prohibited. All rights reserved.

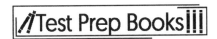

investor now has to pay $100 per share and sell it at $10 (so the potential for large losses is present). To execute such trades, advisors must evaluate their customer's stability because a customer must have the liquidity and net worth to pay for such large losses.

Brokers must also identify the risks of working with certain customers, such as corporate insiders, foreign residents, and broker-dealer employees. This is accomplished through formal programs and customer interviews, allowing the broker to determine who is a valuable customer and who does not serve their best interests. This screening process can include:

- Customer Identification Program (CIP): A result of the Patriot Act, this requires financial institutions to identify and assess anyone wanting to engage in financial activities. The program began in 2003 and is used primarily to verify a customer's identity.

- Know Your Customer (KYC) Forms: This set of documents provides brokers with information on place of residence and citizenship to determine whether the customer is a foreign resident. The forms also assess the customer's assets, knowledge, and willingness to assume the risk of trading securities.

- Identifying Corporate Insiders: Identifying anyone with access to material and non-public knowledge about a corporation, including directors and officers of the company as well as those owning over 10% of the voting shares. These individuals are subject to an additional set of restrictions on all securities transactions.

- Identifying Employees of a Broker-Dealer: Working with broker-dealer employees and competitors is risky. Brokers must identify these prospective customers and receive consent from their employer to proceed.

- Identifying Employees of Self-Regulatory Organizations (SROs): Working with employees of SROs is also risky, and they are subject to certain restrictions. To proceed, the broker must receive consent from the prospective customer's employer.

Prohibited Activities

Market Manipulation

Market manipulation is a deliberate abuse of the market by interfering with the supply or demand of a security.

Securities Act Rule 144 sets standards for selling restricted or controlled securities. The rule provides an exemption depending on how many securities are held, the amount that can be sold at one time, and how the securities are traded or sold to an investor. These sales involve control persons, which are usually considered to be the board of directors and C-suite level management (CEO, CFO, etc.).

A reporting company is the company responsible for reporting requirements to the SEC. If the company that issued the securities is the reporting company, the securities must be held for at least six months (the holding period, which is the required amount of time an investor must hold the securities). Other requirements for restricted securities sales are that current public information about the issuer must be available, no more than 1% of outstanding stock can be sold per quarter by an affiliate, and if an affiliate sells more than 5,000 shares or $50,000 in market value, they must file that sale with the SEC.

This material is provided for exam preparation purposes only and does not indicate an endorsement of any specific scientific, political, or religious point of view. © TPB Publishing. You have been licensed one copy of this document for personal use only. Any other reproduction or redistribution is strictly prohibited. All rights reserved.

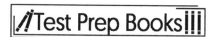

There are several governing bodies with rules regarding spreading market rumors. NYSE Rule 435(5), NYSE Rule 476, FINRA Rule 6140(e), and FINRA Rule 2010 address market rumors. NYSE Rule 435(5) makes a general statement, in that investors and market participants must not circulate rumors that can influence the market. This includes "unsubstantiated" rumors, even if they appear in the main stream. Circulation and the sources of these rumors should be reported by market participants. FINRA Rule 6140 is more specific about guidelines around rumors. Part (a) of this rule states trades cannot be made at prices to induce the market to trade on poor price information. Essentially, this means that participants cannot inflate the price of a stock for their own benefit. The rule also states syndicates and margin accounts can't be used to artificially influence prices. If false and misleading information is used to raise a price of a security which is subsequently sold at a gain, this is known as pump and dump.

Front running occurs when a broker takes advantage of the market for their own benefit while their customers' orders are pending. In such situations, a broker may purchase blocks of shares to drive up prices before executing the trade for a customer. The broker could then sell the new shares at the artificially inflated prices to reap a short-term profit. Traditional front running is more easily detected because regulators can simply compare paper records between a broker and client, but when front running is carried out via computer, it is much harder to detect. In 2001, the SEC changed the pricing of stocks from 1/8 increments to pennies to deter front running by reducing the incentive.

Churning occurs when a broker or salesman executes trades simply to increase their commission. If caught, all commissions and fees must be repaid, as well as any losses incurred on the investment. Fines can be assessed, and licensing can be suspended. SEC Rule 15c1-7 addresses churning. Frequent in and out purchases and high turnover are often indicative of churning. Most mutual funds turn their portfolio over about once a year, so monthly turnover can be evidence of churning and excessive trading.

Reverse churning can also occur; this is when infrequently traded accounts are put into fee-based accounts to maximize the commission. Marking the close is a type of market manipulation that occurs when a large quantity of securities is bought or sold just before the close of trading to influence price. The opposite, or marking the open, is when the same type of activity occurs directly before the market opens.

Backing away is a violation that happens when a securities dealer refuses to honor a firm quote. When a stock is purchased and then sold before it has been paid for, this is known as freeriding. Both of these activities are prohibited.

Insider Trading

Transactions performed by individuals with access to special, non-public information for a company are defined as insider trading activities. Insiders are anyone with access to material and non-public knowledge about a corporation, including directors and officers of the company as well as those owning over 10% of the voting shares. These individuals are subject to an additional set of restrictions on all securities transactions. Material nonpublic information is anything not already released to the public that would have an effect on the value or trading of a security.

Since there are inherent risks associated with these types of transactions, they're subject to SEC regulations. According to the SEC, insider trading violations occur when confidential information is used to perform illegal trades that are "in breach of a fiduciary duty or other relationship of trust and confidence." An example of this would be when friends or business associates trade securities after being "tipped" with information from an officer.

This material is provided for exam preparation purposes only and does not indicate an endorsement of any specific scientific, political, or religious point of view. © TPB Publishing. You have been licensed one copy of this document for personal use only. Any other reproduction or redistribution is strictly prohibited. All rights reserved.

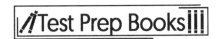

Insiders and any other involved parties can be subject to liability penalties. Civil sanctions and criminal prosecution are both possible punishments for insider trading. Criminal insider trading can include sentencing of up to 20 years imprisonment and maximum amount of fines can be anywhere from $5,000,000 to $25,000,000 depending on whether an individual or a business entity committed the crime.

Other Prohibited Activities

Commingling of funds occurs when an advisor mixes their own funds with those of a client. Commingling makes it difficult to determine to whom specific funds belong. This increases the potential for fraud. If commingling is identified, any losses are allocated to the advisor and any gains are allocated to the client.

Unauthorized transactions are prohibited on most exchanges. This occurs when trades are executed without the permission or authorization from the client. There are some exceptions; a broker may be able to sell a client's securities if a margin call is made, and the client does not have sufficient cash.

FINRA Rule 2010 covers unauthorized transactions. Advisors and brokers are prohibited from making guarantees that gains or losses will occur. FINRA Rule 2150(b) states advisors cannot make a statement guaranteeing that there will be no losses on any securities purchased.

SEC Rule 206(4)-3 covers referral fees. This rule states that an advisor cannot pay a cash fee unless specific conditions are met. If there is a written agreement or if the client is notified in advance that the solicitor is being compensated with a fee, it is legal. An advisor who violates these rules can lose their registration license.

Brokers must have a reasonable basis for recommending the purchase or sale of a security. When making a recommendation, brokers must consider their client's income, net worth, portfolio, investment objectives, liquidity, experience, investment horizon, and their total portfolio. It is also important to have a conversation about a client's ability and willingness to take risks.

Securities industry professionals must avoid conflicts of interest that create the mere appearance of impropriety. For example, model acts do not allow customers to borrow from investment advisers unless the client is also a financial institution such as a broker-dealer, an affiliated entity of an investment adviser, or a firm that is in the business of lending money, like a commercial bank. Model acts also do not permit industry professionals to share customer accounts unless both the financial institution and the client agree in writing to share the account, and the sharing of the account is proportionate to the amount invested by the financial institution and the client.

In addition, over the last decade laws have been passed at the federal and state level in response to the increased abuse of senior citizens in financial matters. An entire body of law known as "elder law" has been established to help vulnerable senior citizens avoid being taken advantage of in all matters—especially financial matters—because senior citizens typically have the most money to lose after a lifetime of earnings, savings, and investments. The financial exploitation of seniors is considered a prohibited activity in the securities industry.

Another common prohibited activity involves individuals employed in securities-related activities without being registered when the model acts require that the individual be properly registered before performing those activities. The process of registering is straightforward and often handled by a financial institution's operational staff. So, there is no excuse for unregistered persons performing

This material is provided for exam preparation purposes only and does not indicate an endorsement of any specific scientific, political, or religious point of view. © TPB Publishing. You have been licensed one copy of this document for personal use only. Any other reproduction or redistribution is strictly prohibited. All rights reserved.

securities-related activities. Investors should confirm that any securities industry professionals they work with are registered before making an investment.

Finally, like most industries, the securities industry prohibits industry professionals from falsifying or withholding documents. Falsifying any document falls under the anti-fraud provisions of the securities acts and represents an intentional misrepresentation of a material fact. Withholding documents can also fall under the anti-fraud provisions of the securities acts as an omission of a material fact.

This material is provided for exam preparation purposes only and does not indicate an endorsement of any specific scientific, political, or religious point of view. © TPB Publishing. You have been licensed one copy of this document for personal use only. Any other reproduction or redistribution is strictly prohibited. All rights reserved.

Glossary

529 College Savings Account	These accounts can pay for approved college expenses. Each state has their own 529 plans with different rules on taxation and contribution limits.
Account Records	Records that reflect purchases and sales of municipal securities, receipts and deliveries of municipal securities, and receipts and disbursements of cash; they also include debits and credits associated with the account.
Acquisition	When one company buys another company usually with money or an exchange of securities of the entities involved
Advisory Account	This is an account for customers working with a financial advisor (to be better informed about investment decisions) but still wanting to retain all rights to authorize purchases. The fee structure for these accounts is asset based, not commission based. This eliminates the broker's incentive to turn a portfolio over or "churn" an account to receive the highest fees.
Ask	The seller's asking price
Bearish	An investor or trader perceives that the security will decrease in value
Bid	The price that buyers are willing to pay for a bond or a share of stock
Bid-Ask Spread (Spread)	The difference between the bid and ask amounts
Bird in Hand Theory	It is better for the investor to receive a dividend, rather than the company retain that cash and invest it back in the company's operations.
Bullish	An investor or trader perceives that the security will increase in value.
Capital Gain	The profit received when assets like stocks, bonds, or real estate are sold
Cash Account	Standard brokerage account in which the customer makes cash deposits for trading purposes
Churning	When a broker or salesman executes trades simply to increase their commission
Commingling	When an advisor mixes their own funds with those of a client
Coverdell Education Savings Account	These accounts have certain tax advantages and can pay for elementary through college education. The contribution limit for a Coverdell ESA is $2,000 per child.
Currency Transaction Reports (CTRs)	All currency transactions exceeding $10,000 must be filed with the federal government by all U.S. financial institutions. Banks typically file these reports electronically for any deposit, withdrawal, exchange, payment, or transfer of more

101

This material is provided for exam preparation purposes only and does not indicate an endorsement of any specific scientific, political, or religious point of view. © TPB Publishing. You have been licensed one copy of this document for personal use only. Any other reproduction or redistribution is strictly prohibited. All rights reserved.

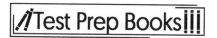

than $10,000 by or through the bank. Multiple currency transactions exceeding $10,000 in a single business day are managed as a single transaction.

Custodial Account	Trust account managed on behalf of a minor. Examples would be Uniform Gifts to Minors Act (UGMA) or Uniform Transfers to Minors Act (UTMA).
Customer Identification Program (CIP)	A result of the Patriot Act, this requires financial institutions to identify and assess anyone wanting to engage in financial activities. The program began in 2003 and is used primarily to verify a customer's identity
Day Order	Expires if criteria is not reached for a trade to occur during that day
Day Trading	This is a designation rather than a type of account. Brokers will label a customer as a "pattern day trader" if they execute four or more day trades within five business days. The "patter day trader" designation only applies to margin accounts. Different SEC rules apply to both cash and margin accounts that are used to day trade.
Delivery Versus Payment (DVP)	A settlement procedure where the buyer's payment for securities is due at the time of delivery. It's also known as delivery against payment (DAP), delivery against cash (DAC), and cash on delivery. The purpose of this transaction is to mitigate settlement risk since both sides of the transaction are executed simultaneously.
Discount Yield	The yield on a Treasury bond sold at a discount (annualized)
Discretionary Account (Managed Account)	Also known as a "managed account," this is created when brokers are given the authority to manage transactions without the customer's consent. This account requires both parties to sign a discretionary disclosure document. Typically, the customer sets up specific parameters (asset class, transaction type, security type, etc.) around what can be traded.
Dividend Payout Ratio	The percentage of earnings paid out as a dividend
Dividend Reinvestment Plan (DRIP)	When a company pay dividends in the form of stock shares (often at a discount to the stock's market value).
Estate Account	Held in the name of the estate of someone who's deceased and is managed by a representative
Exchange Offers	These occur when a company (or parent company) with different asset classes offers an exchange of stock classes, companies' stocks, or securities (i.e., bonds).
Ex-Dividend Date	This is the first day the stock trades without the dividend, which means the amount of the dividend is subtracted from the stock price.
Fee-Based Account	Account where the financial advisor receives a commission based on a percentage of the customer's assets
FINRA Rule 4320	If the short seller has not delivered the securities to the buyer, the seller will not receive payment if the trade is profitable.
Front Running	This occurs when a broker takes advantage of the market for their own benefit while their customers' orders are pending.

This material is provided for exam preparation purposes only and does not indicate an endorsement of any specific scientific, political, or religious point of view. © TPB Publishing. You have been licensed one copy of this document for personal use only. Any other reproduction or redistribution is strictly prohibited. All rights reserved.

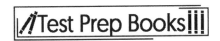

Good-Til-Canceled (GTC)	This means that the order is in place until executed, unless the investor cancels the order.
Individual Retirement Account (IRA)	Investment vehicle provided by most employers and corporations that provide investments with significant tax advantages
Insider Trading	Transactions performed by individuals with access to special, non-public information for a company
Irrevocable Trust	Set up by one party in order to benefit another party; It is not allowed to be amended or cancelled without the beneficiary's approval.
Joint Tenants In Common (JTIC)	This is an account where authorized individuals do not retain control over the account if the joint tenant dies but may receive a portion of the assets as outlined in the deceased's will.
Joint Tenants with Rights Of Survivorship (JTWROS)	Account where authorized individuals have equal authority over the account and retain control even when one of the joint tenants dies.
Know Your Customer (KYC) Forms	This set of documents provides brokers with information on place of residence and citizenship to determine whether the customer is a foreign resident. The forms also assess the customer's assets, knowledge, and willingness to assume the risk of trading securities.
Limit Order	In this, the investor has more control, and the order is not executed if the market price does not fall within the limit range.
Margin Account	An account created when a broker lends money to a customer and uses cash and securities as collateral for the loan. The margin covers some or all of the credit risk for a transaction.
Market Manipulation	Deliberate abuse of the market by interfering with the supply or demand of a security
Market Order	An order that is executed at whatever the market price is
Merger	This is when one company combines with another company to form one new company.
Money Laundering	Deliberate concealment of illegally obtained funds; The process of laundering has three stages: placement, layering, and structuring.
Non-Solicited Order	If the investor or trader contacts the professional affecting the transaction to initiate a transaction
Options Trading (Account)	Higher risk type of trading, with more regulations, where the customer is allowed to hold options; Brokerages require that option traders use a margin account.
Payable Date	The date when the dividend will actually be paid by the corporation
Proxy Voting	When someone delegates their voting power to another party

This material is provided for exam preparation purposes only and does not indicate an endorsement of any specific scientific, political, or religious point of view. © TPB Publishing. You have been licensed one copy of this document for personal use only. Any other reproduction or redistribution is strictly prohibited. All rights reserved.

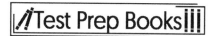
Put Options and Repurchase Agreements	These are records of all written or oral options to sell municipal securities (put options) and any repurchase agreements made.
Qualified Tuition Programs (QTP) (Education Accounts)	Tax-advantaged savings plan or brokerage account used to pay for expenses related to education
Receive Versus Payment (RVP)	A settlement procedure where the buyer's payment for securities is due at the time of receipt. It's also called receive against payment (RAP).
Record Date	This is the date that a stockholder must own the stock in order to receive the dividend.
Records for Agency Transactions	Memorandum of each agency order that includes instructions for the purchase or sale of securities, terms and conditions of the sale, and any other information related to the transaction
Records for Transactions as Principal	This is a memorandum of all municipal transaction securities for a given account. It includes details such as the price and date of execution, the customer's order, and any and all account designations.
Records of Original Entry	Itemized daily record of purchases and sales of municipal securities, receipts showing transactions, and receipts of cash disbursements
Records of Primary Offerings	Records of the description and aggregate par value of securities, terms and conditions, and all orders received for the purchase of securities by any selling group
Retirement Account	Tax-advantaged brokerage account that can be either a cash or margin account; Examples include: IRA, Roth IRA, SEP IRA, and SIMPLE IRA.
Return Of Capital	When an investor receives all or a portion of their original principal invested
Reverse Churning	When infrequently traded accounts are put into fee-based accounts to maximize the commission
Revocable Trust	Set up by one party in order to benefit another party; It allows for alterations, changes, and even cancellation depending on the grantor.
Roth IRA	This is a variation of a traditional IRA, but the tax break occurs when the money is withdrawn, not invested.
Securities Records	These show all positions of municipal securities separately.
SIMPLE IRA	This is similar to a 401(k) or 403(b) plan many employers offer. They can be funded with pretax dollars but are still subject to social security, Medicare, and unemployment taxes. Early withdrawals are taxed at 25 percent.
Simplified Employee Pension IRA (SEP IRA)	Investment instrument used by small businesses to provide tax-free investing for their owners and employees. These funds are taxed at the ordinary rate when withdrawn if the beneficiary has reached the age of 59 1/2. Employees can contribute up to 25 percent of their wages into the SEP IRA.
Solicited Order	If the investor or trader is contacted by a professional affecting a transaction to induce the investor or trader to initiate a transaction

This material is provided for exam preparation purposes only and does not indicate an endorsement of any specific scientific, political, or religious point of view. © TPB Publishing. You have been licensed one copy of this document for personal use only. Any other reproduction or redistribution is strictly prohibited. All rights reserved.

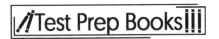

Stock Split	When a company increases the number of outstanding shares; The share price will decline relative to the number of new shares issued.
Stop Order	The trade is only executed when the price surpasses a certain point.
Straddle	An options trading technique that involves an investor buying a put and a call of the same underlying stock with the same strike price and expiration date
Subsidiary Records	Records that reflect municipal securities in transfer, municipal securities to be validated, municipal securities borrowed or loaned, and any municipal securities transactions that weren't completed on the settlement date
Suspicious Activity Reports (SARS)	These must be delivered to the Financial Crimes Enforcement Network (FinCEN) at the U.S. Department of Treasury to report suspicious transactions and individuals. Brokers who identify customers involved in suspicious activity must contact the U.S. Department of Treasury immediately.
Tender Offer	The company proposes to buy a certain number of shares at a certain price from existing shareholders.
The Bank Secrecy Act (BSA)	Financial institutions must maintain accurate records of all cash purchases of negotiable instruments, file all purchases over $10,000, and report suspicious activity that might indicate money laundering, tax evasion, or other criminal activity.
The Office of Foreign Asset Control (OFAC)	Part of the U.S. Treasury Department and is responsible for tracking terrorist activity and uncovering financial activities associated with financing them
Transfer On Death (TOD)	Where an accountholder identifies which assets will be transferred to various parties upon their death without the probate process
Yield To Call (YTC)	The total return that a bond investor can receive if he holds a bond until its call date. Not every bond is callable.
Yield To Maturity (YTM)	The yield an investor can expect to earn if they hold the bond until it matures
Yield To Worst (YTW)	The yield assuming the worst-case scenario for the bond, whether it matures or is called first
Zeros	Bonds that do not pay interest

This material is provided for exam preparation purposes only and does not indicate an endorsement of any specific scientific, political, or religious point of view. © TPB Publishing. You have been licensed one copy of this document for personal use only. Any other reproduction or redistribution is strictly prohibited. All rights reserved.

Practice Quiz

1. Which of the following is NOT a financial factor that an investment advisor should include in their customer's investment profile?
   a. Other assets
   b. Net worth
   c. Political party
   d. Federal tax rate

2. Which of the following is an investment concept that should be applied to a customer's financial profile to determine the best investment for a customer?
   a. Turnover ratio
   b. Total investment portfolio
   c. Current financial status
   d. Risk vs. return

3. Diana and Greg are a newly retired couple. Which of the following would be the most appropriate investment vehicle for them?
   a. Stocks
   b. Options
   c. Roth IRAs
   d. Money market funds

4. Which of the following investments have tax advantages for an investor?
   a. Treasury bonds
   b. Partnerships
   c. Options
   d. Convertible stock

5. What type of brokerage account would need to be opened for a customer who wants to invest long-term without using debt?
   a. Margin Account
   b. Options Trading Account
   c. Cash Account
   d. Day Trading Account

See answers on next page.

106

This material is provided for exam preparation purposes only and does not indicate an endorsement of any specific scientific, political, or religious point of view. © TPB Publishing. You have been licensed one copy of this document for personal use only. Any other reproduction or redistribution is strictly prohibited. All rights reserved.

Answer Explanations

1. C: A customer's political party is not a financial factor that an investment advisor should include in a customer's investment profile. The customer's security holdings, other assets, liabilities, annual income, expenses, net worth, liquid net worth, and federal tax rate are all pieces of information relevant to an investment profile.

2. D: Investment concepts include risk vs. return, potential returns of different investment classes, inflationary effects, and taxability. These should be used in correlation with a customer's profile to determine the best investment for that customer.

3. D: The most appropriate investment choices for retired couples are money market funds and bonds. Options and stocks have more variable swings in the value of investments which is usually not appropriate for a retired couple living on a fixed income. Roth IRAs would not be an appropriate investment because Diana and Greg are already retired.

4. B: Municipal bonds, partnerships, UITs, and annuities all have tax advantages that can be used as part of an investment strategy for investors.

5. C: A cash account would be best for a long-term investor who doesn't want to borrow. There are only two types of brokerage accounts according to the SEC. A cash account is a common type of brokerage account where the customer makes cash deposits to be used in trades. A margin account is used for when a customer borrows money from the broker. In order to invest in options, a customer must open a margin account. Day traders can use cash or margin accounts to invest.

This material is provided for exam preparation purposes only and does not indicate an endorsement of any specific scientific, political, or religious point of view. © TPB Publishing. You have been licensed one copy of this document for personal use only. Any other reproduction or redistribution is strictly prohibited. All rights reserved.

Overview of Regulatory Framework

SRO Regulatory Requirements for Associated Persons

Registration and Continuing Education

SRO Qualification and Registration Requirements

Self-regulatory organizations in the securities industry primarily comprise large nongovernmental organizations that seek to self-govern specific areas where specialized knowledge can more effectively provide an orderly market system. The most well-known SROs in the securities industry are the Financial Industry Regulatory Authority (FINRA) and the most prominent exchanges, such as the New York Stock Exchange. In addition, smaller, regional exchanges such as the Chicago Stock Exchange are considered SROs.

Because SROs are generally operated by industry participants, those participants have the power to determine what steps an entity must take to be considered qualified within the industry as an SRO. Once an entity meets specific qualifications, which are often financially-based, an SRO may be required to register with the Securities and Exchange Commission to empower the SRO to make and enforce rules and regulations intended to provide necessary order to the securities market landscape.

An SRO is not granted SRO status simply because an application is made to become an SRO. This is easy to understand because SROs are responsible for creating literally volumes of rules and regulations that combine with federal and state securities laws to promote equity and fairness in the securities markets. An application to become an SRO may be rejected or delayed if potential members of the SRO are deemed ineligible for the membership or association. In most cases, ineligibility is based on financial inadequacy, criminal histories, or lack of a legitimate purpose. As part of the process to become an SRO, the potential founders must agree to background checks and fingerprinting as part of due diligence in determining the character of an SRO application.

Notwithstanding passing background checks and fingerprinting requirements, sometimes a proposed SRO or an existing SRO will be denied or lose its status if the SRO is in conflict with a statute. In statutory disqualification, the proposed SRO or existing SRO will lose its status regardless of background checks, fingerprinting, or even if everything else about the SRO is in compliance. The statute is said to govern and if the SRO falls under any element of the statute for disqualification, the SRO can be terminated.

Employees involved with securities or investment banking for a Financial Industry Regulatory Authority (FINRA) member firm must register with FINRA. Employees who work in a FINRA member firm in clerical or administrative positions that do not interact with clients or customers may not have to register.

Individuals must pass a Qualification Exam for Principals before they are allowed to register. Principals are employees, directors, sole proprietors, partners, or managers of the member firm who train, solicit, or otherwise engage in or support securities activities or investment banking.

This material is provided for exam preparation purposes only and does not indicate an endorsement of any specific scientific, political, or religious point of view. © TPB Publishing. You have been licensed one copy of this document for personal use only. Any other reproduction or redistribution is strictly prohibited. All rights reserved.

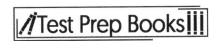

Depending upon the type of exam passed and type of registration, registered persons may engage in certain acts. For example, an individual who passes the Series 6 exam may solicit, purchase, or sell the following products:

- Mutual funds (closed-end funds on the initial offering only)

- Variable annuities

- Variable life insurance

- Unit investment trusts (UITs)

- Municipal fund securities (e.g., 529 College Savings Plans, local government investment pools (LGIPs), and Coverdell Education Savings Accounts)

Series 7 holders may solicit, purchase, or sell the following products:

- Public offerings and/or private placements of corporate securities (stocks and bonds)
- Rights
- Warrants
- Mutual funds
- Money market funds
- Unit investment trusts (UITs)
- Exchange traded funds (ETFs)
- Real estate investment trusts (REITs)
- Options on mortgage-backed securities
- Government securities
- Repos and certificates of accrual on government securities
- Direct participation programs
- Securities traders
- Venture capital
- Sale of municipal securities
- Hedge funds

There are other exams an individual could take based on their position at the member firm and the types of securities business he or she wishes to engage in. Non-registered persons who do not pass the correct exam may not solicit, buy, or sell the securities products that require a Series exam.

State Registration Requirements

While the federal government operating through the Securities and Exchange Commission is the primary and most powerful regulating body in the securities industry, state governments also have their place in regulating the securities industry. Recall that laws enacted by the states are commonly referred to as **blue sky laws**, and they exist to allow states to regulate securities in a manner consistent with their specific situations.

While states may regulate the securities industry, state laws are subject to the Supremacy Clause of the United States Constitution just like any other law enacted by a state. In the securities industry, this typically results in state, blue sky laws that provide additional protections to state residents over the protections provided at the federal level. Notwithstanding state rights to regulate the securities industry

This material is provided for exam preparation purposes only and does not indicate an endorsement of any specific scientific, political, or religious point of view. © TPB Publishing. You have been licensed one copy of this document for personal use only. Any other reproduction or redistribution is strictly prohibited. All rights reserved.

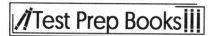

at the state legislature level, most states rely on model securities acts drafted by the North American Securities Administrators Association (NASAA). While each state usually makes some revision to the model acts before enactment, research and review of state blue sky laws will uncover similar laws, rules, and regulations.

For example, states can require additional protections when there is a proposed registration of a securities offering in a state, when an individual is seeking to become licensed as a securities professional in a state, or when a firm is registering to do securities-related business within a state. In addition, states may require more continuing education than federal laws when an individual or firm seeks to continue doing business within a state.

Continuing Education (CE) Requirement

Registered persons must complete what is known as the Regulatory Element on the second anniversary of their registration, and again three years thereafter as part of their continuing education. The content of the Regulatory Element is determined by FINRA.

Registered persons may be required to take the Regulatory Element outside of this timeframe if they break certain securities laws and/or are subject to certain fines or disciplinary action(s).

Each member organization has a responsibility to annually evaluate and assess all employees who directly interact with customers or clients to ensure their securities knowledge is accurate and up-to-date. Written plans must be developed when considering the size, scope, and nature of the member firm's business to ensure the plan is appropriate.

This training plan, at a minimum, must cover the following topics:

- General investment features and associated risk factors

- Suitability and sales practice considerations

- Applicable regulatory requirements

- Training in ethics, professional responsibility, and the requirements of Rule 2241 for registered research analysts and their immediate supervisors

The member firm must administer the written plan it develops and document both the plan and its implementation.

Employee Conduct and Reportable Events

Employee Conduct

Form U4 and Form U5

Form U4 (Uniform Application for Security Industry Registration or Transfer) is filed electronically via the Central Registration Depository by the firms that employ representatives of investment advisors and broker-dealers to register them with FINRA and with the states.

Form U5 (Uniform Termination Notice for Security Industry Registration) is used by investment advisors and broker-dealers to terminate the registrations of representatives with a specific self-regulatory

This material is provided for exam preparation purposes only and does not indicate an endorsement of any specific scientific, political, or religious point of view. © TPB Publishing. You have been licensed one copy of this document for personal use only. Any other reproduction or redistribution is strictly prohibited. All rights reserved.

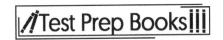

organization or jurisdiction. A number of disclosure questions must be addressed during the filing of the termination.

Filing Misleading Information

Individuals employed in the securities industry must not file misleading information or omit material information in a filing. Information that is filed must be able to be reasonably relied upon by an investor before making an investment decision. If the information that is filed is misleading, an investor cannot reasonably rely on that information in making an investment decision. On the other hand, an investor, by definition, cannot reasonably rely on omitted material information in making an investment decision. Filing misleading information or omitting information from a filing may also violate the anti-fraud provisions of the securities acts.

Customer Complaints

All complaints to the Financial Industry Regulatory Authority (FINRA) must be submitted in writing. FINRA may use a formal or informal process to handle customer complaints depending on the customer making the complaint.

Formal proceedings occur when the customer pursues them to resolve a complaint, and the issue is resolved according to FINRA's code of procedure. In this case, the District Business Conduct Committee (DBCC) has first jurisdiction over the complaint. If the customer is dissatisfied with how the issue is handled, they can appeal the outcome to the FINRA Board of Governors or take the case up to the Supreme Court.

Informal proceedings happen when a complaint is resolved according to FINRA's code of arbitration. At least two arbitrators participate in an informal hearing, and the decision is binding (not open to appeal). Arbitration can be pursued by customers as well as members of FINRA. Mediation is also an option for these types of complaints.

Potential Red Flags

The securities industry is one of the most regulated industries in the world because of the importance of maintaining the integrity of the capital markets. Employees of firms in the securities industry are also strictly regulated. Employee conduct that could potentially impair that integrity should be red flagged. In many cases, suspicious conduct can be identified by common sense. For example, employees that manipulate clients for their benefit, engage in business transactions with clients, possess surprising and confidential information, or behave in a manner that otherwise does not pass the "smell test" should be reported and reviewed to ensure that no unethical or illegal actions or omissions are occurring in the workplace.

Reportable Events

Outside Business Activities

While a Registered Representative (RR) is allowed to execute trades for people employed at another firm, they must exercise reasonable diligence to ensure these trades won't harm their own employer. An RR is required, by law, to disclose outside business activities that would betray an "adverse interest" against the broker's own employer.

This material is provided for exam preparation purposes only and does not indicate an endorsement of any specific scientific, political, or religious point of view. © TPB Publishing. You have been licensed one copy of this document for personal use only. Any other reproduction or redistribution is strictly prohibited. All rights reserved.

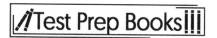

Outside business activities include personal investment accounts that an RR holds outside of their own firm. When an RR has an interest in an account at another firm, the firm must do the following before conducting any transactions:

- Notify the RR's employer in writing
- Deliver duplicate documents for the account
- Notify the RR that these two tasks have been completed

Private Securities Transactions

These transactions occur when the broker sells a security that's not recognized or sold by their own broker-dealer or they receive compensation for the transaction.

Political Contributions

No FINRA member firms, companies, broker-dealers, or securities dealers may ask for, raise, solicit, or otherwise attempt to get political donations from their own employees, investors, customers, or from other FINRA member firms.

This rule applies to political parties of state and local governments, as well as federal governments.

Any payments to political sources must be disclosed to the firm's board or senior executive team and must also be documented. These contributions cannot exceed $250 per person or per political party per year.

The Municipal Securities Rulemaking Board Rule G-37 outlines the parameters around municipal bonds and political contributions. The stipulations include that no dealer can engage in business with an issuer within two years of any contribution to an official made by the dealer, any professional associated with a dealer, or any political action committee (PAC) controlled by the dealer or anyone associated with them.

Contributions less than $250 are exempt from the rule, as well as charitable donations. The intent of the rule is to assure high standards and integrity in the municipal bond industry, to prevent fraudulent activity, to prevent manipulation of political officials for private financial gain or benefit, to promote just and equitable principles of trading municipal bonds, and to protect the public interest.

Gifts and Gratuities

Regulated entities cannot receive more than $100 per person per year if that compensation is related to their activities concerning municipal securities. Exceptions to this rule include bereavement gifts and regular office supplies such as pens and notepads.

FINRA member firms also face this $100 limit per person when dealing with the associates or employees of other firms. Firms who conduct business on behalf of the Cboe Options Exchange or with Cboe are limited to the same restriction, but in a reduced amount of $50 per person per year.

Business Entertainment

The securities industry means big business and big business relationships. However, the securities industry is keenly aware that business relationships can sometimes become averse to the interests of investors in financial markets by affecting the independent judgment of industry professionals. In order to tame the potential abuses, inappropriate business entertainment is considered a reportable event.

This material is provided for exam preparation purposes only and does not indicate an endorsement of any specific scientific, political, or religious point of view. © TPB Publishing. You have been licensed one copy of this document for personal use only. Any other reproduction or redistribution is strictly prohibited. All rights reserved.

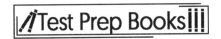

Other Reportable Events

The securities industry often takes a harder stance than other industries toward the crimes and credit histories of the individuals working in the industry. The regulation of securities professionals can include the exclusion of individuals for felonies, securities-related misdemeanors, liens, and credit events such as compromises with creditors and bankruptcies. Depending on the nature of any past crimes committed, an individual can be barred, suspended, or censured. Credit events are typically reportable events that do not bar, suspend, or censure individuals so long as the credit events are sufficiently disclosed to all parties and regulators.

This material is provided for exam preparation purposes only and does not indicate an endorsement of any specific scientific, political, or religious point of view. © TPB Publishing. You have been licensed one copy of this document for personal use only. Any other reproduction or redistribution is strictly prohibited. All rights reserved.

Glossary

Blue Sky Laws	These are recall laws enacted by the state, and they exist to allow states to regulate securities in a manner consistent with their specific situations.
Continuing Education (CE)	Non-credit programs or courses for continual improvement of skills and knowledge, directed toward license holders and working professionals
Form U4	Filed electronically by the firms that employ representatives of investment advisors and broker-dealers to register them with FINRA and with the states
Form U5	Used by investment advisors and broker-dealers to terminate the registrations of representatives with a specific self-regulatory organization or jurisdiction
Municipal Securities Rulemaking Board Rule G-37	Outlines the parameters around municipal bonds and political contributions; The stipulations include that no dealer can engage in business with an issuer within two years of any contribution to an official made by the dealer, any professional associated with a dealer, or any political action committee (PAC) controlled by the dealer or anyone associated with them.
National Association of Securities Dealers (NASD)	This was the original self-regulatory organization that supervised securities trading on behalf of the SEC before merging with another organization to become FINRA.
North American Securities Administrators Association (NASAA)	Agent and firm licensing organization that also provides investment fraud education, investigates state and provincial law violations, and files enforcement actions
Political Action Committee (PAC)	Political committee organized for the purpose of raising and spending money to elect and defeat candidates
Principals	Employees, directors, sole proprietors, partners, or managers of the member firm who train, solicit, or otherwise engage in or support securities activities or investment banking
Registered Representative (RR)	Are allowed to execute trades for people employed at another firm and are required, by law, to disclose outside business activities that would betray an "adverse interest" against the broker's own employer
Regulatory Element	Focuses on compliance, regulatory, ethical and sales practice standards

This material is provided for exam preparation purposes only and does not indicate an endorsement of any specific scientific, political, or religious point of view. © TPB Publishing. You have been licensed one copy of this document for personal use only. Any other reproduction or redistribution is strictly prohibited. All rights reserved.

Practice Quiz

1. Which of the following is NOT considered a self-regulatory organization?
   a. Cboe
   b. FINRA
   c. MSRB
   d. SEC

2. When must registered persons first complete the Regulatory Element?
   a. Before they are allowed to register
   b. On the first anniversary of their registration
   c. On the second anniversary of their registration
   d. On the third anniversary of their registration

3. Which organization determines the contents of the Regulatory Element section for registered members' continuing education (CE)?
   a. The Financial Industry Regulatory Authority (FINRA)
   b. The U.S. Securities and Exchange Commission (SEC)
   c. The Financial Accounting Standards Board (FASB)
   d. The Consumer Financial Protection Bureau (CFPB)

4. Which of the following is a potential red flag that firms should watch for in regards to their registered representatives?
   a. A member offering a client advertisement material regarding certain debt securities.
   b. Clients asking their account advisors for stock recommendations.
   c. A representative asking a client to sign forms that are not required to open an account or purchase securities.
   d. A representative asking for certain private details such as SSN, home address, and phone number.

5. When a representative has an interest in an account at another firm, the firm must do the following before making any transactions:

   I. Notify the firm in writing.
   II. Deliver duplicate account documents to the RR's employer.
   III. Notify the RR.

   a. II, III
   b. I, III
   c. I, II
   d. I, II, III

See answers on next page.

115

This material is provided for exam preparation purposes only and does not indicate an endorsement of any specific scientific, political, or religious point of view. © TPB Publishing. You have been licensed one copy of this document for personal use only. Any other reproduction or redistribution is strictly prohibited. All rights reserved.

Answer Explanations

1. D: The SEC is a government agency that broadly regulates most securities (debt, equity, etc.) and is not considered a self-regulatory organization. The Cboe, MSRB, and FINRA are all considered SROs because they are large nongovernmental organizations that self-govern areas where specialized knowledge is needed.

2. C: Registered persons must complete what is called the Regulatory Element on the second anniversary of their registration and then every three years following that. A qualification exam must be passed before anyone can register.

3. A: FINRA determines the contents of the Regulatory Element for members taking continuing education courses. The SEC, FASB, and CFPB do not determine contents of any CE courses for registered representatives.

4. C: There would be little reason to ask a client to sign forms that do not pertain to opening an account or buying securities. Members handing out promotional material for securities, clients asking for stock advice, and representatives asking for private details (SSN, home address, phone number) are normal activities.

5. D: Firms must notify the representative's employer at the other firm, deliver duplicate account documents to said employer, and notify the representative once both tasks have been completed.

This material is provided for exam preparation purposes only and does not indicate an endorsement of any specific scientific, political, or religious point of view. © TPB Publishing. You have been licensed one copy of this document for personal use only. Any other reproduction or redistribution is strictly prohibited. All rights reserved.

Practice Test #1

1. If a bond has a par value of $1,000 and the conversion ratio is 20, what is the conversion price of the bond?
   a. $50
   b. $100
   c. $20
   d. $10

2. Which of the below items are examples of riders on variable-annuity contracts?

   I. A cost-of-living adjustment
   II. A lump-sum payment of principal
   III. A positive covenant
   IV. A negative covenant

   a. I and II
   b. III and IV
   c. I and III
   d. II and IV

3. Your client, Rick Smith, came into your office recently asking about all of the headlines in national and local newspapers about the second strongest bull market in the history of stock market investing. Mr. Smith is somewhat in shock because he came into your office initially in 2008 when the stock market had just crashed, and the headlines he read then were just the opposite. You are excited to inform him that your advice turned out to be correct back then about investing when the market was at a generational low.

When you persuaded Rick to invest his entire $100,000 portfolio into securities in 2009, you suggested that due to Rick's annual income, net worth, and age, he should invest 70% of his portfolio in equities and 30% in fixed-income securities. Because Rick never opens his mail to read his brokerage statements and doesn't check his accounts online, he is ecstatic when you tell him his $100,000 portfolio is now worth $300,000. Rick is so excited he wants to invest another $100,000 with you solely in stocks because he believes the market will keep going up like it has for the past 10 years. Rick's investor profile has not changed despite his being 10 years older than he was in 2009.

What advice do you give to Rick?
   a. You should advise Rick to keep investing solely in stocks because even though the stock market goes down sometimes, it is the best long-term investment vehicle to choose from in the financial markets.
   b. You should advise Rick to liquidate his portfolio of stocks because they have increased in value so much that he shouldn't be greedy and should take profits while he still can.
   c. You should advise Rick that his current ownership in equities exceeds his initial target portfolio allocation, that investing solely in more stocks will expose Rick to excess risk, and that Rick should actually sell some of his equities even though Rick thinks the stock market will continue to rise.
   d. You should advise Rick to buy financial futures contracts so that he can participate in future market gains without having to invest as much capital.

117

This material is provided for exam preparation purposes only and does not indicate an endorsement of any specific scientific, political, or religious point of view. © TPB Publishing. You have been licensed one copy of this document for personal use only. Any other reproduction or redistribution is strictly prohibited. All rights reserved.

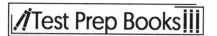

4. Which of the following is the correct sequence when investing in REITs?

        I. Rental income is paid to the REIT.
        II. Investors buy shares.
        III. Distributions to investors
        IV. Acquisitions and capital investment

    a. I, III, II, and IV
    b. IV, III, I, and II
    c. II, I, IV, and III
    d. II, IV, I, and III

5. A registration statement does NOT include what information?
    a. Information on a company's board of directors
    b. Financial information and company history
    c. A background on each of the company's employees
    d. Information on any pending litigation

6. What does the underwriting commitment ensure?
    a. A new issue will be accurately priced.
    b. That all securities being offered will be purchased.
    c. The par value of the offering will be $1 per share.
    d. A syndicate will be formed.

This material is provided for exam preparation purposes only and does not indicate an endorsement of any specific scientific, political, or religious point of view. © TPB Publishing. You have been licensed one copy of this document for personal use only. Any other reproduction or redistribution is strictly prohibited. All rights reserved.

7. You have recently accepted a position in the retirement planning field because of the immense opportunity to assist seniors in maintaining their retirement goals. At one nursing home, a resident informs you that their intelligent son handles all of their finances, so the resident has nothing to worry about concerning the future. While you believe that the resident is telling the truth, you are concerned about how lackadaisical the resident is, and also believe that simply being intelligent does not equate to the experience needed for such a complex situation.

You ask the resident for permission to contact the son, and the resident agrees. During your conversation with their son, you discover that the son has the resident invested 100% in stocks and that there are no planned investments in fixed-income securities or real estate. You truly believe that the resident will eventually not be able to afford the nursing home into the future unless the stock market continues to rise. What advice should you give the nursing home resident and their son?

    a. You should advise the resident and the son that you have a friend who sells long-term care insurance and that the entire portfolio should be liquidated, and the proceeds used to buy long-term care insurance.

    b. You should advise the resident to reduce their one hundred percent exposure to stock market fluctuations and use the proceeds to buy some fixed-income securities to provide some safety from stock market volatility and a steady income. In the event the stock market actually loses value, the resident will be able to afford even less time in the nursing home, creating a new, substantial responsibility for the son.

    c. You should advise the resident that over the last century the stock market has been in an uptrend and that this uptrend almost guarantees that the stock market will continue to rise until the time of their passing.

    d. You should advise the resident that they should only sell approximately 10% of their stock market holdings because you want to ensure that the resident profits from increased stock market valuations while setting aside enough money to pay for the nursing home for two to three years.

8. Which of the following is NOT a role of investment banks?

    a. Help companies raise capital via underwriting commitment

    b. Provide depository accounts, loans, and mortgages

    c. Evaluate company assets while following SEC regulations

    d. Act as broker or intermediary between securities issuers and investors

9. What are convertible preferred shares?

    a. Shares that convert to debt

    b. Preferred equity that can be converted to common stock

    c. Common stock that can convert to preferred shares

    d. Debt that can be called by the issuing company

10. What's the spread between a 10-year Treasury bond yielding 4.8% and a Treasury note yielding 4.2%?

    a. 4.4%

    b. 0.6%

    c. 1.14%

    d. 1.0%

This material is provided for exam preparation purposes only and does not indicate an endorsement of any specific scientific, political, or religious point of view. © TPB Publishing. You have been licensed one copy of this document for personal use only. Any other reproduction or redistribution is strictly prohibited. All rights reserved.

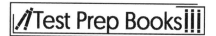

11. When a registered representative (RR) has an interest in an account at another firm, what must the firm do before conducting any transactions?
    a. Notify the RR's employer by phone
    b. Deliver duplicate documents for the account
    c. Notify the Securities and Exchange Commission (SEC)
    d. Make a note in the RR's file

12. The ratings provided by the major rating agencies are intended to reflect which of the following?
    a. The issuer's ability to pay the interest and principal
    b. The value of a bond
    c. The price of a bond
    d. The prepayment risk of a bond

13. What type of account would need to be opened for a customer who makes deposits for trading purposes?
    a. Margin Account
    b. Option Account
    c. Cash Account
    d. Day Trading Account

14. What are American Depositary Receipts (ADRs)?
    a. Shares of U.S. companies sold on foreign stock markets
    b. Deposits similar to CDs
    c. Shares of foreign companies purchased in the US without having to go through foreign stock exchanges
    d. Stock receipts allowing for the purchase of additional shares

15. An arbitrage short selling strategy occurs in which of the following situations?
    a. When an investor owns shares and wants to protect their return in case the stock declines in value
    b. When the investor does not own shares and short sells a stock because he or she feels it is overvalued
    c. When the investor uses a straddle
    d. When the investor wants to take advantage of pricing differences in different markets

16. Which of the following is NOT true regarding customer complaints?
    a. Complaints cannot be resolved using mediation.
    b. Complaints must be submitted in writing.
    c. Complaints can be solved using a formal or informal process.
    d. Complaints are submitted to the Financial Industry Regulatory Authority (FINRA).

17. If a company does a reverse stock split for 30,000 outstanding shares trading at $10 per share, what is the market value of the shares at the time of the split?
    a. $60,000
    b. $600,000
    c. $300,000
    d. $150,000

This material is provided for exam preparation purposes only and does not indicate an endorsement of any specific scientific, political, or religious point of view. © TPB Publishing. You have been licensed one copy of this document for personal use only. Any other reproduction or redistribution is strictly prohibited. All rights reserved.

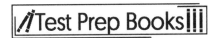

18. Which of the following is a lock-up provision as it applies to investing in hedge funds?
    a. A period of time that investors cannot withdraw their money
    b. The average duration of the fixed income investments the hedge fund holds
    c. The period of time that the hedge fund has been under investigation by the SEC and cannot perform all of the trades it would like
    d. A period of time that investors can withdraw money, and after the lock-up expires, they will no longer be able to do so

19. What is a currency revaluation?
    a. When a government allows its currency value to float
    b. When a government pegs its currency at a value lower than what the open market dictates
    c. When a government prints more currency
    d. When a government artificially pegs its currency at a higher value than what the market dictates

20. What is a fund that accrues a balance for the future redemption of a callable bond by a corporation?
    a. Mutual fund
    b. Money market fund
    c. Sinking fund
    d. Bond fund

21. What are the hours in which employees of a FINRA member firm are prohibited from calling residences?
    a. Before 7 a.m. and after 11 p.m.
    b. Before 8 a.m. and after 9 p.m.
    c. Before 6 a.m. and after 10 p.m.
    d. Before 9 a.m. and after 8 p.m.

22. In a negotiated municipal bond sale, how is the deal structured?
    a. To meet demands of investors and the issuer
    b. At the lowest rate the issuer can receive
    c. To match the municipality's tax revenue
    d. To withstand the worst possible economic downturn

23. Which of the following is true of a money market fund?
    a. Money market funds must be mainly invested in short-term securities with a maturity not exceeding 120 days.
    b. Money market funds are not insured by the Federal Deposit Insurance Corporation (FDIC).
    c. Money market funds cannot have a maturity of more than 12 months.
    d. Money market funds are guaranteed to maintain a net asset value of a dollar.

This material is provided for exam preparation purposes only and does not indicate an endorsement of any specific scientific, political, or religious point of view. © TPB Publishing. You have been licensed one copy of this document for personal use only. Any other reproduction or redistribution is strictly prohibited. All rights reserved.

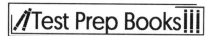
24. Which of the following comprise an option's total value?

       I. Intrinsic value
       II. Exercise price
       III. Time value
       IV. Strike price

    a. I and II
    b. II and IV
    c. II and III
    d. I and III

25. Reports from a firm's research department must be made independent of any influence from which of the following departments?
    a. Bond trading desk
    b. Investment banking department
    c. Compliance department
    d. Board of directors

26. To maintain their tax-free status, closed-end funds must distribute to investors what percent of their income from dividends and interest and what percent of their capital gains?
    a. 98% of income and 90% of capital gains
    b. 50% of income and capital gains
    c. 98% of income and capital gains
    d. 90% of income and 98% of capital gains

27. Which category below is NOT a common stockholder right?
    a. The right to inspect a corporation's financial records, systems, and bookkeeping
    b. The right to evaluate the assets of a corporation
    c. The right to call and reissue shares at a specified price
    d. The right to receive an equal share of dividends (i.e., pro rata dividends)

28. Which of the following is a way to increase information security?
    a. Using password-protected laptops
    b. Encrypting the company website
    c. Sharing software programs between employees
    d. Allowing employees to take files home with them

29. If a mutual fund has a public offering price of $32.56 and a net asset value of $27.18, what is the sales charge?
    a. 19.7%
    b. 18.3%
    c. 16.5%
    d. 5.4%

This material is provided for exam preparation purposes only and does not indicate an endorsement of any specific scientific, political, or religious point of view. © TPB Publishing. You have been licensed one copy of this document for personal use only. Any other reproduction or redistribution is strictly prohibited. All rights reserved.

30. When are taxes incurred on a traditional IRA?
   a. Never
   b. When the initial investment occurs
   c. When the money is withdrawn
   d. Annually, when the beneficiary pays income tax

31. Which of the following is true concerning disclosures and review of public communications?
   a. Records must be kept in a SEC-approved format.
   b. Certain public communications must be filed at least 15 business days before their publication.
   c. Public communication does not have to be approved by a supervisory member of the firm.
   d. Records must include the date and content of the communication.

32. What's the current yield of a bond with a par value of $1,000, a coupon rate of 7%, and a market value of $1,150?
   a. 70%
   b. 7.0%
   c. 6.1%
   d. 11.5%

33. How are the deferred sales charges on unit investment trusts paid?
   a. Upon trust liquidation
   b. Annually
   c. Monthly
   d. Up front

34. At the end of the second quarter, if a company has a stock price of $10 and pays a dividend of $0.50 on a quarterly basis, what is the annualized dividend yield?
   a. 5%
   b. 0.5%
   c. 10%
   d. 20%

35. Which of the following terms describes a trade that is only executed when the price surpasses a certain point?
   a. Day order
   b. Stop order
   c. Market order
   d. Good 'Til Cancelled order

36. Which of the following is an advantage of a Roth IRA when compared to other types of IRAs?
   a. Contributions to the plan are tax-deductible.
   b. Required minimum distributions (RMDs) are not required at the age of 70½ when the original owner is alive.
   c. Funds are taxed as ordinary income when withdrawn in retirement.
   d. There is no provision for catch-up contributions.

This material is provided for exam preparation purposes only and does not indicate an endorsement of any specific scientific, political, or religious point of view. © TPB Publishing. You have been licensed one copy of this document for personal use only. Any other reproduction or redistribution is strictly prohibited. All rights reserved.

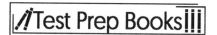

37. Which of the following is an example of return of capital?
    a. When a stock goes from $100 to $150
    b. The amortization of a bond
    c. When a stock pays a dividend of 10%
    d. When a bond makes a coupon payment

38. Which of the following entities would most likely be involved with reverse churning?
    a. Investment bankers
    b. Research analysts
    c. Commission-based brokers
    d. Fee-based brokers

39. What is the correct order of the four key phases of the business cycle?
    a. Peak, expansion, trough, contraction
    b. Contraction, expansion, trough, peak
    c. Expansion, trough, contraction, peak
    d. Expansion, peak, contraction, trough

40. What is the primary difference between closed-end mutual funds and open-ended ones?
    a. Closed-end funds are limited to 10 investors.
    b. Closed-end funds do not raise or accept new capital contributions after their IPO.
    c. Closed-end funds invest in fixed income securities while open-ended mutual funds only invest in stocks and ETFs.
    d. Closed-end funds have a different tax treatment of their dividends and returns of capital.

41. Which of the following is NOT a rule of an auction market?
    a. All transactions are secret.
    b. The first bid has priority.
    c. Bids and offers must be audible.
    d. New bids are entered when all bids at a certain price have been exhausted.

42. If an asset is not sold quickly and requires a significant reduction in price to be sold, which of the following types of risk occurs?
    a. Credit risk
    b. Liquidity risk
    c. Prepayment risk
    d. Price risk

43. Which of the following requires financial institutions to submit five types of reports intended to detect money laundering activities?
    a. Suspicious Activity Reports (SARS)
    b. The Office of Foreign Asset Control (OFAC)
    c. Currency Transaction Reports (CTRs)
    d. The Bank Secrecy Act (BSA)

This material is provided for exam preparation purposes only and does not indicate an endorsement of any specific scientific, political, or religious point of view. © TPB Publishing. You have been licensed one copy of this document for personal use only. Any other reproduction or redistribution is strictly prohibited. All rights reserved.

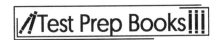

44. Which of these individuals is considered to have a control relationship with Company X?
    a. A wife of the CEO of Company X
    b. The chairman of the board of Company X
    c. A low-level HR recruiter working at Company X for more than five years
    d. A retail investor owning 1% of Company X's common stock

45. Which of the following would be an example of a preventive measure included in a Business Continuity and Disaster Recovery (BC/DR) Plan?
    a. Having one server where all customers access their accounts
    b. Backing up data once a quarter
    c. Having home phone numbers as the primary contact number for employees
    d. Having computer and customer files backed up to a location offsite

46. What type of security is typically assumed to have no credit risk (i.e., the probability that the full principal will not be repaid is 0%)?
    a. Municipal bonds
    b. Asset-backed securities
    c. Corporate bonds
    d. Treasury bonds

47. Which of the following forms is used to terminate the registrations of representatives with a specific self-regulatory organization or jurisdiction?
    a. Form U4
    b. EMMA
    c. Form U5
    d. TRACE

48. What are Blue Sky Laws?
    a. State securities laws
    b. SEC regulations that apply to foreign investments
    c. Laws governing American Depositary Receipts and their custodians
    d. Credits that investors may receive for supporting clean energy projects, such as wind and solar

49. Which of the following is a non-profit retirement plan?
    a. 529
    b. 457(b)
    c. 401(k)
    d. 403(b)

50. A rights offering allows which of the following?
    a. A stock issuer to call the stock back for reissuance
    b. An investor to retire shares when they want
    c. An existing shareholder to purchase shares at a discount
    d. A bond holder the right to receive stock dividends

This material is provided for exam preparation purposes only and does not indicate an endorsement of any specific scientific, political, or religious point of view. © TPB Publishing. You have been licensed one copy of this document for personal use only. Any other reproduction or redistribution is strictly prohibited. All rights reserved.

51. What do the horizontal and vertical axis of the capital asset pricing model (CAPM) represent?
    a. Horizontal: assets; Vertical: rate
    b. Horizontal: equities; Vertical: bonds
    c. Horizontal: risk; Vertical: expected return
    d. Horizontal: volatility; Vertical: willingness

52. Which best describes how a puttable bond works?
    a. It grants the issuer the obligation to "put" bonds back to the investor at a lower rate.
    b. It grants the issuer the right to change the rate on the bonds they've issued.
    c. It grants the investor the right to "put" the bonds back to the issuer.
    d. It ensures that the corporation can no longer issue new debt.

53. What agency protects clients of brokers in the event of financial failure or bankruptcy?
    a. The FDIC
    b. The Federal Reserve
    c. The US Treasury
    d. The SIPC

54. Which of the following is true of continuing education for registered persons?
    a. There are three elements: regulatory, firm, and personal.
    b. Organizations who employ registered persons must evaluate members' securities knowledge biannually.
    c. Organizations must document their written plan and its implementation.
    d. FINRA details specific points that must be covered in the training plan.

55. What does the acronym RAP stand for?
    a. Reverse Away Payment
    b. Recapture Account Pension
    c. Receive Against Payment
    d. Remit Against Payor

56. When do LEAPS expire?
    a. On the first Tuesday in November
    b. Every two years
    c. The last day of the year
    d. The third Friday of every January

57. How much money is an employee allowed to contribute to their 401(k) on a pre-tax basis if they are under 50 years of age?
    a. $5,500
    b. $15,000
    c. $20,500
    d. $10,000

58. Who has first jurisdiction over a complaint filed using formal proceedings?
    a. District Business Conduct Committee (DBCC)
    b. Supreme Court
    c. FINRA Board of Governors
    d. Securities and Exchange Commission (SEC)

This material is provided for exam preparation purposes only and does not indicate an endorsement of any specific scientific, political, or religious point of view. © TPB Publishing. You have been licensed one copy of this document for personal use only. Any other reproduction or redistribution is strictly prohibited. All rights reserved.

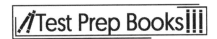

59. The City of Tranche has been experiencing explosive economic growth over the last five years since a major online retailer named the city as the location for its global headquarters. When the online retailer announced that it was moving to Tranche, the company also announced the creation of 50,000 new jobs at the Tranche location. The influx of new workers moving to the area caused a spike in home construction and existing home sales in Tranche. The Tranche Community Bank originated thousands of mortgages to support the economic growth in Tranche. While the Tranche Community Bank made millions of dollars on the loans, the bank's risk management officer now feels that the bank's portfolio of loans is too concentrated and fears what may happen if the online retailer cuts jobs in an economic downturn. The risk management officer has contacted Wall Street investment banks to inquire about potential methods to reduce the bank's risk.

What is the best course of action for the risk management officer attempting to reduce his bank's mortgage risk?
   a. The risk management officer should immediately stop originating mortgage loans in the local area because economic downturns happen fast and without warning.
   b. The risk management officer should not be concerned with making additional mortgage loans because housing prices rarely decline, and the bank is safe without further action.
   c. The risk management officer should determine if there is a market for his bank's loans and sell the loans to a firm with specialized expertise in securitization so that the bank holds fewer concentrated mortgages.
   d. The risk management officer should purchase a substantial amount of the bank's free cash flow in interest rate futures contracts to protect the bank in the event that interest rates decline.

60. A customer is considered a corporate insider if they own more than what percentage of the voting shares of a company?
   a. 1.50%
   b. 10%
   c. 5%
   d. 8%

61. Under the Investment Company Act of 1940 Rule 3c1, which of the following would violate the tax-exemption status of a hedge fund?
   a. Retaining more than 10% of its income
   b. Having more than one hundred beneficial shareholders
   c. Distributing more than 98% of capital gains
   d. Having more than 100 pension funds investing in their shares

62. Which of the following are examples of political risk?

   I. A new law forces a company to change the way it does business.
   II. A currency fluctuates in value.
   III. A regulator requires banks to change the way they market loans to customers.
   IV. A CEO launders money from the company.

   a. I, II, and III
   b. III and IV
   c. I and III
   d. II and IV

127

This material is provided for exam preparation purposes only and does not indicate an endorsement of any specific scientific, political, or religious point of view. © TPB Publishing. You have been licensed one copy of this document for personal use only. Any other reproduction or redistribution is strictly prohibited. All rights reserved.

63. John and Sarah are a married couple. They wish to open an account with a broker that allows them to both have authority over the account. They also would like to be able to continue to have control over the account if the other spouse dies. What type of account should the broker recommend?
    a. Joint Tenants in Common (JTIC) Account
    b. Marital Account
    c. Transfer on Death (TOD) Account
    d. Joint Tenants with Rights of Survivorship (JTWROS) Account

64. Which of the following would be expected to earn a risk-free rate?
    a. Short-term treasury bonds
    b. Equities
    c. Options
    d. Commodities

65. What is the MAIN benefit of allowing for the shelf registration of securities?
    a. It does not require registration with the SEC.
    b. Less company disclosure is required.
    c. The debt can be more easily converted to equity.
    d. There is better flexibility when issuing debt and equity.

66. Which of the following is true of the yield curve?
    a. The yield curve is a predictor of expansion.
    b. The yield curve is part of the index of leading indicators.
    c. The yield curve becomes peaked to indicate a recession.
    d. The yield curve typically has a downward slope.

67. Which of the following is true of Keynesian Economic Theory?
    a. It calls for the government to regulate the money supply.
    b. It calls for the government to spend tax money on projects to stimulate the economy.
    c. It calls for the government to stay out of the market.
    d. It calls for the government to decrease demand for products.

68. In reference to REITs, what does DRIP stand for?
    a. Dividend repurchase insurance program
    b. Divisible retained income purchase
    c. Division real estate income plan
    d. Dividend reinvestment program

69. The S&P 500 return for a time period was 7%. Maggie, a fund manager, had a benchmark in the S&P 500 that returned 9%. What was the Alpha generated?
    a. 2%
    b. -2%
    c. 14%
    d. 9%

This material is provided for exam preparation purposes only and does not indicate an endorsement of any specific scientific, political, or religious point of view. © TPB Publishing. You have been licensed one copy of this document for personal use only. Any other reproduction or redistribution is strictly prohibited. All rights reserved.

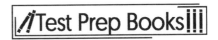

70. What do direct participation programs (DPPs) typically invest in?
    a. Real estate, futures, and mutual funds
    b. Other private-equity funds
    c. Real estate, energy, futures/options, and equipment leases
    d. Commercial paper, short-term treasury bonds, and other short-term debt

71. What is an indication of interest?
    a. When an investment bank shows interest in representing a company in an IPO
    b. When the SEC displays interest in having a company issue shares
    c. When a company indicates they will be issuing a dividend
    d. When an investor shows interest in a company's stock before the company has received clearance from the SEC

72. Nancy and Bob Barkley are meeting with their investment advisor representative later this week to discuss any recommendations for rebalancing their portfolio because they have both decided to retire at the end of the year. The Barkleys have tried to keep their portfolio at 65% invested in stocks, 25% in fixed-income securities, and 10% cash for their emergency fund.

At the meeting, the Barkleys' investment advisor representative suggests that the Barkleys liquidate 45% of their stock portfolio and reinvest those proceeds in fixed-income securities. The Barkleys have always liked to hold their fixed-income securities in their lockbox at their local bank; they have never felt comfortable investing in bond mutual funds because they seem too complex to understand when reading the prospectuses.

While acknowledging the Barkleys desire to physically hold their fixed-income securities, their investment advisor representative feels that he would be remiss if he didn't discuss some revolutionary new products in the fixed-income investment space. Because the Barkleys reiterated their concern about bond mutual funds, their investment advisor introduces the Barkleys to the idea of investing in exchange-traded notes.

How should the investment advisor representative go about reconciling the Barkleys' concerns and their legitimate retirement needs?
    a. The investment advisor representative should explain that the exchange-traded notes are perfect substitutes for the liquidated stock portion of the portfolio because they can be traded like the stock on a securities exchange.
    b. The investment advisor representative should invest the liquidated stock portfolio entirely in exchange-notes because exchange-traded notes do not represent ownership in a company like the stock does, and this reduces the Barkleys' risk.
    c. The investment advisor representative should explain to the Barkleys that the exchange-traded notes pay coupons and return the principal of the debt at maturity, so they are as close as the Barkleys can get to holding the new investment in the lockbox at their local bank.
    d. The investment advisor representative should explain that the exchange-traded notes would be a good addition to the portfolio when investing the stock proceeds because the Barkleys already own some debt securities with coupon payments and that the benchmark tracking feature of the exchange-traded notes is a nice complement to the standard debt securities that the Barkleys already own.

129

This material is provided for exam preparation purposes only and does not indicate an endorsement of any specific scientific, political, or religious point of view. © TPB Publishing. You have been licensed one copy of this document for personal use only. Any other reproduction or redistribution is strictly prohibited. All rights reserved.

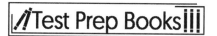

73. Which of the following is true about political donations by FINRA member firms?
    a. Payment to political sources must be disclosed to FINRA.
    b. Payments to local governments do not count towards the donation limit.
    c. Political contributions cannot exceed $250 per person.
    d. Payments to political sources must be documented.

74. By holding cash, an investor increases and decreases their exposure, respectively, to which of the following risks?
    a. Reinvestment risk and currency risk
    b. Currency risk and default risk
    c. Credit risk and capital risk
    d. Inflation risk and capital risk

75. Regulated entities cannot receive more than how much money per person per year if the compensation is related to municipal securities?
    a. $100
    b. $50
    c. $200
    d. $150

This material is provided for exam preparation purposes only and does not indicate an endorsement of any specific scientific, political, or religious point of view. © TPB Publishing. You have been licensed one copy of this document for personal use only. Any other reproduction or redistribution is strictly prohibited. All rights reserved.

Answer Explanations #1

1. A: The conversion ratio formula is:

$$conversion\ ratio = \frac{Bond\ par\ value}{Conversion\ price}$$

By substituting the bond par value and the conversion ratio, the conversion price can be found:

$$20 = \frac{\$1,000}{Conversion\ price} \rightarrow Conversion\ price = \$50$$

2. A: Cost-of-living adjustments adjust the payments to assure the investor is receiving payments to cover their cost of living, usually adjusted by an inflationary index. Lump-sum payments assure principal will be returned in its entirety. Disability riders assure payment should the owner of the annuity become ill. Positive and negative covenants apply to bonds, not annuities.

3. C: The gains in Rick's portfolio have created an asset allocation that is no longer consistent with Rick's target allocation. Rick should rebalance his portfolio to meet the initial target even if this means he will not participate in future stock market gains. Rick should be advised that the stock market does not always go up and that even if it does, the risk that he is taking by owning more equities is not worth the potential reward given his asset allocation target.

4. D: Investors buy shares in an IPO, the REIT acquires and invests in properties, tenants pay rent to the REIT, and a percentage of that money is distributed back to the shareholders in the form of dividends.

5. C: There is information about the company's management and board of directors, but not about each employee at the company. All the other answers are legally required parts of a registration statement.

6. B: The commitment ensures all shares will be purchased, or "best efforts" will be made to sell all of the securities, but it is not a guarantee by the syndicate to purchase any unsold securities. The commitment has nothing to do with deal pricing or the par value. The commitment is set up after the syndicate has been formed.

7. B: The realities of the expensive costs of living in a nursing home require a healthy mix of participating in the stock market and having exposure to fixed-income securities for safety and income to help pay for the nursing home. However, staying 100% invested in the stock market is much too risky for a resident of a nursing home. While the stock market may continue to rise into the future, the nursing home resident may have a financial need at a time when the market is significantly down which could impair the ability of the resident to meet nursing home financial obligations. The resident should rebalance the portfolio to assist with owning an effective mix of assets to meet potential financial obligations.

8. B: Investment banks do not provide depository accounts (checking or savings accounts), nor do they offer loans or home mortgages like a traditional bank does. Their main purpose is to help raise capital, evaluate assets, and act as broker or intermediary between securities issuers and investors.

9. B: Equity shares can't convert to debt in most cases. Convertible preferred equity are shares that can convert to common stock. Common stock normally can't convert to preferred shares. Choice *D* is referred to as a callable bond.

This material is provided for exam preparation purposes only and does not indicate an endorsement of any specific scientific, political, or religious point of view. © TPB Publishing. You have been licensed one copy of this document for personal use only. Any other reproduction or redistribution is strictly prohibited. All rights reserved.

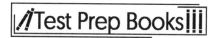

10. B: The spread between two bonds is the difference between their yields:

$$4.8\% - 4.2\% = 0.6\%$$

11. B: The firm must deliver duplicate documents for the account. They must also notify the RR's employer in writing rather than by phone. Notifying the SEC and making a note in the RR's file are not one of the steps that a firm must take when a RR has a personal investment account outside of their firm.

12. A: A bond rating reflects the issuer's ability to pay interest and principal on its outstanding debt. The rating has nothing to do with a bond's value, price, or prepayment risk.

13. C: A cash account is a common type of brokerage account with the customer making cash deposits to be used in trades. A margin account is used for when a customer borrows money from the broker. An option account is an account in which the customer can hold options. A day trading account is used to trade securities in the same day.

14. C: American Depositary Receipts (ADRs) are shares of foreign companies purchased in the US without having to go through a foreign stock exchange.

15. D: Arbitrage is when an investor wants to sell shares short in a market that has advantageous pricing from a different market. When an investor owns shares and wants to protect themselves through short selling, it is known as hedging. Short selling without owning the stock is known as speculation. A straddle uses options, not short selling.

16. A: Complaints can be solved using mediation if it is an informal proceeding. Complaints are submitted to FINRA in writing and are solved using either formal or informal proceedings.

17. C: The market value of $\$10 \times 30{,}000 = \$300{,}000$ will be the same before and after the stock split.

18. A: A lock-up provision prevents investors from withdrawing any money from the fund. These provisions allow the hedge fund to pursue its strategy without redemptions interfering. This is important, since many funds pursue strategies that take several years to play out and see results.

19. D: Currency revaluation is when a government artificially increases the value of its currency. A floating currency has its value determined by supply and demand. A devaluation is an intentional lowering of a currency's value.

20. C: A sinking fund accrues a balance that's used to redeem bonds or preferred stock. Mutual funds are investment vehicles used by investors. A money market fund has short-term investments. A bond fund is a portfolio of individual, fixed-income securities.

21. B: Salespeople and employees of FINRA member firms may not make outbound telephone calls to any residence before 8 a.m. or after 9 p.m. unless there is already an established business relationship with that person.

22. A: These deals are set up to meet the needs of the investor and the issuer. The lowest rate is not necessarily the best deal for the investor. Tax revenue may be considered but is not part of the actual structuring of the deal. Economic downturns are also not part of the deal structure.

This material is provided for exam preparation purposes only and does not indicate an endorsement of any specific scientific, political, or religious point of view. © TPB Publishing. You have been licensed one copy of this document for personal use only. Any other reproduction or redistribution is strictly prohibited. All rights reserved.

23. B: Money market funds are not insured by the FDIC. Also, there is no guarantee that that they will maintain a net asset value of a dollar; therefore, Choice *D* is incorrect. They must be mainly invested in short-term securities with an average maturity of no greater than 90 days, rather than 120 days. The maturity cannot be more than 13 months, instead of 12 months; thus, Choice *C* is incorrect.

24. D: An option's total value is comprised of its intrinsic value, usually the value if the option were to be exercised immediately, and its time value, which is derived from the probability it will exceed the strike price before expiring.

25. B: Research reports, the individuals doing the research, their compensation, and all other aspects of a firm's research should be completely and totally separate from the firm's investment banking department. This is to avoid conflicts of interest that could result from a firm providing favorable research in exchange for investment banking opportunities. The compliance department and board of directors oversee all compliance and operations at a company but are not expressly forbidden from interacting with research reports by regulators, although it would be unusual for them to do so.

26. D: To maintain their tax-exempt status, closed-end funds must distribute 90% of income and 98% of capital gains to their shareholders.

27. C: The right to call and reissue shares at a specified price is a company's right when issuing a callable bond. It is not a common stockholder right.

28. A: Using password-protected laptops would be one possible measure that would help protect confidential information. Encrypting the company website would not be helpful, but encrypting email interactions would increase information security. Software programs should be password-protected to help protect data. Allowing employees to take files home with them would not increase information security.

29. C: Using the sales charge formula, the public offering price and the net asset value can be substituted:

$$Sales\ charge = \frac{(Public\ offering\ price - Net\ asset\ value)}{Public\ offering\ price}$$

$$\frac{(32.56 - 27.18)}{32.56} = \frac{5.38}{32.56}$$

$$0.165 = 16.5\%$$

30. C: Taxation occurs when the money is withdrawn. People invest already-taxed income into Roth IRAs. No IRAs require annual taxation.

31. D: Accurate records of all public communications including the date and content of the communication must be kept in a FINRA-approved format. Certain public communications must be filed with FINRA at least 10 business days prior to their use. All public communication must be approved by a supervisory member of the firm.

This material is provided for exam preparation purposes only and does not indicate an endorsement of any specific scientific, political, or religious point of view. © TPB Publishing. You have been licensed one copy of this document for personal use only. Any other reproduction or redistribution is strictly prohibited. All rights reserved.

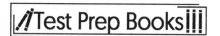

32. C: The coupon rate of 7% equates to an annual payment of $70. Substituting $70 for the interest and $1,150 for the price, the current yield can be found:

$$\frac{\$70}{\$1,150} = 6.1\%$$

33. C: Deferred sales charges are paid monthly.

34. D: The dividend yield formula calls for dividing the annual dividend by the current stock price. The company has been paying a quarterly dividend of $0.50, so the annual rate is $2.00 which is 20% of $10.

35. B: A stop order is a trade that is only executed when the price surpasses a certain point. A day order expires if criteria is not reached for a trade to occur during that day. A market order is simply an order that is executed at whatever the market price is. Finally, a Good 'Til Cancelled (GTC) order means the order is in place until executed unless the investor cancels the order.

36. B: An advantage of a Roth IRA is that required minimum distributions (RMDs) are not required at the age of 70½ when the original owner is alive. The other options listed are not advantages of Roth IRAs.

37. B: Amortization is when portions of the principal are paid back, which is return of capital. The appreciation of a stock's value, dividends, and interest payments are returns on capital.

38. D: Reverse churning occurs with fee-based accounts, where brokers have no incentive to trade for a customer because they are simply earning a fixed fee. Commission-based brokers have the incentive to churn, not reverse churn. If commission-based brokers do not trade for customers, they earn less money.

39. D: The correct order of the four key phases of the business cycle is expansion, peak, contraction, and trough. Expansion starts with strong economic indicators and moves to the peak, which is the high point of the expansion phase. Next, is the contraction which is usually a recession or even a depression. The trough phase is last. This is when downtrends begin to level off which allows for the cycle to begin again with expansion.

40. B: A closed-end fund is closed because after its initial public offering, no more capital will be contributed to the fund. The investments inside the fund are not rolled over, and once expired, the profits, losses, and capital will be returned to investors. Due to this lack of liquidity, if demand for the fund wanes, it can begin to trade below NAV. Closed-end funds are not restricted on their number of investors, nor must they only buy fixed income securities. Private placements and some business structures have a limit on how many investors can be involved, but mutual funds of any type do not have such a restriction.

41. A: None of the transactions in an auction market can be secret. The first bid does have priority. Bids and offers must be audible. New bids occur when all others have been exhausted.

42. B: This situation poses a liquidity risk. If an asset requires a significant reduction in price in order to be sold, the asset or security is said to be illiquid. Credit risk refers to the risk that a borrower cannot pay the interest or principal on debt. Prepayment risk is the risk that a loan will be paid back before its scheduled maturity. Price risk is the risk incurred when a security is purchased that fluctuates in value.

This material is provided for exam preparation purposes only and does not indicate an endorsement of any specific scientific, political, or religious point of view. © TPB Publishing. You have been licensed one copy of this document for personal use only. Any other reproduction or redistribution is strictly prohibited. All rights reserved.

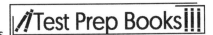
43. D: The Bank Secrecy Act (BSA), also called The Currency and Foreign Transactions Reporting Act, is intended to help prevent and find money laundering activities through certain rules and regulations. Suspicious Activity Reports (SARs) and Currency Transaction Reports (CTRs) are both included under this act. The Office of Foreign Asset Control (OFAC) is used to track terrorist activity and their financing.

44. B: Control relationships stem from individuals, such as C-suite level management, board of directors, and other individuals who have a large amount of control and influence over publicly traded corporations. Control relationships must be disclosed in public filings and during an IPO, usually in the prospectus. Retail investors do not usually have control relationships and can hold their shares in their broker's name to avoid publicity.

45. D: Having computer and customer files backed up to a location offsite is one possible preventive measure included on a BC/DR plan. Having more than one server where customers can access their data would help ensure access during a disaster situation. Regular backups of data are another preventive measure, but completing them more than once a quarter would be more appropriate. In the event of a disaster, mobile phone numbers would be better contact numbers to reach employees.

46. D: Municipal bonds may not have principal paid in full if there isn't a significant tax base in that municipality. Asset-backed securities have credit risk because borrowers may stop paying their loans. Corporate bonds have credit risk because companies can go bankrupt and not have enough assets to pay back all of their creditors if liquidated. Treasury bonds are usually assumed to have zero credit risk since they're backed by the full faith of the US government.

47. C: Form U5 is used to terminate the registrations of representatives with a specific self-regulatory organization or jurisdiction. Form U4 is used to register representatives. EMMA is the system that tracks information about municipal securities. TRACE is the system by which all broker-dealers must report the information pertaining to trades involving certain fixed income securities that are traded over-the-counter, on the secondary market, or not on a regulated exchange.

48. A: Blue Sky Laws are state-specific securities laws that need to be followed by investors and firms operating in that state. Most of the securities laws discussed in this guide are federal laws that apply regardless of what state a firm resides in or operates out of.

49. D: Non-profit organizations have 403(b)s as retirement plans, 457(b)s are government-sponsored plans, and 401(k)s are found in the private sector.

50. C: A rights offering can be one way for a company to raise capital as it encourages existing shareholders to purchase additional, newly issued shares at a discount.

51. C: The vertical axis of the CAPM represents the expected return given the amount of volatility, or risk, they are willing to accept, which is what is represented on the horizontal axis.

52. C: A puttable bond grants the investor the right—not the obligation—to "put" the bond back to the issuer.

53. D: The SIPC provides services in the case of a broker failing. Financial assistance may be provided by the US Treasury if SIPC funds are not adequate. They organize the distribution of cash and securities when this occurs. The FDIC insures bank deposits. The Federal Reserve institutes monetary policy and provides some bank oversight and regulation.

This material is provided for exam preparation purposes only and does not indicate an endorsement of any specific scientific, political, or religious point of view. © TPB Publishing. You have been licensed one copy of this document for personal use only. Any other reproduction or redistribution is strictly prohibited. All rights reserved.

54. C: Member organizations must document their written plan and its implementation. Continuing education includes two elements, regulatory and firm. Organizations must assess employees' knowledge annually. FINRA provides a minimum number of topics that must be covered in training plans but not specific points.

55. C: RAP is an acronym for Receive Against Payment which signifies that a buyer's payment for securities must be paid at the time of receipt. It is also known as Receive Versus Payment (RVP). The other three choices do not represent actual acronyms.

56. D: LEAPS expire on the third Friday of every January and have expiration dates up to three years.

57. C: For 2022, a person can contribute up to $20,500 per year to a 401(k) on a pre-tax basis without any income tax being paid on that money.

58. A: The District Business Conduct Committee (DBCC) has first jurisdiction over a complaint filed using formal proceedings. If the customer is unhappy with how the complaint is handled, the next step is to appeal to the FINRA Board of Governors or even to the Supreme Court. The SEC is not generally involved in this process.

59. C: The risk management officer should attempt to sell the bank's loans to a firm specializing in securitization. If the officer can sell some of the bank's loans to a party willing to package the loans and sell them in a primary market of their own, then the bank can reduce risk and continue to originate additional mortgage loans according to the prevailing market conditions.

60. B: A customer that owns over 10% of a company's voting shares is considered a corporate insider. Directors and officers of a corporation, as well as those that are privy to material and non-public knowledge about a corporation, are also considered corporate insiders.

61. B: To maintain their tax-exempt status, hedge funds cannot have more than 100 beneficial investors. REITs can't retain more than 10% of income. They must distribute 90% of income to maintain their REIT status.

62. C: The introduction of laws and regulations poses a political risk outside of the course of normal business. Currency fluctuations are simply currency risk that investors incur when they invest internationally. The risk of a CEO laundering money is a business risk.

63. D: John and Sarah would need to open a Joint Tenants with Rights of Survivorship (JTWROS) Account to meet their specifications. The Joint Tenants in Common (JTIC) Account would not allow them to retain control of the account in the event of a joint tenant death. A Marital Account allows for marital property and trust accounts to be controlled by a trustee. A Transfer on Death (TOD) Account helps with the transfer of assets upon the accountholder's death.

64. A: Short-term treasury bonds and highly rated money market funds would be expected to earn a risk-free rate. Equities, options, and commodities experience more volatility in their returns.

65. D: With shelf registration, companies can issue securities under the most favorable market conditions more easily. The shares still must be registered with the SEC. The company must still make all of the relevant disclosures that would occur with normal issuance of securities. Shelf registration has nothing to do with the capability to convert debt.

This material is provided for exam preparation purposes only and does not indicate an endorsement of any specific scientific, political, or religious point of view. © TPB Publishing. You have been licensed one copy of this document for personal use only. Any other reproduction or redistribution is strictly prohibited. All rights reserved.

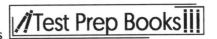

66. B: The yield curve is measured and included in the Conference Board Leading Economic Index. The yield curve is a predictor of recession. The yield curve flattens to indicate a recession and typically has an upward slope.

67. B: Keynesian Economic Theory suggests that to support the economy, the federal government should spend tax money on projects that stimulate the economy. Choices *A* and *C* are true of Monetarist Economic Theory. Choice *D* is not suggested by either economic theory.

68. D: DRIP stands for dividend reinvestment program. Under this plan, existing shareholders can purchase more shares when a dividend is paid at a discount to the current share price.

69. A: The Alpha is the excess return that fund managers generate against an index benchmark. The Alpha is the return of the fund manager less the return of the selected index: $9\% - 7\% = 2\%$.

70. C: DPPs invest in real estate, energy, futures/options, and equipment leases (as well as oil and gas). They do not invest in mutual funds. Funds that invest in other private-equity funds are funds-of-funds. Money-market funds invest in short-term debt instruments.

71. D: This is when a potential investor shows interest before a company has issued its shares. Choices *A* and *B* have no formal term. Choice *C* could be considered a corporate action or corporate resolution.

72. D: Adding exchange-traded notes with part of the proceeds from the stock portfolio is the best answer because the notes add a layer of additional diversification within the fixed-income portion of the Barkleys' overall portfolio. Choice *A* is incorrect because whether or not exchange-traded notes are a good fit for a particular portfolio does not significantly depend on whether they can be traded on an exchange like stocks. Choice *B* is incorrect because the reduction of ownership of an underlying asset is not the primary concern when deciding to add exchange-traded notes to part of a fixed-income portfolio. Choice *C* is incorrect because exchange-traded notes do not pay coupons.

73. D: Payments to political sources must be documented and disclosed to the firm's board of directors or senior executive team. Payments to local, state, and federal governments are all included in prohibited political donations. Contributions cannot exceed $250 per person or per political party per year.

74. D: By holding cash, investors expose themselves to the risk that inflation will erode the purchasing power of their cash. They have no exposure to capital risk because cash carries no risk of losing its principal value.

75. A: Regulated entities cannot receive more than $100 per person per year if that compensation is based on their activities concerning municipal securities.

This material is provided for exam preparation purposes only and does not indicate an endorsement of any specific scientific, political, or religious point of view. © TPB Publishing. You have been licensed one copy of this document for personal use only. Any other reproduction or redistribution is strictly prohibited. All rights reserved.

Practice Test #2

1. Which statement about account types is correct?
   a. A cash account is an account with which a customer pays for all transactions in full.
   b. A margin account is an account with which a customer does not pay for a transaction in full but borrows up to 90% of the transaction amount from the member firm.
   c. A cash account may have a short sale made in it.
   d. A margin account must have payments made promptly, no later than T+1.

2. Which statement about the process of exercising an option is correct?
   a. The exchange notifies the holder of the expiration date.
   b. The holder's broker-dealer identifies a counterparty who will fulfill the option.
   c. It begins with the holder informing the holder's broker-dealer of their intention to exercise the contract.
   d. The broker-dealer that receives the exercise notice fulfills the option without notifying the writer.

3. What is a typical characteristic of equity-indexed contracts (EICs) but NOT a typical characteristic of variable contracts?
   a. "Bonus" additions in excess of the cash amount invested, as the basis for calculating death benefits and annuitization
   b. Income tax deferral
   c. Payments for the life of the annuitant, who is usually the owner
   d. Death benefits for one or more beneficiaries

4. Which statement about corporate actions is correct?
   a. An exchange offer occurs when the party making the offer would provide another security's shares in exchange for the desired shares.
   b. A rights offer is not approved by a board of directors. Its purpose is to raise additional capital by offering current shareholders the opportunity to purchase shares adequate to maintain the same proportional ownership as previously held.
   c. An acquisition may be approved by a board of directors in order to combine the company with another company.
   d. A merger may be approved by a board of directors in order to purchase another company.

5. Which of the following is true regarding discretionary and nondiscretionary accounts?
   a. The investor with a nondiscretionary account must authorize a discretionary order in writing.
   b. The investor must open a discretionary account in order to authorize the representative to make discretionary trades.
   c. A discretionary order placed in a discretionary account must be approved by the supervisory principal within two days after the trade is made.
   d. A discretionary order placed in a discretionary account must be approved by the supervisory principal before the end of the month in which the trade is made.

This material is provided for exam preparation purposes only and does not indicate an endorsement of any specific scientific, political, or religious point of view. © TPB Publishing. You have been licensed one copy of this document for personal use only. Any other reproduction or redistribution is strictly prohibited. All rights reserved.

6. Which statement about expiration of options is correct?
   a. Listed American stock index options may be exercised on any day on or before the expiration date.
   b. Listed foreign currency options may be exercised on any day on or before the expiration date.
   c. Listed American stock options may be exercised on any day on or before the expiration date.
   d. Unlisted American stock options expire on the second Friday of the expiration month.

7. A municipal 529 program is established for which of the following purposes?
   a. Municipal tax calculations
   b. College savings plans
   c. Municipal bond interest estimates
   d. Municipal securities registrations

8. Which statement about settlement that may vary from regular-way settlement is correct?
   a. If the seller is not able to provide ownership in the regular-way time frame, the trade is always reversed as if it never happened.
   b. The purchaser or seller may not settle on the trade date.
   c. The purchaser or seller may agree, before the trade takes place, to settle during other than regular-way (special settlement).
   d. The purchaser or seller may agree, after the trade takes place, to settle during other than regular-way (special settlement).

9. Which of the following is a characteristic of Keynesian theory?
   a. A balanced federal budget, except in time of economic stability
   b. A focus on governments adjusting money supply
   c. Deficit spending
   d. A focus on governments adjusting available credit

10. Which of the following is NOT required in FINRA Rule 4530 – Reporting Requirements?
   a. Quarterly summary reports of investor complaints made in writing
   b. Compensation for each registered representative
   c. Immediate reports (within 30 days after the firm could have been expected to know) of specified significant events
   d. Copy of certain criminal and civil actions

11. Which statement about municipal bond credit ratings or rating firms is correct?
   a. The credit rating of a special tax bond is not affected by what is being taxed.
   b. The credit rating of a transit system may be affected by whether the municipality is highly dependent on public transportation.
   c. Rating firms need not scrutinize healthcare or hospital bond issues, as a low portion of municipal bonds in default are in this sector.
   d. Investors can focus on characteristics of revenue bonds other than whether the projects are essential because rating firms ensure that all municipal bonds will fulfill debt service.

12. Which order type is certain to be fulfilled?
   a. Market
   b. Buy stop
   c. Limit
   d. Sell stop-limit

This material is provided for exam preparation purposes only and does not indicate an endorsement of any specific scientific, political, or religious point of view. © TPB Publishing. You have been licensed one copy of this document for personal use only. Any other reproduction or redistribution is strictly prohibited. All rights reserved.

13. Which order type is appropriate for liquid securities?
    a. Sell stop (loss)
    b. Market
    c. Limit
    d. Sell stop-limit

14. Which statement is correct?
    a. Long positions, also called covered positions, are conservative.
    b. Long positions, also called naked positions, are conservative.
    c. Short positions, also called covered positions, are aggressive.
    d. Short positions, also called naked positions, are conservative.

15. Which definition of the asking price is correct?
    a. It is the amount the buyer asks the broker-dealer to obtain for a stock.
    b. It is the amount the buyer's broker-dealer asks the clearing broker to accept for the stock.
    c. It is the amount the market maker requires in order to sell the stock to the buyer.
    d. It is the amount the seller's broker-dealer negotiates for the stock.

16. An investor has made a long purchase. How would this investor most likely react if the market price declined afterward?
    a. The investor would make a short sale in the security.
    b. The investor would wait for the market price to rise above the price at which the security was purchased.
    c. The investor would gift the security to an investment club for educational purposes.
    d. The investor would file a complaint with FINRA against the broker-dealer who helped with the long purchase.

17. What is an advantage that a company gains by using rights to sell stock?
    a. It provides an opportunity to invest excess cash to get a better return than through expansion.
    b. It enlarges the number of investors holding stock, and it fosters goodwill among the investing public.
    c. It provides a secret way to issue additional shares by communicating only with current shareholders.
    d. It eliminates the cost of hiring an investment banker or syndicate to prepare paperwork for the SEC.

18. Which act established packaged products that could provide investors with diversification without personally researching each investment?
    a. Investment Company Act of 1940
    b. Trust Indenture Act of 1939
    c. Securities Exchange Act of 1934
    d. Securities Act of 1933

This material is provided for exam preparation purposes only and does not indicate an endorsement of any specific scientific, political, or religious point of view. © TPB Publishing. You have been licensed one copy of this document for personal use only. Any other reproduction or redistribution is strictly prohibited. All rights reserved.

19. Which statement about notations on the order record is correct?
   a. Every solicited order must be indicated as solicited on the order, but a discretionary order placed in a nondiscretionary account doesn't need to be indicated as discretionary on the order.
   b. A solicited order doesn't need to be indicated as solicited on the order, and a discretionary order placed in a nondiscretionary account doesn't need to be indicated as discretionary on the order.
   c. Every solicited order must be indicated as solicited on the order, and a discretionary order placed in a nondiscretionary account must be indicated as discretionary on the order.
   d. A solicited order doesn't need to be indicated as solicited on the order, but a discretionary order placed in a nondiscretionary account must be indicated as discretionary on the order.

20. Which of the following is a bank draft?
   a. Short-term debt instruments
   b. Commercial paper
   c. Bankers' acceptance
   d. Money market instruments

21. Suppose that a bond has the following characteristics:

$$\text{Years to call} = 5$$

$$\text{Coupon rate} = 3\%$$

$$\text{Face value} = \$1,000$$

$$\text{Call premium} = \$30$$

$$\text{Call value} = \text{face value } \$1,000 + \text{call premium } \$30 = \$1,030$$

$$\text{Purchased price} = \$1,100$$

The following calculation is made:

$$\frac{\left(\dfrac{(Coupon\ Rate \times Face\ Value \times Years\ to\ Call) + (Call\ Value - Purchase\ Price)}{Years\ to\ Call}\right)}{\left(\dfrac{Call\ Value\ to\ be\ Received + Purchase\ Price}{2}\right)}$$

$$\frac{\left(\dfrac{(0.03 \times 1,000 \times 5) + (1,030 - 1,100)}{5}\right)}{\left(\dfrac{1,030 + 1,100}{2}\right)}$$

$$\frac{\left(\dfrac{150 + (-70)}{5}\right)}{1,065} = \frac{\left(\dfrac{80}{5}\right)}{1,065} = \frac{16}{1,065} = 15\%$$

What is being calculated?
   a. Current yield
   b. Nominal yield
   c. Yield to maturity (YTM)
   d. Yield to call (YTC)

This material is provided for exam preparation purposes only and does not indicate an endorsement of any specific scientific, political, or religious point of view. © TPB Publishing. You have been licensed one copy of this document for personal use only. Any other reproduction or redistribution is strictly prohibited. All rights reserved.

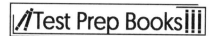

22. Which share class is most appropriate for an investor just starting to get acquainted with mutual funds and unsure of their time horizon?
    a. Class A
    b. Class B
    c. Class C
    d. Class T

23. Which self-regulatory organization (SRO) participates in the securities industry?
    a. Financial Planning Association (FPA)
    b. Chicago Board Options Exchange, Inc. (CBOE)
    c. American Council of Life Insurers (ACLI)
    d. American Institute of Certified Public Accounts (AICPA)

24. What is a characteristic of municipal bond insurance?
    a. In case of inadequate revenue for a revenue bond, the insurance company offers to purchase all of that bond issue from the investors.
    b. GO bonds with insurance typically have lower credit ratings than uninsured GO bonds.
    c. Insured bonds typically sell at a lower price than uninsured bonds.
    d. More bonds may be sold if the issue is insured.

25. Which act is also known as the Truth in Securities Act?
    a. 1933 Securities Act
    b. 1934 Securities Exchange Act
    c. 1940 Investment Company Act
    d. 2002 Sarbanes-Oxley (SOX) Act

26. Which of the following is NOT true of a unit investment trust (UIT)?
    a. The invested assets are eventually sold, with the proceeds going to the investors.
    b. A UIT has no stated termination date.
    c. A UIT has no investment manager after the investments are initially chosen.
    d. UITs issue shares of beneficial interest (SBIs).

27. When a company issues additional new securities and/or securities to previous shareholders, this is referred to as which of the following?
    a. Initial public offering (IPO)
    b. Contingent value rights (CVR)
    c. Private placement
    d. Follow-on public offering (FPO)

28. Which statement about the 1934 Act Section 15 – Rules Relating to Over-the-Counter Markets is correct?
    a. The broker-dealer reads the risk disclosure document aloud to the customer and maintains the document after it has been read aloud.
    b. The broker-dealer informs the customer of a way to learn the bid and ask prices and the quantity of penny stock shares for each price.
    c. The broker-dealer must be certain the specific penny stock order is possible and receive written approval of the trade from the investor.
    d. The broker-dealer must inform the customer of the percentage of the transaction that the firm and its broker will receive for the trade.

This material is provided for exam preparation purposes only and does not indicate an endorsement of any specific scientific, political, or religious point of view. © TPB Publishing. You have been licensed one copy of this document for personal use only. Any other reproduction or redistribution is strictly prohibited. All rights reserved.

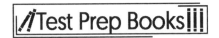

29. Which of the following is calculated based upon the proportion of shares held by a stockholder, compared to all outstanding shares?
    a. Preemptive rights clause
    b. Anti-dilution provision
    c. Rights issue ratio
    d. Right of first refusal

30. The Federal Reserve may adjust interest rates in which of the following ways?
    a. Adjusting rates on credit cards
    b. Adjusting rates on home mortgages
    c. Adjusting the rate the Fed charges for overnight loans
    d. Adjusting rates on corporate bonds

31. Which is a correct statement about Form U4 (Uniform Application for Broker-Dealer Registered) or Form U5 (Uniform Application for Broker-Dealer)?
    a. Firms typically submit Form U4 information on paper through the mail or by fax.
    b. Form U5 is used by an associated person's firm to end the registrations of the associated person with self-regulatory organizations.
    c. Form U5 information is available to the public through the BrokerCheck website, https://brokercheck.finra.org/.
    d. Firms typically submit Form U5 information on paper forms through the mail or by fax.

32. Which statement about the intention of securities regulation is correct?
    a. No investor will be able to sue the investor's broker-dealer.
    b. Every investor will have enough of the right information to make an informed decision regarding a purchase or sale.
    c. No investor will make more than a fair profit on any pair of buy/sell transactions.
    d. Every investor will realize enough profit to cover the commissions involved in the pair of buy/sell transactions.

33. Which sentence most accurately describes fractional reserve banking?
    a. Banks loan money deposited by depositors in the proportion allowed by regulators.
    b. Banks allow depositors to withdraw only a certain proportion of their account balance on a given day.
    c. Banks are required to hold a certain fraction of their depositors' funds in gold bullion.
    d. Banks loan a depositor's funds back to that depositor up to a certain fraction of the depositor's account balance.

34. A mortgage-backed pass-through certificate entitles its owner to which of the following?
    a. Monthly cash flow of principal and interest payments, less administrative costs
    b. Upon maturity, face value plus accrued interest, less administrative costs
    c. Monthly cash flow of interest payments, less administrative costs, and the face value at maturity
    d. Discounted present value of total interest payments and face value that would be paid at maturity

This material is provided for exam preparation purposes only and does not indicate an endorsement of any specific scientific, political, or religious point of view. © TPB Publishing. You have been licensed one copy of this document for personal use only. Any other reproduction or redistribution is strictly prohibited. All rights reserved.

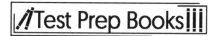

35. What is the limited liability advantage of common equity securities?
   a. The stockholder has no personal liability for the firm's liabilities, neither at liquidation, even if liabilities are in excess of assets, nor at any time prior to liquidation.
   b. The stockholder has no personal liability for the firm's liabilities at liquidation, but prior to liquidation the board of directors may make an assessment of stockholders, limited to the par value of the stock owned.
   c. The stockholder has no personal liability for the firm's liabilities, unless the firm defaults on loan covenants on mortgages held by banks, in which case personal liability is limited to the par value of stock owned.
   d. The stockholder has no personal liability for the firm's liabilities, unless the board of directors is found to have committed illegal acts, in which case personal liability is limited to twice the par value of the stock owned.

36. Which share class may serve as a short-term investment, even though it is included in a variable annuity?
   a. Class B
   b. Class C
   c. Class L
   d. Class T

37. Which statement about the effect of interest on federal income tax on municipal bonds is correct?
   a. Interest payments on bonds used to build facilities not used by the general public are typically exempt from federal income tax.
   b. Interest payments on hospital bonds are typically exempt from federal income tax.
   c. Interest payments on municipal bonds that are exempt from federal income tax do not affect the portion of social security benefits subject to federal income tax.
   d. Interest payments on bonds to help replenish an underfunded retirement pension plan are exempt from federal income tax.

38. Which is the correct statement about guidelines under MSRB Rule G-20 – Gifts, Gratuities and Non-cash Compensations for non-cash compensation for representatives who sell municipal securities?
   a. Gifts are allowed, if not linked to sales, up to $500 per person per year.
   b. Promotional items of nominal value that display the issuing entity's business or other corporate logo are allowed.
   c. Non-frequent meals or tickets to entertainment events are not allowed.
   d. Personal gifts for a birth or a wedding are allowed, up to $100 each.

39. Which statement about options is correct?
   a. They are debt securities that are only issued by corporations.
   b. They are equity securities that are only developed by hedge funds.
   c. They are derivative instruments that may be developed by traders.
   d. They trade with less volume than stock warrants.

This material is provided for exam preparation purposes only and does not indicate an endorsement of any specific scientific, political, or religious point of view. © TPB Publishing. You have been licensed one copy of this document for personal use only. Any other reproduction or redistribution is strictly prohibited. All rights reserved.

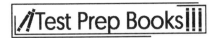

40. Which statement about dividends is correct?
    a. A board of directors chooses when the stock will begin to trade without a right to a declared dividend (ex-dividend date or ex-date).
    b. The ex-dividend date or ex-date is typically the first business day or first trading day after the date of ownership (record date), which determines which owners will be paid the dividend.
    c. The price of the stock will typically increase by the amount of the dividend on the ex-date.
    d. A board of directors may declare a dividend in cash or with stock.

41. Which statement best describes how a market maker receives compensation?
    a. The market maker earns compensation on the difference between the bid and ask prices, as well as receiving 50% of the commission paid by the buyer and seller to their respective broker-dealers.
    b. The market maker earns compensation on the difference between the bid and ask prices, as well as receiving 25% of the commission paid by the buyer and seller to their respective broker-dealers.
    c. The market maker earns compensation on the difference between the bid and ask prices, as well as one half of the difference between the historical price the market maker paid for a security and the price for which it is later sold.
    d. The market maker earns compensation on the difference between the bid and ask prices, as well as the difference between the historical price the market maker paid for a security and the price for which it is later sold.

42. Which statement about a prospectus is correct?
    a. The primary disclosure document may be one of two kinds, either a statutory prospectus or a summary prospectus.
    b. The representative may mark on the prospectus to emphasize items of particular importance.
    c. The prospectus is not to be relied upon by the investor to make an informed choice.
    d. The representative's professional opinion about which share class to purchase is to be the only basis for the investor's decision.

43. Under FINRA Rule 2251 – Forwarding of Proxy and Other Issuer-Related Materials, which event would require the broker to send proxy materials?
    a. The issuer provides payment in advance for the cost of the forwarding process.
    b. The issuer identifies stockholders who own at least a round lot (100 shares).
    c. The issuer does not object to distribution of proxy materials.
    d. The issuer provides enough copies of proxy materials.

44. In which of the following FINRA By-Laws Articles are member broker-dealer firms required to make annual payments and other payments as determined?
    a. FINRA By-Laws Article I – Definitions
    b. FINRA By-Laws Article III – Qualifications of Members and Associated Persons
    c. FINRA By-Laws Article IV – Membership
    d. FINRA By-Laws Article V – Registered Representatives and Associated Persons

This material is provided for exam preparation purposes only and does not indicate an endorsement of any specific scientific, political, or religious point of view. © TPB Publishing. You have been licensed one copy of this document for personal use only. Any other reproduction or redistribution is strictly prohibited. All rights reserved.

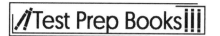
45. Which of the following is correct regarding statements made in FINRA By-Laws Article XV – Limitations of Power?
    a. FINRA may make political contributions to state officials' campaigns but not federal officials' campaigns.
    b. FINRA may use its name for a political purpose, as authorized by FINRA's governors.
    c. FINRA's rules regarding municipal securities will not be in effect for member firms or their associated persons if not consistent with Section 15 of the Securities Exchange Act of 1934, which establishes the Municipal Securities Rulemaking Board (MSRB).
    d. FINRA's governors and committee members may serve with conflicts of interest if the conflicts are fully disclosed and approved.

46. Which of the following is a function of Congress?
    a. Control international balance of payments.
    b. Control monetary policy by directly stimulating the economy through open market activities.
    c. Control fiscal policy by directly stimulating the economy through deficit spending.
    d. Make decisions primarily based upon economic analysis.

47. Which organization guarantees all listed options?
    a. Financial Industry Regulatory Authority (FINRA)
    b. Securities Exchange Commission (SEC)
    c. Options Clearing Corporation (OCC)
    d. Chicago Board Options Exchange (CBOE)

48. An equity indexed contract holder has chosen a minimum guaranteed rate of 4%, along with a limited upside potential of 80% of the increase in the S&P Index, up to a maximum of 8%. If the S&P Index increases by 12%, what would the contract be credited with?
    a. 4%
    b. 8%
    c. 9.6%
    d. 12%

49. Which statement about short-term debt instruments is correct?
    a. Short-term debt instruments are defined as having a term of less than two years.
    b. A variety of short-term debt instruments are typically used by a firm with a long-term cash need.
    c. The primary goal of a purchaser of short-term debt is a high tax-effective interest rate.
    d. A purchaser of short-term debt is typically most concerned with stability of value and certainty of repayment.

50. Which statement about total return is correct?
    a. It is a dollar value that equals the proceeds when disposed of by sale or maturity, less the cost of the investment.
    b. It is a dollar value that equals the proceeds, when disposed of by sale or maturity.
    c. It is a percentage calculated with the numerator being the cash received, plus or minus gain or loss on the sale, less the purchase cost of the investment, and the denominator being the purchase cost of the investment.
    d. It is a percentage calculated with the numerator being the cash received and the denominator being the purchase cost of the investment.

This material is provided for exam preparation purposes only and does not indicate an endorsement of any specific scientific, political, or religious point of view. © TPB Publishing. You have been licensed one copy of this document for personal use only. Any other reproduction or redistribution is strictly prohibited. All rights reserved.

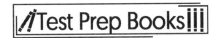

51. Which description of financial statements is correct?
    a. Their purpose depends upon the audience for which they are prepared.
    b. They name future expectations of management regarding profitability.
    c. They recommend whether to buy or sell stock of the company issuing them.
    d. They are not used for income tax purposes.

52. Which statement about the Municipal Securities Rulemaking Board (MSRB) is correct?
    a. It does not regulate initial issuance of municipal securities, which are regulated by the SEC.
    b. It requires a municipal securities dealer to offer prices that are lower than the general market.
    c. It promotes municipal securities as generally having higher nominal interest rates than corporate bonds.
    d. It seeks to issue rules to promote a fair and organized market, with protections for those involved.

53. The North American Securities Administrators Association (NASAA) includes securities administrators from which of the following?
    a. The 50 states and the District of Columbia, Canada, Mexico, and Greenland
    b. The 50 states and the District of Columbia, Puerto Rico, Canada, and Mexico
    c. The 50 states and the District of Columbia, the US Virgin Islands, Puerto Rico, Canada, and Mexico
    d. The 50 states, the District of Columbia, the US Virgin Islands, Canada, and Mexico

54. Why did Section 4 of the Securities Exchange Act of 1934 establish the Securities and Exchange Commission (SEC)?
    a. To encourage investors to provide capital by educating investors regarding the risks and benefits of each security
    b. To encourage investors to provide capital by enforcing laws and regulations to inform and protect investors
    c. To encourage investors to provide capital by restricting the varieties of securities available in the secondary market
    d. To encourage investors to provide capital by setting a maximum number of securities available in the secondary market

55. What is one reason that a firm would likely include a provision to call a bond issue?
    a. Under certain conditions and at certain times, the bondholders would be able to convert the bonds to common stock.
    b. In case interest rates decline, the issue could be replaced by one with a lower interest rate.
    c. This provision could increase the demand for the bonds.
    d. The SEC requires a certain percentage of each corporation's bonds to have a call provision.

56. Which statement about a mutual fund family is correct?
    a. After purchasing shares in one fund, the transfer fee to move from one investment choice to another is typically 1%.
    b. A front-end sales load cannot be used to compensate representatives for soliciting the investor.
    c. A 12b-1 fee typically increases as a percentage of net asset value (NAV) during the time the investor owns the fund's shares.
    d. If purchasing a large number of shares, an investor should consider purchasing shares with an up-front sales load.

This material is provided for exam preparation purposes only and does not indicate an endorsement of any specific scientific, political, or religious point of view. © TPB Publishing. You have been licensed one copy of this document for personal use only. Any other reproduction or redistribution is strictly prohibited. All rights reserved.

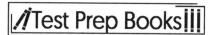

57. Which statement about prepaid tuition plans (PTPs) is correct?
    a. PTPs are not considered to be municipal fund securities.
    b. PTPs invest in conservative equity and debt securities.
    c. PTPs cover no more than two years of qualified educational expenses.
    d. PTPs offer the donor a choice of investment vehicles.

58. Which definition of the spread is correct?
    a. It is the profit realized by the investor.
    b. It is the amount the ask price changes during a period of time.
    c. It is the amount by which the market maker may be persuaded to change the price.
    d. It is the difference between the ask price and the bid price provided by a market maker at a given point in time.

59. Which sentence accurately describes a relationship between purchases of Treasury securities and their interest rate (yield) and the US economy, or investors' perception of the US economy?
    a. Prevailing interest rates determine the stated or nominal interest rates for government securities.
    b. The interest rates for government securities do not materially affect prevailing interest rates.
    c. High demand for government securities results in increased yields.
    d. Purchases of Treasury securities suggest how investors assess the strength of the US economy.

60. Which statement about put warrants is true?
    a. Expired put warrants provide voting rights.
    b. Expired put warrants receive dividends when declared and paid.
    c. Expired put warrants receive monetary value upon liquidation of the company.
    d. Until put warrants are exercised, the seller receives all dividends declared and paid.

61. Which statement about variable contracts is correct?
    a. As the investment account balance grows, it enjoys tax-deferral if the contract is not part of a qualified retirement account.
    b. The purchaser of a variable contract typically receives no investment advice.
    c. Investments are always limited to the IRS retirement fund contribution limits.
    d. The investment options of variable contracts are all fixed income investments.

62. Which compliance statement regarding American Depositary Receipts (ADRs) is correct?
    a. No matter what level of compliance, unsponsored ADRs may not trade in the OTC market.
    b. Level II compliance does not allow ADRs to trade on the New York Stock Exchange (NYSE).
    c. No sponsored ADRS may issue shares in the US.
    d. ADRs are considered to have risks that stocks in American companies do not.

63. Which of the following is NOT listed in FINRA Rule 1220 Registration Categories?
    a. Research principal
    b. General securities representative
    c. Securities administrative assistant
    d. General securities principal

This material is provided for exam preparation purposes only and does not indicate an endorsement of any specific scientific, political, or religious point of view. © TPB Publishing. You have been licensed one copy of this document for personal use only. Any other reproduction or redistribution is strictly prohibited. All rights reserved.

64. The Securities Exchange Act of 1934 was primarily focused on investors being adequately informed to make reasonable decisions, not allowing market participants to unreasonably manipulate prices, and keeping fraud to a minimum in which market?
   a. Primary market, involving initial issuance of securities by an issuing firm
   b. Secondary market
   c. Third market
   d. Fourth market (sometimes called "Dark Pools")

65. Which of the following is NOT regulated by FINRA Rule 2120 – Commissions, Mark Ups and Charges?
   a. Commissions received by a broker-dealer acting in an agency capacity for a market order on the New York Stock Exchange (NYSE)
   b. Markup received by a broker-dealer acting in a principal capacity
   c. Markdown received by a broker-dealer acting in a principal capacity
   d. Sale of securities sold at the specific public offering price when a prospectus or offering document is mandated to be provided to the investor (primary market)

66. If the board of directors of a company declares and pays dividends for common shareholders, what else must it also do?
   a. Redeem subordinated debentures.
   b. Declare and pay dividends on preferred stock.
   c. Reduce the market value of the common stock.
   d. Hold a special stockholders meeting.

67. Which of the following is true regarding the term of Treasury securities?
   a. All Treasury securities have maturities of one year or more.
   b. Treasury bills (T-bills) have maturities of one year.
   c. Treasury notes (T-notes) have maturities or two, four, six, eight, or ten years.
   d. Treasury bonds (T-bonds) have maturities of more than ten years.

68. Which statement about Section 529A Plans (529 ABLE) is correct?
   a. Earnings withdrawn for non-qualified expenses are taxable at ordinary rates, with no additional tax penalty.
   b. Medicare or Social Security payments and state benefits will be reduced if the ABLE savings account balance exceeds $10,000.
   c. The Achieving a Better Life Experience (ABLE) Act allows families to make before-tax contributions (for federal income tax purposes) to a state-managed savings account and use that account to supplement future private insurance and government benefits.
   d. Contributions of up to $15,000 annually, and totaling no more than $500,000, may be deposited in an ABLE account.

69. Which definition of a short sale is correct?
   a. It is a sale of a security that is borrowed but not owned.
   b. It is a sale that is settled on the trade date.
   c. It is a sale of stock with fewer than 100 shares (a round lot).
   d. It is a sale on behalf of a minor in a UGMA or UTMA account.

This material is provided for exam preparation purposes only and does not indicate an endorsement of any specific scientific, political, or religious point of view. © TPB Publishing. You have been licensed one copy of this document for personal use only. Any other reproduction or redistribution is strictly prohibited. All rights reserved.

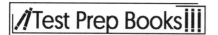

70. Which statement about requirements of the Investment Company Act of 1940 is true?
    a. A mutual fund may not trade securities.
    b. A company controlled by a mutual fund may not trade securities.
    c. A portfolio affiliate of a mutual fund may not trade securities.
    d. A mutual fund may not purchase securities from, or sell securities to, another mutual fund if it is likely that the purchase or sale will harm the fund.

71. Which order is to be completed at the best available price, as soon as reasonably practical, and expires at the end of the current trading day if NOT completed?
    a. Market order
    b. Stop order
    c. Limit order
    d. Good-til-canceled (GTC) order

72. Which of the following is generally considered a lagging indicator?
    a. Unemployment rate
    b. Average weekly hours worked in manufacturing
    c. Level of new business start-ups
    d. Consumer Price Index (CPI), intended to reflect the cost of living

73. Which statement about cost basis is true?
    a. From the point of view of the IRS, the oldest shares purchased may need to be designated as the shares sold.
    b. Cash received is usually included in the calculation of the cost basis.
    c. Only the purchase price is included, not the cost of acquisition.
    d. If stock dividends have been declared, this does not affect the calculation of cost basis per share.

74. Which statement about the distinction regarding registered and non-registered persons and their activities is correct?
    a. A registered person is a person who has registered to sit for a FINRA registration exam.
    b. A non-registered person may not invite members of the public to a meeting for which the firm is responsible.
    c. Without being engaged by a member broker-dealer firm, a registered person may encourage a person to buy or sell securities.
    d. A non-registered person may, without close supervision, ask whether a member of the public is interested in receiving printed materials about investments.

75. Which statement about municipal securities is correct?
    a. Municipal bonds may be issued only by the federal government.
    b. Municipal bonds may not be issued by Puerto Rico.
    c. Private activity bonds are one category of municipal bonds that is subject to the alternative minimum tax, whereas most municipal bond interest is exempt from federal income tax.
    d. Municipal bond interest is always exempt from state or local income tax.

This material is provided for exam preparation purposes only and does not indicate an endorsement of any specific scientific, political, or religious point of view. © TPB Publishing. You have been licensed one copy of this document for personal use only. Any other reproduction or redistribution is strictly prohibited. All rights reserved.

Answer Explanations #2

1. A: Choice *A* is correct because all transactions in a cash account are paid with cash. Choice *B* is incorrect because Federal Reserve Board Regulation T requires that the customer must pay at least 50% (or the amount over $500) of the cost of a security purchased on margin. Choice *C* is incorrect because Federal Reserve Board Regulation T requires that short sales must be made in a margin account. Choice *D* is incorrect because Federal Reserve Board Regulation T provides that payments be made promptly, not later than T+2, for securities purchased with cash accounts or margin accounts.

2. C: Choice *C* is correct because the holder must decide to exercise, and then they must notify their broker-dealer of that intention. Choice *A* is incorrect because the exchange does not typically notify the holder of the expiration date, which is the third Friday of the expiration month. Choice *B* is incorrect because the holder's broker-dealer notifies the OCC. Choice *D* is incorrect because the broker-dealer that receives the exercise notice from the OCC uses one several processes to select a customer and assign the notice to that customer: first-in, first-out (FIFO), random selection, or another alternative selection process.

3. A: Choice *A* is correct because some EICs provide "Bonus" additions in excess of the cash amount invested as the basis for calculating death benefits and annuitization. Choice *B* is incorrect because both EICs and variable contracts offer income tax deferral. Choice *C* is incorrect because both EICs and variable contracts typically offer annuitization options, one of which is payments for the life of the contract owner. Choice *D* is incorrect because both EICs and variable contracts offer death benefits for one or more beneficiaries.

4. A: Choice *A* is correct because an exchange offer is a type of tender offer in which the party making the offer would provide another security's shares in exchange for the desired shares. This is not necessarily approved by the board of directors. Choice *B* is incorrect because a rights offer must be approved by the board of directors. Choice *C* is incorrect because an acquisition is a decision by a board of directors to purchase another company. Choice *D* is incorrect because a merger is a decision by a board of directors to combine the company with another company.

5. A: Choice *A* is correct because the investor has not yet provided discretionary authority to the representative. Choice *B* is incorrect because the investor may authorize a discretionary order in writing without opening a discretionary account. Choices *C* and *D* are incorrect because a discretionary order placed in a discretionary account must be approved by the supervisory principal on the date the trade is made.

6. C: Choice *C* is correct because all listed American stock options use American style exercise, which allows exercise on or before the expiration date. Choices *A* and *B* are incorrect because listed stock index and foreign currency options generally use European style exercise, which only allows exercise on the expiration date. Choice *D* is incorrect because options expire on the third Friday of the expiration date.

7. B: Choice *B*, 529 plans, may be either college savings plans or prepaid tuition plans. Choices *A, C,* and *D* are not related to 529 plans.

8. C: Choice *C* is correct because the purchaser or seller may wish to settle during other than regular-way (special settlement). If so, this is agreed to before the trade takes place. Choice *A* is incorrect

151

This material is provided for exam preparation purposes only and does not indicate an endorsement of any specific scientific, political, or religious point of view. © TPB Publishing. You have been licensed one copy of this document for personal use only. Any other reproduction or redistribution is strictly prohibited. All rights reserved.

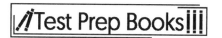

because, if the seller is not able to provide ownership in the regular-way time frame, the seller may request the settlement be done with extended time (seller's option). Choice *B* is incorrect because, if the purchaser and seller agree, a cash trade (cash settlement) may settle on the trade date (T). Choice *D* is incorrect because special settlement is agreed to by the buyer and seller before the trade takes place.

9. C: Choice *C* reflects the economic theory of John Maynard Keynes, which recommends governments adjust taxation and spending to stimulate the economy through deficit spending. Choice *A* is the opposite of deficit spending. Choices *B* and *D* are associated with monetary theory.

10. B: Choice *B* is correct because regular reporting of compensation to FINRA is not required. Choices *A*, *C*, and *D* are incorrect because they are all required by the rule.

11. B: Choice *B* is correct because if the municipality is highly dependent on public transportation, the municipality may more readily raise rates to assure debt service. Choice *A* is incorrect because the credit rating for a special tax bond could be affected by what is being taxed and whether its tax base or usage is expected to remain steady or change. This can be affected by changes in the economy and whether the population is increasing or decreasing. Choice *C* is incorrect because a significant portion of municipal bonds in default are in the healthcare and hospital sector. Choice *D* is incorrect because if a rating service assigns a low credit rating for a revenue bond issue on the grounds that the project is not essential, investors should have a higher level of concern regarding the provision for debt service and make their own judgment regarding how essential the project is.

12. A: Choice *A* is correct because a market order is to be fulfilled as soon as practical at the current market price. Choices *B*, *C*, and *D* are incorrect because they have conditions that may not be fulfilled before the end of day, and at that point they would expire unless they were good-til-canceled (GTC) orders. In that situation, it is still not certain that any of these orders would be fulfilled because the market price may never reach the specified price targets in the orders.

13. B: Choice *B* is correct because a market order is fulfilled as soon as practical at the best available price. Choices *A*, *C*, and *D* are incorrect because these have conditions that are especially important for more illiquid securities.

14. A: Choice *A* is correct because long (covered) positions are conservative ones in which the customer buys the security prior to selling it. The maximum possible loss is equal to the amount paid for the security were it to become worthless. This is called a bullish position, taken with the expectation that the price will increase. Choice *B* is incorrect because long positions are called covered, not naked. Choice *C* is incorrect because short positions are called naked, not covered. Choice *D* is incorrect because short (naked) positions are aggressive ones in which the customer borrows the security and sells it, rather than owning it before selling it. A short (naked) position is called a bearish position, taken with the expectation that the price will decrease.

15. C: Choice *C* is correct because the market maker offers an asking price for what the market maker is willing to sell a security for. Choices *A*, *B*, and *D* are incorrect because the market maker offers the asking price, which is the price the buyer pays.

16. B: Choice *B* is correct because, of the choices presented, it is the action that a prudent investor would typically follow. One other possibility, not listed among the answer choices here, is to sell the security at a loss. Choice *A* is incorrect because a short sale involves selling a security that is not owned. That would not be likely, as the investor could sell the security that they already own. Choice *C* is

152

This material is provided for exam preparation purposes only and does not indicate an endorsement of any specific scientific, political, or religious point of view. © TPB Publishing. You have been licensed one copy of this document for personal use only. Any other reproduction or redistribution is strictly prohibited. All rights reserved.

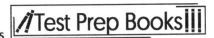

incorrect because gifting a security in decline is not a decision that an investor would typically make, not when the investor can either sell it and invest in something else or hold the security longer in hopes that the security's price will rise. Choice D is incorrect because, unless the broker-dealer violated some regulation, the broker-dealer is not responsible for a decline in market value of a purchased security.

17. D: Choice D is correct because using rights to sell stock avoids the cost of an investment banker as the shares are only offered to current shareholders and are not offered to the public. Choice A is incorrect because using rights to sell stock is usually done by a company in need of cash. Choice B is incorrect because using rights to sell stock typically only involves offering stock at a price below market price to current shareholders and does not increase the number of shareholders. The market price typically declines because future dividends will be distributed among a larger number of shares, unless the proceeds enable the company to expand profits proportionate to the additional shares issued. The investing public would typically choose to pay less for outstanding shares after the announcement of a rights offering. Choice C is incorrect because rights issues do not provide a secret way to issue new shares, as they are publicly announced.

18. A: Choice A is correct because the Investment Company Act of 1940 established unit investment trusts, closed-end investment companies, and open-end investment companies. The most popular of these is open-end investment companies. Choice B is incorrect because the Trust Indenture Act of 1939 dealt with bond issues of more than $5 million. It requires a legal agreement specifying details of the bond agreement, including selection of a trustee to protect bondholders. Choice C is incorrect because the Securities Exchange Act of 1934 regulated the resale of individual stocks after their initial issues in the secondary market, largely traded on exchanges. Choice D is incorrect because the Securities Act of 1933 regulates initial public offerings (IPOs), requiring them to be registered with the Securities Exchange Commission (SEC).

19. C: Choice C is correct because a solicited order must be indicated as solicited on the order, and a discretionary order placed in a nondiscretionary account must be indicated as discretionary on the order. Choices A, B, and D are therefore incorrect.

20. C: Choice C is correct because a banker's acceptance is a bank draft. It obligates the issuing institution to pay the owner of the instrument the amount on the instrument on a specific date. This is usually 90 days from the issue date, but it may be from one to 180 days from the issue date. Choice A is incorrect because, while some or all bank drafts (banker's acceptances) are short-term instruments that typically have terms of less than one year, not all short-term instruments are bank drafts. Choice B is incorrect because commercial paper is not a bank draft. It is a short-term loan issued by a bank that is unsecured and sold at a discount. Choice D is incorrect because, though banker's acceptances, which are bank drafts, are money market instruments, other money market instruments, such as repurchase agreements, are not bank drafts.

21. D: Choice D is correct because factors used include years to call, call premium, and call value. Choice A is incorrect because current yield is the nominal interest rate divided by the market value of the bond. Choice B is incorrect because the nominal yield is the coupon interest rate stated in the bond issue. Choice C is incorrect because years to maturity is not used.

22. C: Choice C is correct because these shares may or may not have an up-front sales load (sometimes 1%, if any), typically have a permanent 12 b-1 fee, and typically they have a 1% CDSC if sold within one year of purchase. This combination of fees may limit the total fees if the investment is sold within a few years. Choice A is incorrect because the up-front sales load of these shares may result in higher fees for

153

This material is provided for exam preparation purposes only and does not indicate an endorsement of any specific scientific, political, or religious point of view. © TPB Publishing. You have been licensed one copy of this document for personal use only. Any other reproduction or redistribution is strictly prohibited. All rights reserved.

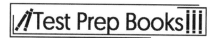
an investment sold within a few years. Choice B is incorrect because the higher CDSC of these shares may result in higher fees for an investment sold within a few years. Choice D is incorrect because the up-front sales load of these shares may result in higher fees for an investment sold within a few years.

23. B. Choice B, the Chicago Board Options Exchange, Inc. (CBOE), is in the securities industry. Choices A, C, and D are not in the securities industry.

24. D: Choice D is correct because investors find the increased safety of an insured bond issue attractive. Choice A is incorrect because the insurance company indemnifies the bondholders for default but does not offer to purchase the bonds. Choice B is incorrect because the increased safety of insured bonds results in higher credit ratings than the same bond if uninsured. Choice C is incorrect because insured bonds typically sell at a higher price based on the attraction of increased financial security.

25. A: Choice A, the 1933 Securities Act, which established standards for disclosure regarding initial public offering of securities, is also known as the Truth in Securities Act. Choice B established the Securities and Exchange Commission (SEC), and it regulates the trading of stock after its initial issuance. Choice C established regulations for investment companies (including mutual funds). Choice D, whose formal name is the Public Company Accounting Reform and Investor Protection Act of 2002, clarified audit rules and established accountability of chief executive officers (CEOs) for the accuracy of their company's financial statements.

26. B: Choice B is correct because a UIT has a stated termination date, which may be decades after inception. Choice A is incorrect because the invested assets of a UIT are eventually sold, with the proceeds being paid to the investors. Choice C is incorrect because no significant change is made to the investments after inception until dissolution. Choice D is incorrect because UITs issue shares of beneficial interest (SBIs).

27. D: Choice D refers to offering the public some shares held by early shareholders.. Choice A refers to newly-issued shares offered to the public by the company. Choice B refers to a benefit that shareholders of a company may receive if a specific situation arises, such as a reorganization or an acquisition by a second company. Choice C, also known as a non-public offering, refers to securities sold to a few chosen investors, such as acquaintances, relatives, accredited investors, and large institutions who invest in several companies.

28. C: Choice C is correct because Section 15 – Rules Relating to Over-the-Counter Markets requires that broker-dealers explain the risks, provide adequate information about penny stocks trading, and determine whether the customer may appropriately invest in penny stocks. One aspect of that required process is to make certain that a particular penny stock order may be placed and receive the customer's written approval. Choice A is incorrect because the broker-dealer must provide the customer with the risk disclosure document that explains the risks of trading in penny stocks. Choice B is incorrect because the broker-dealer must let the customer know the bid and ask prices and the number of shares that apply to such bid and ask prices for the penny stock. Choice D is incorrect because the broker-dealer must explain to the customer the dollar value of fees the firm and its broker will receive for the trade.

29. C: The rights issue ratio, Choice C, determines the number of rights a shareholder receives to allow maintenance of the same proportion of ownership when a new common stock issue is made. Choices A and B are names for the provision, if used, usually included in original issue of common stock. Choice D names the right given to previous shareholders, that is, the first right to purchase new shares of common stock.

This material is provided for exam preparation purposes only and does not indicate an endorsement of any specific scientific, political, or religious point of view. © TPB Publishing. You have been licensed one copy of this document for personal use only. Any other reproduction or redistribution is strictly prohibited. All rights reserved.

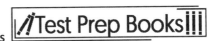

30. C: Choice *C*, adjusting the rate the Fed charges for overnight loans, is setting the federal funds rate. Choices *A, B,* and *D* are not actions of the Federal Reserve.

31. B: Choice *B* is correct because firms use Form U5 to end the registration of an associated person and answer some questions regarding the circumstances of the ending registration. Choice *A* is incorrect because firms typically submit U4 information electronically on the Central Registration Depository. Choice *C* is incorrect because the information that is available to the public through the BrokerCheck website is for Form U4, not Form U5. Choice *D* is incorrect because member firms typically submit U5 information electronically on the Central Registration Depository.

32. B: Choice *B* is correct because, after the stock market crash of 1929, Congress established laws and organizations to aid investors by giving them adequate information to make informed decisions about trades. Choice *A* is incorrect because, though lawsuits can be minimized by broker-dealers following securities laws and regulations, securities laws in general are not intended to end all lawsuits against broker-dealers. Choices *C* and *D* are incorrect because securities regulation is not intended to guarantee any specific outcome of a pair of buy/sell transactions.

33. A: Choice *A* reflects the ability to loan depositors' funds up to the limit set by regulation. Choices *B* and *C* are not elements of fractional reserve banking. Choice *D* is not an element of fractional reserve banking, which places no limit on a bank making loans to a depositor based upon that depositor's account balance.

34. A: Choice *A* is correct because owners of mortgage-backed pass-through certificates are entitled to share in the monthly cash flow made by homeowners in the pool of mortgages and interest payments and principal, less administrative costs. Choice *B* is incorrect because mortgage-backed pass-through certificates provide monthly payments of interest and principal. Mortgage principal balances are decreasing each month, so no payment would be expected at a maturity date, other than the final mortgage payment(s). Choice *C* is incorrect because, though monthly cash flow of interest payments, less administrative costs, is received by the bond holders, the monthly payments also include amortized principal repayment. Choice *D* is incorrect because, depending upon prevailing interest rates, default risk, credit risk, repayment risk, and the general economic outlook, the approximate present value of total interest payments and face value that would be paid at maturity could only be obtained by selling the bond on the open market.

35. A: Choice *A* accurately describes the advantage of the limited liability of common equity securities to stockholders. Choices *B, C,* and *D* are incorrect.

36. C: Choice *C* is correct because, though a variable annuity is typically a long-term investment, Class L shares are for an investor who wants to treat them as a short-term investment. The Class L shares do not have an up-front sales charge, but they do have a surrender period of three to four years, compared with the average surrender period of six to eight years for variable annuities. Class L shares allow payment to begin after three or four years, which is earlier than other share classes. Choices *A, B,* and *D* are incorrect because they are not offered in variable annuities with the option to begin payment as early as Class L shares.

37. B: Choice *B* is correct because interest payments on hospital bonds are typically exempt from federal income tax because the facilities are used by the general public. Other examples of revenue bonds serving the general public are those used to build bridges, airports, and toll roads. Choice *A* is incorrect because interest on bonds used to build facilities not used by the general public is generally not exempt

155

This material is provided for exam preparation purposes only and does not indicate an endorsement of any specific scientific, political, or religious point of view. © TPB Publishing. You have been licensed one copy of this document for personal use only. Any other reproduction or redistribution is strictly prohibited. All rights reserved.

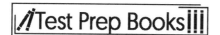

from federal income tax. Choice *C* is incorrect because municipal bond interest that is exempt from federal income tax is included in the modified adjusted gross income (MAGI) when calculating what proportion of Social Security benefits is subject to federal income tax. Choice *D* is incorrect because interest payments on bonds to help replenish an underfunded retirement pension plan or bonds related to the Build America Bonds (BAB) program are not exempt from federal income tax.

38. B: Choice *B* is correct because Rule G-20(d) excludes such promotional items from restrictions. Choice *A* is incorrect because the annual limit per person is $100. Choice *C* is incorrect because nonfrequent meals or tickets to entertainment events are allowed, so long as they are not costly enough to seem inappropriate, nor linked to a certain level of sales. Choice *D* is incorrect because Rule G-20(d)(vi) provides for personal gifts given upon the occurrence of infrequent life events, such as a wedding or birth of a child, and are not subject to the $100 limit so long as the gift(s) do not otherwise give rise to any apparent or actual material conflict of interest.

39. C: Choice *C* is correct because options are derivative instruments tracking the value of an underlying asset, such as an equity security or debt security. Options may be developed by traders. Choice *A* is incorrect because, although options may be issued by corporations, they may be developed by traders. Choice *B* is incorrect because options may be issued by corporations or developed by traders. Choice *D* is incorrect because options trade with more total volume than stock warrants.

40. D: Choice *D* is correct because a board of directors has the choice of declaring a dividend in cash or with stock. Unless future earnings increase proportionately to the increase in shares, stock dividends may dilute the value of existing stock because future dividends will be distributed over a larger number of shares. Choice *A* is incorrect because the rules of the exchange on which the stock is traded determine the ex-dividend date or ex-date. Choice *B* is incorrect because the ex-date is typically the first business day or first trading day before the date of ownership (record date) because one business day is needed in order to settle trades. Choice *C* is incorrect because the price of the stock will typically decrease by the amount of the dividend on the ex-date because an investor purchasing the stock on or after the ex-date will not be entitled to receive the dividend.

41. D: Choice *D* is correct because the market maker earns compensation by the spread (the difference between the bid and ask prices), as well as the difference between the historical price the market maker paid for a security and the price for which it is later sold. it is later sold. Choices *A* and *B* are incorrect because market makers do not typically receive any of the commission paid by the buyer or seller to their respective broker-dealers. Choice *C* is incorrect because the market maker receives compensation that includes the full amount of the difference between the historical price the market maker paid for a security and the price for which it is later sold.

42. A: Choice *A* is correct because both the statutory prospectus and the summary prospectus have the necessary information about objectives, risks, fees and expenses, and past performance. The summary prospectus is provided by some mutual funds. The statutory prospectus also includes the fund's investment managers and how to buy and sell shares. Choice *B* is incorrect because the representative is not allowed to mark on the prospectus. Choice *C* is incorrect because the investor is encouraged to read the prospectus in order to make an informed choice. Choice *D* is incorrect because, though the representative is expected to recommend the class of shares that matches the investor's needs, the investor is encouraged to read the prospectus in order to make an informed choice and not rely only on the representative's suggestion.

This material is provided for exam preparation purposes only and does not indicate an endorsement of any specific scientific, political, or religious point of view. © TPB Publishing. You have been licensed one copy of this document for personal use only. Any other reproduction or redistribution is strictly prohibited. All rights reserved.

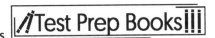

43. D: Choice *D* is correct because the rule states that, in order for the broker to be obligated to forward proxy materials, the issuer must provide enough copies of proxy materials (the proxy vote form and explanatory materials, such as annual reports and information statements) to the member firm. Choice *A* is incorrect because advance payment of the cost of the forwarding process is not required in the rule. Rather, the issuer must provide assurance that payment will be made for the cost of the forwarding process. Choice *B* is incorrect because the rule does not limit proxy distribution to stockholders who own 100 shares. Every shareholder is to receive proxy materials from the broker if the named events occur. Choice *C* is incorrect because the issuer is to request that the proxy materials be forwarded to the shareholders.

44. C: Choice *C* is correct because Article IV describes the application for membership, which includes the agreement to make required payments, including annual amounts and others as determined. Choice *A* is incorrect because Article I defines dozens of terms used throughout the bylaws but does not provide for payments by member firms to FINRA. Choice *B* is incorrect because Article III describes, in general, registration and other qualifications that may be established, activity in the profession, standards of behavior, and reporting requirements. However, it does not provide for payments by member firms to FINRA. Choice *D* is incorrect because Article V requires member firms to only allow qualified persons, who are not subject to disqualification, to perform securities activities or investment banking activities.

45. C: Choice *C* is correct because the MSRB oversees municipal securities and related firms and individuals in a way that is similar to FINRA's oversight of non-municipal securities and related firms and individuals. The MSRB's jurisdiction was originally defined by Congress to include banks and broker-dealers that handled transactions involving municipal securities. In 2010, Congress added the oversight of municipal advisors, which are firms and their qualified individuals, who advise governmental and other municipal organizations about offering municipal securities. FINRA specifically excludes itself from areas in which the MSRB exercises oversight. Choice *A* is incorrect because FINRA By-Laws Article XV states that FINRA will not make political contributions. Choice *B* is incorrect because FINRA By-Laws Article XV states that FINRA will not use its name for any political purpose. Choice *D* is incorrect because FINRA By-Laws Article XV states that FINRA's governors and committee members will avoid conflicts of interest.

46. C: Choice *C* correctly reflects Congress's action in controlling fiscal policy, which is stimulating the economy by authorizing more in expenditures than what is collected through taxes. Choice *A* is not directly determined by Congress, as the balance of payments is the net inflow or outflow of funds from imports and exports. Choice *B* reflects action by the Federal Reserve. Choice *D* is incorrect; Congress is responsive to constituencies and their political preferences, so they take action with broad goals.

47. C: Choice *C* is correct because the OCC guarantees all options traded on registered American exchanges, known as listed options. Choice *A* is incorrect because FINRA does not guarantee listed options, though it does regulate options. Choice *B* is incorrect because the SEC does not guarantee listed options, though it has overall responsibility for oversight of domestic exchange activity. Choice *D* is incorrect because the CBOE does not guarantee listed options, though it is the largest option exchange in the United States.

48. B: Choice *B*, 8%, is correct because, though 80% of 12% equals 9.6%, the contract would be credited with 8%, which is the maximum upside potential. Choice *A*, 4%, is incorrect because the allowed increase of 8% is greater than the minimum of 4%. Choice *C*, 9.6%, is incorrect because maximum credit is 8%. Choice *D*, 12%, is incorrect because, though the S&P Index increased by 12%, the contract is

This material is provided for exam preparation purposes only and does not indicate an endorsement of any specific scientific, political, or religious point of view. © TPB Publishing. You have been licensed one copy of this document for personal use only. Any other reproduction or redistribution is strictly prohibited. All rights reserved.

credited with 80% of 12% (which equals 9.6%) only if the resulting amount is no more than 8%, which is the maximum upside potential.

49. D: Choice *D* is correct because the holder of short-term debt expects to need the funds within a year or less and cannot wait for recovery of market value during a trough in the business cycle, which could take a number of years. Choice *A* is incorrect because short-term instruments are defined as having a term of less than one year. Choice *B* is incorrect because short-term instruments are used to match a party having a short-term excess of cash with a party having a short-term need for cash. A firm with a long-term cash need typically uses long-term debt instruments. Choice *C* is incorrect because the primary goal of a purchaser of short-term debt is the ability to receive the principal value upon resale or maturity. Interest income is generally a lesser concern.

50. C: Choice *C* is correct because this correctly calculates the cash received plus or minus the realized gain or loss, with the result divided by the purchase. Choice *A* is incorrect because this calculates the realized gain or loss. Choice *B* is incorrect because this is merely the proceeds at the time of sale or maturity. Choice *D* is incorrect because this calculates the current yield at the time of purchase.

51. A: Choice *A* correctly states that the purpose of financial statements depends upon the audience for which they are prepared, whether to determine compensation for executives or employees, to satisfy SEC reporting requirements, or, in the case of insurance companies, to reflect their ability to pay claims. Choice *B* refers to statements that are historical in nature. Choice *C* refers to comments that may be made by investment analysts but not by a company in its financial statements. Choice *D* is incorrect because financial statements may be used for income taxes; however, some elements of the financial statement, such as depreciation, may be reported differently for federal tax purposes than for generally accepted accounting principles (GAAP).

52. D: Choice *D* is correct because the MSRB seeks to issue rules to promote a fair and organized market, with protections for those involved. MSRB Rule G-17 requires firms and individuals advising municipalities regarding new issues to be honest. MSRB Rule G-30 mandates that municipal securities dealers use reasonable and fair prices. Choice *A* is incorrect because the MSRB does regulate the initial issuance of municipal securities and requires those involved to honestly serve the sellers and buyers. Choice *B* is incorrect because MSRB Rule G-30 mandates that municipal securities dealers use reasonable and fair prices. A low price may not be reasonable or fair. Choice *C* is incorrect because municipal securities generally have lower nominal interest rates than corporate bonds. As the investor's marginal income tax rate increases, the tax-effective interest rate may become quite competitive, especially for municipal general obligation bonds, which are backed by the full faith and credit of a taxing authority.

53. C: Choice *C* is correct because the North American Securities Administrators Association (NASAA) includes the 50 states, the District of Columbia, Puerto Rico, the US Virgin Islands, Mexico, and Canada. Choice *A* includes Greenland, which is not a member of the NASAA. Choice *B* is missing the US Virgin Islands, which are part of the NASAA, and Choice *D* is missing Puerto Rico.

54. B: Choice *B* best explains the reason for establishing the Securities and Exchange Commission (SEC). Choice *A* explains only part of the ultimate reason; it describes informing investors but not protecting them. Choice *C* is not correct, though one effect of the SEC's activities may be to prevent the establishment of types of investments that are deemed inappropriate, but not because of any goal to restrict the numerical count or variety of investment types. Choice *D* is not correct, as no maximum

This material is provided for exam preparation purposes only and does not indicate an endorsement of any specific scientific, political, or religious point of view. © TPB Publishing. You have been licensed one copy of this document for personal use only. Any other reproduction or redistribution is strictly prohibited. All rights reserved.

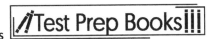
number of securities is set, though enforcement of laws and regulations may limit the quantity of securities in a specific issue.

55. B: Choice *B* is correct because a firm would likely include a provision to call in a bond issue in case interest rates decline. In that case, the company could decrease its interest costs by replacing the original issue with a new issue that has a lower interest rate. Choice *A* is incorrect because conversion occurs with a convertible bond, not a callable bond, unless the callable bond is also convertible. Choice *C* is incorrect because this would likely decrease the demand for the bonds, as a call provision is a benefit to the firm and provides reinvestment risk to the investor. Choice *D* is incorrect because the SEC has no requirement that any corporation have a call provision on any bond issue.

56. D: Choice *D* is correct because breakpoint purchases may allow lower total sales charges over the time period of the investment. Purchasing a large total value of shares would result in a reduced up-front sales charge, which does not continue, and lower ongoing 12b-1 fees, if any. Choice *A* is incorrect because subsequent to the initial purchase, transfers between funds are typically made as net transactions at net asset value (NAV), without any reductions for transfer fees or sales charges. Choice *B* is incorrect because a front-end sales load is the main way a mutual funds company compensates a soliciting representative. Choice *C* is incorrect because 12b-1 fees typically do not increase as a percentage of NAV during the time an investor owns the fund's shares. If the NAV of the fund rises over time, the nominal dollar amount would increase, even though the percentage does not increase.

57. A: Choice *A* is correct because PTPs are not considered to be municipal fund securities, as they are not typical instruments that can be traded, either on an exchange or over-the-counter. Some PTPs are intended to prepay tuition at public institutions of higher learning and freeze the cost for future students at current levels. Choice *B* is incorrect because PTPs do not invest in securities. Choice *C* is incorrect because PTPs may provide from one to five years of qualified education expenses. Choice *D* is incorrect because donors to PTPs have no choices regarding investment vehicles.

58. D: Choice *D* is correct because the spread is the compensation for the market maker's services. Choice *A* is incorrect because the spread is the compensation for the market maker. The spread at any given time may not be the same as the profit realized by the investor because the ask and bid prices change throughout the trading day and from day to day. The profit realized by the investor may be quite different from the spread on any given day. Choice *B* is incorrect because the spread is the difference between the bid and ask price at any given time, which is the compensation for the market maker. Choice *C* is incorrect because the market maker does not typically negotiate with a buyer's broker-dealer or a seller's broker-dealer.

59. D: Choice *D* is correct because purchases of Treasury securities suggest how investors assess the strength of the US economy and the creditworthiness of the US government. Lower levels of purchases suggest the economy is growing slowly, or that purchasers are concerned about the government defaulting on its payments. Choice *A* is incorrect because prevailing interest rates do not determine the stated or nominal interest rates for government securities, as these are set by the government. Choice *B* is incorrect because the interest rates for government securities influences other interest rates, such as home mortgages. Choice *C* is incorrect because high demand for government securities, which may lead to higher prices, results in decreased yields or effective interest rates.

60. D: Choice *D* is correct because shares of stock held by the seller of a stock put warrant receive dividends when they are declared and paid until the stock put warrant is exercised. This exercise results in the stock being sold to the buyer/holder of the stock put warrant. The buyer/holder of the stock put

This material is provided for exam preparation purposes only and does not indicate an endorsement of any specific scientific, political, or religious point of view. © TPB Publishing. You have been licensed one copy of this document for personal use only. Any other reproduction or redistribution is strictly prohibited. All rights reserved.

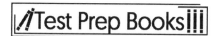

warrant then begins receiving dividends when declared and paid. Choice *A* is incorrect because stock put warrants have no voting rights, so expired stock put warrants have no voting rights. However, the stock related to the expired put warrants will have voting rights before and after expiration of the warrants. Choice *B* is incorrect because expired stock put warrants receive no dividends. However, the stock related to the warrants will continue to receive dividends. Choice *C* is incorrect because expired warrants receive no monetary value upon liquidation of the company. However, the stock related to the warrants may receive monetary value upon liquidation of the company.

61. A: Choice *A* is correct because the investment grows on a tax-deferred basis whether or not the contract is part of a qualified retirement account. Choice *B* is incorrect because the purchaser of a variable contract, also known as a variable annuity or a variable annuity contract, typically receives information about investment choices and the advice of a person with a securities registration and an insurance license. Choice *C* is incorrect because if the variable annuity contract is not in a qualified retirement plan, contributions may be made in excess of the limits for qualified retirement accounts. Choice *D* is incorrect because variable contracts typically have equity investment options.

62. D: Choice *D* is correct because ADRs have currency risk, and American companies' stock do not. ADRs may also have more political risk than American companies have. Choice *A* is incorrect because some unsponsored ADRs with Level I compliance may trade over the counter. Choice *B* is incorrect because sponsored ADRs may trade on the New York Stock Exchange (compliance Level II). Choice *C* is incorrect because some sponsored ADRS may issue shares in the US (Level III) to raise capital for business expansion.

63. C: Choice *C* is correct because securities administrative assistant is not listed in the FINRA Rule 1220 Registration Categories. An unregistered person may perform many administrative responsibilities. Choices *A, B,* and *D* are incorrect because they are listed in the FINRA Rule 1220 Registration Categories.

64. B: Choice *B* is correct because the secondary market involves the trading of securities on exchanges following their original issue. Choice *A* refers to initial public offerings, which is the focus of the Securities Act of 1933. Choice *C* refers to securities listed on a national exchange when they are traded somewhere other than the exchange. Choice *D* refers to companies trading in an over-the-counter market where trade occurs directly without an intermediary.

65. D: Choice *D* is correct because FINRA Rule 2120 – Commissions, Mark Ups and Charges regulates compensation on the resale of securities (the secondary market). The sale of securities sold at the specific public offering price when a prospectus or offering document is mandated to be provided to the investor is considered the primary market. Choice *A* is incorrect because this is a transaction in the secondary market, which is regulated by FINRA Rule 2120. Choices *B* and *C* are incorrect because a broker-dealer acting in a principal capacity is buying from, or selling to, an investor in the secondary market, which is regulated by FINRA Rule 2120.

66. B: Choice *B* is correct because if common dividends are declared and paid, preferred dividends, including any preferred dividends in arrears, must be declared paid. Choice *A* is incorrect because subordinated debentures are not required to be redeemed in the event of common dividends being declared and paid. Choice *C* is incorrect because the board cannot directly reduce the market value of the common stock, but declaring common dividends may result in the market value being reduced by approximately the number of dividends, whether common or preferred. Choice *D* is incorrect because typically the board does not need to call a special stockholders meeting when declaring dividends.

This material is provided for exam preparation purposes only and does not indicate an endorsement of any specific scientific, political, or religious point of view. © TPB Publishing. You have been licensed one copy of this document for personal use only. Any other reproduction or redistribution is strictly prohibited. All rights reserved.

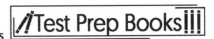

67. D: Choice *D* is correct because Treasury bonds (T-bonds) have maturities of more than 10 years. Their market value is more sensitive to fluctuations in the prevailing interest rates than Treasury securities with shorter terms. Choices *A* and *B* are incorrect because some T-bills have maturities of less than one year, so their market value is less sensitive to changes in prevailing interest rates. Choice *C* is incorrect because T-notes have maturities of two, three, five, seven, or ten years.

68. D: Choice *D* is correct because contributions of up to $15,000 annually, and totaling no more than $500,000, may be deposited in an ABLE account. Choice *A* is incorrect because earnings withdrawn for non-qualified expenses are taxable at ordinary rates, and a 10% tax penalty applies. Choice *B* is incorrect because Medicare or Social Security payments and state benefits will not be reduced because of the ABLE savings account, so long as it equals $100,000 or less. Choice *C* is incorrect because the Achieving a Better Life Experience (ABLE) Act allows families to make after-tax contributions (for federal income tax purposes) to a state-managed savings account and use that account to supplement future private insurance and government benefits.

69. A: Choice *A* is correct because a short sale is the sale of a security that is borrowed in the expectation that the price will decline. At that point, the security may be purchased and provided to the borrower, who realizes a profit. Choice *B* is incorrect because a short sale has nothing to do with the time to settle. Choice *C* is incorrect because a short sale has nothing to do with the quantity of shares in the transaction. Choice *D* is incorrect because a short sale has nothing to do with a uniform gift to minors account (UGMA) or uniform transfer to minors account (UTMA), which allow an adult to manage assets for a minor.

70. D: Choice *D* is correct because Investment Company Act of 1940 17a-7 – Exemption of Certain Purchase or Sale Transactions Between an Investment Company and Certain Affiliated Persons Thereof is intended to allow purchasing and selling of securities between mutual funds and specific affiliated persons if it is unlikely that the purchase or sale will harm the fund. Choices *A, B,* and *C* are incorrect because the Investment Company Act of 1940 17a-6 – Exemption for Transactions with Portfolio Affiliates provides that a mutual fund, a company controlled by a mutual fund, and a portfolio affiliate of the mutual fund may trade securities, so long as none of a list of persons close to the fund is a party to the trade or would benefit financially from the trade.

71. A: Choice *A* is correct because a market order has no price specified by the investor. The intention is to execute the order immediately at the best possible price. This is also known as a "day order," or a "good-til-day" order, and it expires at the end of the trading day if not complete. Choice *B* is incorrect because a stop order is only to be carried out if a certain market price is reached, known as the stop price. A stop order typically expires at the end of the day if not completed. Choice *C* is incorrect because a limit order is only to be carried out if it can be completed at a price that is at least as good as the price chosen by the investor. A limit order typically expires at the end of the day if not completed. Choice *D* is incorrect because a good-til-canceled (GTC) order does not expire at the end of the day. It does not expire until it is either fulfilled or canceled by the investor.

72. D: Choice *D*, the Consumer Price Index (CPI), is intended to reflect the cost of living by summarizing the costs of essential needs. The change in the CPI is a primary measure of inflation. This measure is generally agreed to typically lag behind changes in the economy. Choices *A* and *B* are considered to be coincident indicators. Choice *C* is considered to be a leading indicator.

73. A: Choice *A* is correct because the IRS may consider first-in, first-out (FIFO) an appropriate identification of securities sold. In the case of a rising market, this may increase the tax liability, in

This material is provided for exam preparation purposes only and does not indicate an endorsement of any specific scientific, political, or religious point of view. © TPB Publishing. You have been licensed one copy of this document for personal use only. Any other reproduction or redistribution is strictly prohibited. All rights reserved.

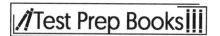

contrast to choosing securities that have not been held as long. Choice *B* is incorrect because cash received is usually taxed in the year received. Choice *C* is incorrect because the cost of acquisition is typically included in the calculation of cost basis. Choice *D* is incorrect because if multiple purchases have been made, if stock dividends have been declared, or if the firm has returned capital in some way, the identification of the cost basis may be more involved.

74. D: Choice *D* is correct because a person doesn't need to be registered to ask whether a member of the public is interested in receiving printed materials about investments. Choice *A* is incorrect because a registered person is a person who has passed a FINRA registration exam. Choice *B* is incorrect because a non-registered person may, without close supervision, invite members of the public to a meeting for which the firm is responsible. Choice *C* is incorrect because a registered person is authorized to encourage a person, according to securities laws and regulations regarding suitability and other considerations, to buy or sell a security appropriate to the representative's registration only when engaged by a FINRA member broker-dealer firm.

75. C: Choice *C* is correct because municipal bond interest is usually exempt from federal income tax. Private activity bonds, which are not for the benefit of the public but are focused on a private project, are subject to the alternative minimum tax. Municipal bond interest is generally exempt from state income tax, depending upon the state. Some states may tax interest on their own bonds but may make an exception for a specific bond issue. Some states may not tax interest on other states' bonds. Income from municipal bonds may be exempt from local income tax. Choice *A* is incorrect because municipal bonds are not issued by the federal government. Choice *B* is incorrect because municipal bonds may be issued by territories and possessions of the US. Since Puerto Rico is a territory, it may issue municipal bonds. Choice *D* is incorrect because municipal bond interest is generally, but not always, free from state income tax by the state in which it is issued.

This material is provided for exam preparation purposes only and does not indicate an endorsement of any specific scientific, political, or religious point of view. © TPB Publishing. You have been licensed one copy of this document for personal use only. Any other reproduction or redistribution is strictly prohibited. All rights reserved.

Practice Test #3

1. Which equation is an expression of a basis point, which may be used to refer to the yield of an investment, especially a debt security?
   a. $0.1\% = one\ basis\ point$
   b. $0.01\% = one\ basis\ point$
   c. $0.001\% = one\ basis\ point$
   d. $1\% = one\ basis\ point$

2. Which broker-dealer is acting in the trade capacity as principal?
   a. A broker-dealer who fulfills an unsolicited order
   b. A broker-dealer who fulfills a solicited order
   c. A broker-dealer who fulfills a good-til-canceled order
   d. A broker-dealer who sells a security to a buyer

3. Which statement about college savings plans is correct?
   a. Contributions to college savings plans are tax-deductible.
   b. Investments grow tax-deferred.
   c. College savings plans always have a large selection of investments.
   d. Income from investments is typically tax-exempt at the state level and taxable at the federal level.

4. Which list of characteristics could apply to one order?
   a. Day, market, GTC, and solicited
   b. Market, GTC, non-discretionary, and unsolicited
   c. Market, GTC, sell stop (loss), and unsolicited
   d. Buy-stop, market, non-discretionary, and unsolicited

5. Section 10b-18 of which of the following acts attempts to aid the investing public by limiting a company's purchases of its own stock?
   a. 1933 Securities Act
   b. 1934 Securities Exchange Act
   c. 1986 Consumer Protection Act
   d. 2002 Sarbanes-Oxley (SOX) Act

6. What is stated on a bond issue?
   a. Current yield
   b. Nominal yield
   c. Yield to maturity (YTM)
   d. Yield to call (YTC)

7. Which area on the business cycle chart refers to the strongest phase of the economy?
   a. Peak
   b. Expansion
   c. Trough
   d. Contraction

This material is provided for exam preparation purposes only and does not indicate an endorsement of any specific scientific, political, or religious point of view. © TPB Publishing. You have been licensed one copy of this document for personal use only. Any other reproduction or redistribution is strictly prohibited. All rights reserved.

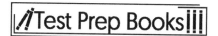

8. The Securities Investor Protection Act of 1970 (SIPA) established the Securities Investor Protection Corporation (SIPC) in response to which situation?
   a. Broker-dealers began selling options, as well as stocks and bonds.
   b. The quantity of broker-dealers increased more than expected.
   c. Broker-dealers generally declined to provide financial disclosures to customers.
   d. Several broker-dealers declared bankruptcy.

9. Which statement about money market instruments is correct?
   a. Certificates of Deposit (CDs) are money market instruments.
   b. Mutual funds typically do not invest in money market instruments.
   c. State governments issue most money market instruments.
   d. Money market instruments are used to obtain a stable value and not for a high interest rate.

10. Which statement about municipal bonds is correct?
   a. Revenue bonds typically benefit the general public.
   b. Rating agencies typically rate revenue bonds higher than general obligation (GO) bonds.
   c. A general obligation (GO) bond must have voter approval.
   d. A revenue bond must have voter approval.

11. Suppose that $100 of interest is received while a security was held over a period of two years, $1,050 is received at the sale at the end of two years, total costs are $50, and the amount paid was $1,000. The calculation is as follows:

$$\frac{\$100 + \$1,050 - \$50 - \$1,000}{\$1,000} = \frac{\$100}{\$1,000} = 10\%$$

What is being calculated in this example?
   a. Realized gain
   b. Unrealized gain
   c. Internal rate of return (IRR)
   d. Return on investment (ROI)

12. Which statement about regular-way trade settlement is correct?
   a. This is the time (in business days) between the order being placed and its fulfillment.
   b. This is the same number of days for all debt instruments.
   c. This is the time (in business days) after the trade is agreed to (transaction date or trade date) until the seller's broker-dealer receives the purchase price and the purchaser's broker-dealer has received ownership of the security by having the purchaser entered as owner on the books of the issuer (settlement date).
   d. This is the same number of days for corporate bonds and Treasury bonds.

13. Which definition of the bid price is correct?
   a. It is the amount the seller asks the broker-dealer to obtain for a stock.
   b. It is the amount the seller's broker-dealer asks the clearing broker to obtain for the stock.
   c. It is the amount the market maker asks in order to sell the stock to the buyer.
   d. It is the amount the buyer pays for the stock.

This material is provided for exam preparation purposes only and does not indicate an endorsement of any specific scientific, political, or religious point of view. © TPB Publishing. You have been licensed one copy of this document for personal use only. Any other reproduction or redistribution is strictly prohibited. All rights reserved.

14. Which statement about an investor's consideration of a municipal bond purchase is correct?
    a. Lower-rated bonds usually pay higher interest rates.
    b. All lease rental bonds have a permanent legislative commitment for debt service.
    c. Revenue bonds typically pay a lower interest rate than general obligation (GO) bonds.
    d. GO bonds usually involve a feasibility study to justify the issue.

15. Which statement about the purpose of corporate bonds is correct?
    a. A firm typically sells bonds at a discount and pays the face amount at maturity.
    b. A firm typically does not provide monetary value to bond holders at liquidation.
    c. A firm may receive proceeds for investing in the firm's growth by selling bonds.
    d. A firm diversifies its ownership by selling bonds.

16. What is one of the main reasons that mutual funds provide investors with a selection of share classes?
    a. So investors can select the lowest up-front sales load
    b. So investors can select a sales charge, including 12b-1 fees, appropriate to their investment horizon
    c. So investors will purchase more shares in that mutual funds family
    d. So investors will obtain a higher return in their first 12 months after purchase

17. SEC Rule 415 provides for an issuer to issue securities that cannot be sold for up to two years later. What is this issue called?
    a. Shelf registration
    b. Deferred registration
    c. Private registration
    d. Immediate registration

18. Which statement about American Depositary Receipts (ADRs) is correct?
    a. Non-Americans can purchase American stock on foreign markets using ADRs.
    b. American investors receive dividends on ADRs in American dollars.
    c. A foreign company issues unsponsored ADR shares by paying an American bank to issue its ADRs.
    d. Sponsored ADRs may not trade in the over-the-counter (OTC) market.

19. Which of the following is true regarding debt certificates issued by a face-amount certificate company?
    a. They pay a set interest rate.
    b. Investments occur only in a lump sum.
    c. They receive no interest payments until maturity.
    d. Redemptions prior to maturity receive face value with no interest.

20. Which statement about commercial paper is correct?
    a. It is secured by equipment.
    b. It is issued by a bank.
    c. It is sold at face value.
    d. It typically has a term of less than one year.

This material is provided for exam preparation purposes only and does not indicate an endorsement of any specific scientific, political, or religious point of view. © TPB Publishing. You have been licensed one copy of this document for personal use only. Any other reproduction or redistribution is strictly prohibited. All rights reserved.

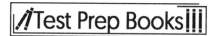

21. Which annuitization option is NOT included in equity-indexed contracts (EICs) or in variable contracts?
    a. Payments for the life of the owner when the owner is not the annuitant
    b. Payments for the combined life of the annuitant and one other person
    c. Payments for the life of the contract owner or for a certain minimum period of time
    d. Payments for the life of the contract owner with the remaining value at death passing to a beneficiary, either in a lump sum or in periodic payments

22. Under FINRA Rule 8312 – FINRA's BrokerCheck Disclosure, what is FINRA NOT required to disclose?
    a. Data from the most recently-submitted registration forms
    b. Summary data regarding some arbitration awards against a member firm related to a dispute with a public customer
    c. Comments provided by the person who is a subject of the data
    d. Dates of qualification exams failed

23. Which statement about the respective rules of FINRA and the Municipal Securities Rulemaking Board (MSRB) is correct?
    a. FINRA Rule 0100 Series – General Standards states that FINRA will coordinate with the MSRB regarding registration and supervision of municipal securities brokers and municipal advisors.
    b. FINRA Rule 1122 – Filing of Misleading Information as to Membership or Registration specifies the manner in which to provide misleading information to FINRA.
    c. MSRB Rule G-2 – Standards of Professional Qualifications provides for non-registered persons to handle municipal securities transactions when closely supervised by a qualified principal.
    d. MSRB Rule G-3 – Professional Qualification Requirements establishes qualification testing requirements but no continuing education requirements.

24. Which share class is associated with a letter of intent and rights of accumulation?
    a. Class A
    b. Class B
    c. Class C
    d. Class T

25. Which statement about agencies of the federal government and government-sponsored enterprises (GSEs) is correct?
    a. Agencies and GSEs borrow money by issuing bond securities.
    b. The US Treasury issues agency bond securities.
    c. Agency bond securities pay a lower interest rate than Treasury bonds.
    d. GSE bond securities are formally backed by the "full faith and credit" of the United States.

26. Which rule requires municipal bond sales to be fulfilled in the sequence determined by the municipality issuing the bonds if the municipality has NOT authorized sales in a different sequence?
    a. MSRB Rule G-11 – Primary Offering Practices
    b. MSRB Rule G-32 – Disclosures in Connection with Primary Offerings
    c. FINRA Rule 2266 – SIPC Information
    d. MSRB Rule G-34 – CUSIP Numbers, New Issue, and Market Information Requirements

This material is provided for exam preparation purposes only and does not indicate an endorsement of any specific scientific, political, or religious point of view. © TPB Publishing. You have been licensed one copy of this document for personal use only. Any other reproduction or redistribution is strictly prohibited. All rights reserved.

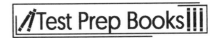

27. Which of the following is NOT a correct statement about FINRA rules on compensation?
    a. FINRA Rule 2121 – Fair Prices and Commissions allows a member broker-dealer to adjust what it charges a customer for handling a security transaction based on the type of security being traded.
    b. FINRA Rule 2122 – Charges for Services Performed provides that charges for services, including handling cash or trading securities, can be reduced for customers it has served for more than 12 months.
    c. FINRA Rule 2124 – Net Transactions with Customers states that disclosure of a net transaction for a non-institutional investor must include the price difference involved.
    d. FINRA Rule 2124 – Net Transactions with Customers states that disclosure of a net transaction for an institutional investor may satisfy notification requirements with a negative consent letter.

28. Which of the following is NOT a distinguishing characteristic of a discretionary order because it is chosen by the representative and NOT by the investor?
    a. Price
    b. Asset
    c. Amount
    d. Action

29. In which corporate action is the shareholder provided with more new shares in exchange for fewer old shares?
    a. Buyback
    b. Stock split
    c. Reverse stock split
    d. Tender offer

30. Which statement about compensation is correct?
    a. Commissioned registered representatives receive a transaction-based commission when a customer acts on their advice.
    b. Commissioned registered representatives may charge for their advice.
    c. Fee-based industry professionals may charge for their advice only if a trade is completed.
    d. Fee-based industry professionals may charge for their advice but not receive a transaction-based commission when a customer acts on their advice.

31. Which self-regulatory organization (SRO) has jurisdiction over banks that handle municipal securities?
    a. FINRA
    b. MSRB
    c. FDIC
    d. SEC

This material is provided for exam preparation purposes only and does not indicate an endorsement of any specific scientific, political, or religious point of view. © TPB Publishing. You have been licensed one copy of this document for personal use only. Any other reproduction or redistribution is strictly prohibited. All rights reserved.

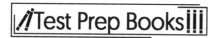

32. What is NOT included in the penny stock risk disclosure document?
    a. An explanation of market risk for penny stocks in both primary offerings (IPOs) or secondary markets
    b. An explanation of a guarantee that the broker-dealer will indemnify the customer for any realized losses due to market decline if notified within 24 hours
    c. An understandable explanation of how a dealer market conducts trades where a dealer either buys the security from, or sells a security to, a customer, the meaning of bid and ask prices, and the spread for penny stocks.
    d. A toll-free telephone number for inquiries about regulatory violations

33. What is likely to have the LEAST effect on the credit rating of an education municipal bond?
    a. Rating firm's estimate of the trend in the percentage of female students enrolled
    b. Rating firm's expectation that public universities will have financial challenges if tuition is not increased in proportion to the rise in expenses
    c. Rating firm's expectation that the level of student aid or grants may be affected by government budget adjustments
    d. Rating firm's perception of the school's reputation and resultant ability to maintain stable enrollment

34. Which of the following relates to a rights offering in which the issuer may NOT receive the full issue proceeds?
    a. Direct rights offering
    b. Standby rights offering
    c. Insured rights offering
    d. Backstop purchaser

35. What does an investor expect will happen after they complete a long purchase?
    a. The investor expects the exchange to halt trading for 15 minutes.
    b. The investor expects the exchange to halt trading for the remainder of the day.
    c. The investor expects the market value of the security to rise.
    d. The investor expects a stock split in the security.

36. Which is the correct statement about options that are not guaranteed?
    a. They all exclusively have standardized terms, which cannot be negotiated.
    b. They have no risk of non-performance by either the buyer or seller.
    c. They have a greater quantity of trades, making a counterparty easier to find.
    d. They trade in the over-the-counter market.

37. Which statement about background checks, fingerprinting, and hiring is NOT true?
    a. Each member firm must have a documented process for background checks before asking to register a person with FINRA.
    b. SEC Rule 17f-2 – Fingerprinting of Securities Industry Personnel only requires fingerprinting of a non-registered person who handles cash and securities.
    c. A member firm may never hire a person who has had disciplinary action taken by the Commodity Futures Trading Commission.
    d. A member firm is not allowed to hire a person who was convicted of certain offenses, no matter the time period when the offenses occurred.

This material is provided for exam preparation purposes only and does not indicate an endorsement of any specific scientific, political, or religious point of view. © TPB Publishing. You have been licensed one copy of this document for personal use only. Any other reproduction or redistribution is strictly prohibited. All rights reserved.

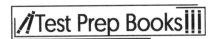

38. Which statement about direct participation programs (DPPs) is correct?
    a. DPPs are non-traditional investments, that is, different from cash, stocks, and bonds.
    b. DPPs must be listed securities.
    c. DPPs do not provide diversification because their values correlate with the market for bonds and stocks.
    d. DPPs are not regulated by the Securities Exchange Commission (SEC) or the Financial Industry Regulatory Authority (FINRA).

39. Under FINRA 4512 – Customer Account Information, which data is NOT required to be kept by the broker-dealer firm?
    a. Contact information
    b. Whether of legal age
    c. For a corporation, an alternative contact
    d. Signature of the supervisor approving the establishment of the account

40. What is a requirement of the FINRA rule regarding quotations and offers at stated prices?
    a. FINRA 5210 – Publication of Transactions and Quotations requires that any published quote of a purchase or sale of any security must be based on a member's understanding that the bid price or asked price of the security is a real bid for, or offer of, the security.
    b. MSRB G-13 – Quotations requires that municipal securities quotes published by dealers must present actual prices and amounts of securities at the prices in the last purchase or sales transaction of that security by the quoting dealer.
    c. FINRA 6438 – Displaying Priced Quotations in Multiple Quotation Mediums requires members that publish real-time quotations for an over-the-counter equity security in more than one market to publish the bid price of the last sale transaction and the ask price of the last purchase transaction in each market, except in some cases for a customer limit order.
    d. FINRA 5220 – Offers at Stated Prices requires that a member must only make an offer to buy a security from, or sell a security to, someone at a stated price of the last purchase or sale of that security.

41. Which statement about market value is true?
    a. Market value of common stock is affected primarily by anticipated growth in earnings and dividend policy.
    b. Market value of non-convertible preferred stock is affected primarily by anticipated growth in earnings.
    c. Market value of stock rights and warrant rights generally tracks with the related stocks.
    d. Market value of American Depositary Receipts (ADRs) generally tracks with the credit rating of the issuing foreign company.

This material is provided for exam preparation purposes only and does not indicate an endorsement of any specific scientific, political, or religious point of view. © TPB Publishing. You have been licensed one copy of this document for personal use only. Any other reproduction or redistribution is strictly prohibited. All rights reserved.

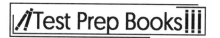

42. Suppose that a bond has the following characteristics:

$$Years\ to\ maturity = 8$$

$$Coupon\ rate = 3\%$$

$$Face\ value = \$1,000$$

$$Purchased\ price = \$1,100$$

The following calculation is made:

$$\frac{\left(\dfrac{(Coupon\ Rate \times Face\ Value \times Years\ to\ Maturity) + (Face\ Value - Purchase\ Price)}{Years\ to\ Maturity}\right)}{\left(\dfrac{Face\ Value\ at\ Maturity + Purchase\ Price}{2}\right)}$$

$$\frac{\left(\dfrac{(0.03 \times 1,000 \times 8) + (1,000 - 1,100)}{8}\right)}{\left(\dfrac{1,000 + 1,100}{2}\right)}$$

$$\frac{\left(\dfrac{240 + (-100)}{8}\right)}{1,050} = \frac{\left(\dfrac{140}{8}\right)}{1,050} = \frac{17.50}{1,050} = 1.67\%$$

What is being calculated?
a. Current yield
b. Nominal yield
c. Yield to maturity (YTM)
d. Yield to call (YTC)

43. Which term describes the selling and purchasing of securities by the Federal Reserve?
a. Open market activities
b. Direct action
c. Lobbying activities
d. Public comment

44. Which of the following is true of stock rights?
a. Expired stock rights provide voting rights.
b. Expired stock rights receive dividends when declared and paid.
c. Expired stock rights receive monetary value upon liquidation of the company.
d. Stock received after rights are exercised receive dividends when declared and paid.

45. In the event that a company is liquidated, which individuals would be last in line to receive financial value?
a. Senior bondholders
b. Holders of subordinated debentures
c. Preferred stockholders
d. Common shareholders

This material is provided for exam preparation purposes only and does not indicate an endorsement of any specific scientific, political, or religious point of view. © TPB Publishing. You have been licensed one copy of this document for personal use only. Any other reproduction or redistribution is strictly prohibited. All rights reserved.

//Test Prep Books!!!

46. Which statement about a long sale is correct?
    a. It is a sale of a security that is owned.
    b. It is a sale of a security with a quantity greater than 100 shares (a round lot).
    c. It is a sale of securities which takes longer than the usual settlement time of T+2.
    d. It is a sale of securities held by a group of persons, such as an investment club.

47. Which act is Rule 144 part of?
    a. Securities Act of 1933
    b. Securities Exchange Act of 1934
    c. Trust Indenture Act of 1939
    d. Investment Company Act of 1940

48. What is a benefit of trading in the over-the-counter (OTC) market?
    a. Securities are obtained directly from the issuer with a "satisfaction/money-back" guarantee.
    b. Prices of over-the-counter transactions do not affect prices on national exchanges.
    c. Broker-dealers are never involved.
    d. Some aspects of the purchases and sales are private.

49. Which of the following is a characteristic of both a variable contract and an equity-indexed contract (EIC)?
    a. They both typically allow exposure to equity-based investment returns.
    b. Neither prevents the investor from having a decline in account value.
    c. Neither can be expected to closely match the returns of the stock included in the S&P 500.
    d. Both typically limit the positive returns to a predetermined maximum.

50. What does cumulative voting allow?
    a. A creditor may vote to increase the interest rate on all mortgages outstanding.
    b. A bond holder may vote for a reduction in the interest rate on all bonds outstanding.
    c. A preferred shareholder may cast votes multiplied by the number of past years when they did not vote for a single candidate for the board of directors.
    d. A common shareholder may vote for a candidate for director using all their votes.

51. An investor chooses to make a long sale of a security that the investor had previously made a long purchase of at a lower price. What is likely to happen?
    a. The counterparty buyer makes a short sale at the same time.
    b. The investor's broker-dealer shares in the gain or loss by increasing or decreasing the commissions retroactively.
    c. The quantity of shares sold is greater than the quantity of shares purchased.
    d. The investor realizes a profit, less any commissions on the transactions.

52. Which of the following would be considered a secured bond?
    a. Debenture
    b. Convertible unsecured bond
    c. Mortgage bond
    d. Convertible preferred stock

This material is provided for exam preparation purposes only and does not indicate an endorsement of any specific scientific, political, or religious point of view. © TPB Publishing. You have been licensed one copy of this document for personal use only. Any other reproduction or redistribution is strictly prohibited. All rights reserved.

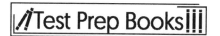

53. Which statement about the manner of delivery of notices regarding corporate actions is correct?
    a. An exchange does not provide notices for shares traded on its exchange.
    b. Notices regarding corporate actions are provided prior to approval by the board of directors.
    c. The New York Stock Exchange (NYSE) provides notices for shares traded over-the-counter (OTC) to meet the appropriate deadlines.
    d. The Financial Industry Regulatory Authority (FINRA) communicates the notices for shares traded over-the-counter (OTC) to meet the appropriate deadlines.

54. Which of the following is an example of public comment by the Federal Reserve?
    a. Buying government securities in a quantity expected to reduce the money supply
    b. Buying corporate bonds in a quantity expected to reduce the money supply
    c. Raising the discount rate to a level that is expected to slow down inflation
    d. Releasing a statement mentioning that the economy is expanding too fast

55. Which statement about derivatives is correct?
    a. Common stock is a derivative.
    b. Stock index options are not derivatives.
    c. A derivative's market value is equal to its intrinsic value.
    d. Their value is based on an underlying security.

56. Which of the following is true of unit investment trusts (UITs), closed-end investment management companies, and open-end investment management companies?
    a. They are governed by a board of directors.
    b. They have ongoing management fees.
    c. They are actively managed portfolios.
    d. They are governed by the Investment Company Act of 1940.

57. Which statement about FINRA By-Laws Article XII – Disciplinary Proceedings is correct?
    a. The specific violation must be stated.
    b. No provision is given for the person who is the subject of the process to speak or to have someone, such as an attorney, speak to the accusation.
    c. No record is kept of the disciplinary process.
    d. Any decision made is not necessarily announced.

58. Which of the following is true of a prospectus for an issue of an SEC-registered security?
    a. It may be for hedge funds domiciled outside the US.
    b. It doesn't need to have information on the financial strength of the issuer.
    c. It is not required to be provided until the time the security is purchased.
    d. It doesn't need to be filed with the SEC until the first sale of the issue is made.

59. Which statement about the completion of an order to buy a security is correct?
    a. The investor typically asks a broker-dealer to complete a buy order. The broker-dealer contacts an introducing broker, who works with a market maker, who offers an ask price.
    b. The investor typically asks a broker-dealer to complete a buy order. The broker-dealer contacts an introducing broker, who works with a market maker, who offers a bid price.
    c. The investor typically asks a broker-dealer to complete a buy order. The broker-dealer contacts a clearing broker, who works with a market maker, who offers an ask price.
    d. The investor typically asks a broker-dealer to complete a buy order. The broker-dealer contacts a clearing broker, who works with a market maker, who offers a bid price.

This material is provided for exam preparation purposes only and does not indicate an endorsement of any specific scientific, political, or religious point of view. © TPB Publishing. You have been licensed one copy of this document for personal use only. Any other reproduction or redistribution is strictly prohibited. All rights reserved.

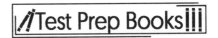

60. Which statement is true?
    a. The gross national product (GNP) is greater than the gross domestic product (GDP).
    b. The gross domestic product (GDP) is greater than the national debt.
    c. Exchange rates are the differences between the GDP and the GNP.
    d. A trade surplus is certain to be healthy for a nation over a long period of time.

61. Which statement about FINRA continuing education requirements is correct?
    a. Regulatory Element training is developed by FINRA. It must be completed within 120 days after the third anniversary of registration and within 120 days of every third anniversary after that.
    b. All persons having communication with customers, whether registered or not, must complete the Firm Element.
    c. Firm Element training is developed by FINRA.
    d. Firm Element training is developed each year by each member firm.

62. According to FINRA Rule 2267 – Investor Education and Protection, which information is NOT required to be provided to each customer annually?
    a. FINRA BrokerCheck Hotline Number
    b. FINRA website address
    c. Notice of the opportunity to obtain a document that describes FINRA BrokerCheck
    d. Continuing education scores of the customer's representative

63. What typically happens when interest rates decline?
    a. Bond values decline.
    b. Cyclical stocks decline.
    c. There is a broad stock market advance.
    d. Defensive stocks decline.

64. Which statement is true regarding interest paid on Treasury securities and bonds created by brokerage firms that are backed by government securities?
    a. T-bills pay interest in semiannual payments.
    b. Treasury receipts make no interest payments before maturity.
    c. Similar to corporate bonds, T-notes pay a fixed interest rate in quarterly payments.
    d. T-bonds make no interest payments before maturity.

65. Which statement about a discretionary order is correct?
    a. If an investor calls to suggest a trade, and the representative later wishes the quantity to be doubled, the investor must have given prior written approval for a discretionary order.
    b. If an investor calls to suggest that a trade be made today, and the representative later wishes the trade to be made the following day, the trade is a discretionary order and requires prior written approval.
    c. If an investor calls to suggest that a trade be made at the current market price, and the representative later prefers that the order be entered at a different time for a more favorable price than that suggested by the investor, the trade is a discretionary order and requires prior written approval.
    d. If an investor calls to suggest that a trade be made tomorrow, and the representative later wishes the trade to be made today, the trade is a discretionary order and requires prior written approval.

173

This material is provided for exam preparation purposes only and does not indicate an endorsement of any specific scientific, political, or religious point of view. © TPB Publishing. You have been licensed one copy of this document for personal use only. Any other reproduction or redistribution is strictly prohibited. All rights reserved.

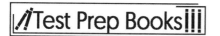

66. What is an advantage of writing a covered stock call option?
    a. The writer can choose to not sell the stock when the stock call option is exercised.
    b. Any time before exercise, the writer can choose the quantity of shares of stock to sell.
    c. The writer has a limited maximum possible loss.
    d. The writer may change the expiration date any time before the stock call option is exercised.

67. Which statement about general obligation (GO) bonds is correct?
    a. GO bonds account for less than half of all municipal bonds sold.
    b. The most popular use for GO bonds is transportation.
    c. Private activity GO bonds lower interest rates for companies.
    d. Moral obligation GO bonds make the state legislature morally, but not legally, obligated to cover shortfalls in revenue.

68. Which of the following is NOT a form of municipal fund securities?
    a. 529A plans
    b. Local government investment pools (LGIPs)
    c. Municipal bond
    d. 529 college savings plan

69. Which statement about conditional orders is correct?
    a. A buy limit order is typically set at a price above the current market.
    b. A sell limit order is typically set at a price below the current market.
    c. A buy stop-limit order is typically set at a price 10% above the current market.
    d. A sell stop-limit order is typically set at a price above the current market.

70. Which statement about closed-end investment companies is correct?
    a. Orders to buy or sell their shares may be placed during the trading day, but orders are only executed after the end of trading for the day.
    b. The buy or sell price is based on the net asset value (NAV), adjusted for sales charge, in the case of purchases, and sometimes a redemption fee, in the case of sales.
    c. They issue common stock when organized, similar to public companies offering their initial public offering.
    d. They do not issue preferred stock.

71. Which of the following revenue bonds typically benefit a private company's facility?
    a. Utility revenue bonds
    b. Education revenue bonds
    c. Housing revenue bonds
    d. Industrial revenue bonds (IDR bonds)

This material is provided for exam preparation purposes only and does not indicate an endorsement of any specific scientific, political, or religious point of view. © TPB Publishing. You have been licensed one copy of this document for personal use only. Any other reproduction or redistribution is strictly prohibited. All rights reserved.

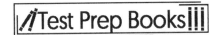
72. Which is the correct statement about MSRB Rule G-37 – Political Contributions and Prohibitions on Municipal Securities Business?
   a. If a firm is assisting, or seeking to assist, an issuer with its municipal securities issue, its municipal financial professionals (MFPs) are not allowed to make political contributions to campaigns of persons of the issuing governmental unit; however, they may request political contributions or assist persons of the issuer in obtaining political contributions.
   b. Payments made to non-political accounts are not regulated, even though those payments might free up funds for political activities.
   c. If a municipal financial professional makes a payment to a person associated with an issuer of municipal securities, the firm of the payer may be prohibited from participating in municipal securities business for two years.
   d. A political action committee (PAC) administered by the firm or its persons may make political contributions without MSRB oversight.

73. Which statement about 12b-1 fees is correct?
   a. No-load funds may have a 12b-1 fee.
   b. A load fund may have a 12b-1 fee of up to 0.75% of the fund's net assets per year for shareholder service.
   c. 12b-1 fees may be deducted from the NAV only one time each year.
   d. Management companies selling no-load funds to investors typically compensate representatives who solicit investors at the time of purchase and recover the expense from the 12b-1 fees over a period of time.

74. What is attractive about buying an option?
   a. The purchaser of a call option knows that a profit will be made when the option is exercised, and the underlying asset is sold.
   b. The contents of the option disclosure document (ODD) will not apply to the transaction.
   c. The purchaser has a limited maximum possible loss.
   d. Buying an option can result in a profit without selling the option or buying or selling any other security.

75. Which statement about the intention of securities regulation regarding the execution of orders to buy or sell securities is correct?
   a. Caveat emptor ("let the buyer beware") is the principle stating that the investor bears the risk for orders that are not executed as authorized.
   b. Larger orders should be executed before smaller orders.
   c. An investor's decision to buy or sell should be carried out in a way that matches the investor's intent.
   d. If the security in the order is not available, a similar security of at least as promising a possible return should be purchased or sold, rather than disappoint the investor.

This material is provided for exam preparation purposes only and does not indicate an endorsement of any specific scientific, political, or religious point of view. © TPB Publishing. You have been licensed one copy of this document for personal use only. Any other reproduction or redistribution is strictly prohibited. All rights reserved.

Answer Explanations #3

1. B: Choice *B* is correct because .01 of 1% equals one basis point. Choices *A, C,* and *D* are incorrect because .01 of 1% equals 1 basis point.

2. D: Choice *D* is correct because the broker-dealer is a party to the transaction. Choices *A, B,* and *C* are incorrect because the broker-dealer is not named as being a party to the transactions.

3. B: Choice *B* is correct because college savings plans grow tax-deferred. Choice *A* is incorrect because contributions to college savings plans are made with after-tax dollars. Choice *C* is incorrect because some college savings plans offer a choice from a limited number of investments. Choice *D* is incorrect because college savings plans are tax-exempt at the federal level. At the state level, they may or may not be tax-exempt.

4. B: Choice *B* is correct because it lists types of order that do not conflict with each other. A day order expires at the end of the trading day if not fulfilled. A market order is placed at the current market price as soon as practical. A good-til-canceled (GTC) order does not expire until fulfilled or canceled by the investor. A non-discretionary order is one in which the representative was authorized to determine characteristics other than the timing and price. An unsolicited order is one that is the client's idea.

These four characteristics—market, GTC, non-discretionary, and solicited—are independent of each other. They do not conflict with each other, and they can all describe different dimensions of one order. Choice *A* is incorrect because a day order expires at the end of the day if not fulfilled, whereas a GTC order does not. Therefore, these characteristics are mutually exclusive. Choice *C* is incorrect because a market order is to be fulfilled at the current market price, whereas the sell stop (loss) order depends upon the market price reaching a certain level before being fulfilled. Therefore, these characteristics are mutually exclusive. Choice *D* is incorrect because a buy-stop order depends upon the market level reaching a certain price, whereas a market order is to be fulfilled at the current market price. Therefore, these characteristics are mutually exclusive.

5. B: Choice *B,* the 1934 Securities Exchange Act, requires a company's purchases of its own stock to be made from only one broker or dealer on any specific day, limits the time in some cases, limits the price, and limits volume of purchases. Choice *A* regulates primary offerings of the issuing company to the public. Choice *C* regulates investment companies (including mutual funds). Choice *D* clarifies audit rules and CEOs' responsibility for accuracy of financial statements.

6. B: Choice *B* is correct because a bond is issued with a stated interest rate and schedule of interest payments. The annual interest is calculated by multiplying the stated or nominal interest rate times the face amount of the bond, then dividing by the number of interest payments each year to determine the dollar amount of each interest payment. Choice *A* is incorrect because the current yield is calculated by dividing the nominal interest rate by the current market value. Therefore, the current yield may change. Choices *C* and *D* are incorrect because yield to maturity (YTM) and yield to call (YTC) are affected by purchasing the bond at a premium, a discount, or a market value different from the face amount and may vary from the nominal yield.

7. A: Choice *A* refers to the highest point on the chart when the economy is the strongest. Choice *B* refers to the rising portion of the chart when economic activity is increasing. Choice *C* refers to the

This material is provided for exam preparation purposes only and does not indicate an endorsement of any specific scientific, political, or religious point of view. © TPB Publishing. You have been licensed one copy of this document for personal use only. Any other reproduction or redistribution is strictly prohibited. All rights reserved.

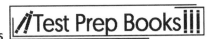

lowest part of the chart when the economy is at its smallest magnitude. Choice *D* refers to the period when economic activity is decreasing.

8. D: Choice *D* is correct. Choice *A* was not the reason for establishing SIPC, even though options may involve more risk than stocks. Choice *B* was not the reason for establishing SIPC since the increase in broker-dealers would not be a problem if they were solvent. Choice *C* was not the reason for establishing SIPC, though a broker-dealer's refusal to provide financial disclosures would be suspect activity.

9. D: Choice *D* is correct because money market instruments are used for cash that will likely be needed in a few days. A small difference in interest rate is relatively unimportant, compared with the need for liquidity and a stable principal value. Choice *A* is incorrect because CDs are usually issued by a bank. They usually pay a higher interest rate than a demand savings account. They are typically issued for a certain period of time, ranging from months to years. Therefore, they are not generally appropriate for investing cash that is expected to be needed in a few days. Choice *B* is incorrect because mutual funds may invest in money market instruments while waiting for an investment opportunity of a long-term nature. Choice *C* is incorrect because state governments typically do not issue money market instruments.

10. C: Choice *C* is correct because a general obligation (GO) bond is guaranteed by the full faith and credit of the taxing authority and must have voter approval. Choice *A* is incorrect because revenue bonds typically benefit only the persons paying for the benefits of the bond issue. Choice *B* is incorrect because rating agencies typically rate GO bonds higher than revenue bonds because GO bonds are backed by the full faith and credit of the taxing authority. The credit rating of a revenue bond will depend upon the terms of the bond issue, such as whether it has a gross pledge or a net pledge. A gross pledge commits to pay debt service prior to operating and other expenses. A net pledge commits to pay debt service after payment of operating and other expenses. Choice *D* is incorrect because a revenue bond has a revenue source other than the full faith and credit of the taxing authority and, therefore, does not need voter approval.

11. D: Choice *D* is correct because an investor's return on investment (ROI) or return on capital is calculated by adding cash received (such as interest or dividends) during the time the investor holds the security to proceeds from the sale (realized gain or loss), less the cost of the investment, less expenses such as commissions, and dividing the result by the cost of the investment. ROI may be calculated either before income tax or after income tax. The example given did not mention income tax, so it would be before tax ROI. Since different taxpayers have different effective and marginal tax rates, the after-tax calculation may be different for different investors. Choice *A* is incorrect because realized gain is a component of the calculation of ROI when the investment is sold. Choice *B* is incorrect because unrealized gain is a component of the calculation of ROI when the investment has not been sold. Choice *C* is incorrect because IRR is the annual growth rate and is only roughly equal to the ROI when the length of time the investment is held is one year.

12. C: Choice *C* is correct because this is the time in business days between trade date (T) and settlement date. For example, if this occurs in two days, it is designated as T+2. Choice *A* is incorrect because trade settlement does not start counting until the order has been fulfilled. Choice *B* is incorrect because commercial paper and bank certificates of deposit (CDs) settle regular-way on the trade date (T), whereas Treasury bonds, Treasury bills, mutual funds, and option trades settle regular-way one day after the trade date (T + 1). Choice *D* is incorrect because Treasuries settle regular-way one day after the trade date (T+1), whereas corporate bonds settle regular-way two business days after the trade date (T

This material is provided for exam preparation purposes only and does not indicate an endorsement of any specific scientific, political, or religious point of view. © TPB Publishing. You have been licensed one copy of this document for personal use only. Any other reproduction or redistribution is strictly prohibited. All rights reserved.

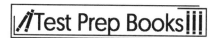

+ 2). Corporate stocks and municipal funds specified by MSRB rule G-15 also settle regular-way two business days after the trade date (T + 2).

13. D: Choice *D* is correct because the seller sells the stock to the market maker at the bid price set by the market maker. Choices *A*, *B*, and *C* are incorrect because the bid price is set by the market maker and is the price the seller receives for the stock.

14. A: Choice *A* is correct because the lower credit rating indicates a higher risk, leading investors to require a higher interest rate in order to accept the increased risk. Choice *B* is incorrect because some bonds require legislative action for each budget cycle. If the legislature does not appropriate adequate funds for a budget cycle, the bonds could default. Choice *C* is incorrect because revenue bonds have a higher level of risk than GO bonds, so investors require a higher interest rate in order to accept the increased risk. Choice *D* is incorrect because GO bonds are backed by the full faith and credit of the issuing authority, so investors do not have the need for a feasibility study.

15. C: Choice *C* is correct because a firm may prefer to finance its growth by selling bonds in order to maintain current proportions of ownership, expecting the return on investment (ROE) on the bond proceeds to surpass the interests and administrative costs of debt service. Choice *A* is incorrect because a firm typically sells bonds at the face value, makes regular interest payments, and repays the face value at maturity. Choice *B* is incorrect because, at liquidation, bondholders have a prior claim to monetary compensation of the face value and accrued interest prior to stockholders receiving any monetary compensation. Choice *D* is incorrect because bonds do not provide any benefits of ownership to their purchasers.

16. B: Choice *B* is correct because the share classes have different combinations of up-front sales load, 12b-1, and contingent deferred sales charge (CDSC) to allow investors to select a combination appropriate to their time horizon, whether it be short-term, medium-term, or long-term. Choices *A*, *C*, and *D* are incorrect because, though any one of these answers may be true in a given scenario, Choice *B* gives a more comprehensive explanation of the reason for the various choices of share classes.

17. A: Choice *A* enables the issuer to select a time to sell when the share price is higher than at registration time. Since this shelf registration is public knowledge, it may affect the share price. The company is required to file reports with the SEC while waiting to sell the issue. Choices *B*, *C*, and *D* are incorrect.

18. B: Choice *B* is correct because dividends on ADRs are paid in American dollars. Choice *A* is incorrect because ADRs allow for the purchasing and selling of shares in foreign companies on American markets. Choice *C* is incorrect because shares issued by an American depositary bank after payment by the shares' issuer are called "sponsored" ADRs. Choice *D* is incorrect because sponsored ADRs may trade in the OTC market. However, unsponsored ADRs may not trade on the NYSE or Nasdaq. Depending upon the level of compliance, unsponsored ADRs may trade in the OTC market.

19. A: Choice *A* is correct because debt certificates issued by a face-amount certificate company pay a set interest rate. Choice *B* is incorrect because investments may be made in installments. Choice *C* is incorrect because they receive fixed interest payments if held until maturity. Choice *D* is incorrect because redemptions before maturity receive a discounted surrender value.

20. D: Choice *D* is correct because commercial paper typically lasts less than 270 days and may last only a few days. Choice *A* is incorrect because commercial paper is unsecured. Choice *B* is incorrect because

This material is provided for exam preparation purposes only and does not indicate an endorsement of any specific scientific, political, or religious point of view. © TPB Publishing. You have been licensed one copy of this document for personal use only. Any other reproduction or redistribution is strictly prohibited. All rights reserved.

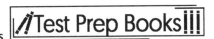

commercial paper is typically issued by corporations for expenses due immediately, such as payroll and inventory purchases. Choice *C* is incorrect because commercial paper is bought and sold at a discount from face value.

21. A: Choice *A* is correct because neither equity-indexed contracts (EICs) nor variable contracts make payments determined on the life of the owner if the owner is not the annuitant. Choice *B* is incorrect because EICs and variable contracts typically offer, as one annuitization choice, payments for the combined life of the annuitant and one other person. Choice *C* is incorrect because EICs and variable contracts, as one annuitization choice, typically offer payments for the life of the contract owner, or for a certain minimum period of time. This assumes the contract owner is the annuitant. This choice is called "life and period certain." Choice *D* is incorrect because some EICs and some variable contracts, as one annuitization choice, offer payments for the life the contract owner with the remaining value at death passing to a beneficiary, either in a lump sum or in periodic payments. This assumes the contract owner is the annuitant.

22. D: Choice *D* is correct because FINRA Rule 8312 does not require the release of the date of failed qualification exams. Choice *A* is incorrect because FINRA Rule 8312 requires the release of any data from the most recently-submitted registration forms. Choice *B* is incorrect because FINRA Rule 8312 requires the release of summary data regarding some arbitration awards against a member firm related to a dispute with a public customer. Choice *C* is incorrect because FINRA Rule 8312 requires the release of the relevant portion of the most current comment provided by the person who is a subject of the data.

23. A: Choice *A* is correct because FINRA and the MSRB perform similar oversight, with the MSRB providing rules for municipal securities, their dealers, and their dealers' representatives. Choice *B* is incorrect because FINRA Rule 1122 prohibits member firms and their associated persons from providing false information in filings with FINRA. Choice *C* is incorrect because MSRB Rule G-2 requires that only qualified persons handle municipal securities transactions. Choice *D* is incorrect because MSRB Rule G-3 establishes continuing education requirements, as well as qualification testing requirements.

24. A: Choice *A* is correct because both a letter of intent and rights of accumulation allow purchasers of Class A shares to reduce the up-front sales load, which will likely result in a lower combination of up-front sales load, 12b-1 fees, and CDSC, as compared with other share classes. By signing a letter of intent, an investor can receive a reduced up-front sales charge based on intended purchases over the next 13 months. Rights of accumulation allow an investor to receive a discount on the up-front sales charge when purchasing additional shares, either in the same fund or in other funds of the same funds family. Choices *B, C,* and *D* are incorrect because a letter of intent and rights of accumulation are not associated with these share classes.

25. A: Choice *A* is correct because agencies of the federal government and government-sponsored enterprises (GSEs) borrow money by issuing securities, which have face amounts and make regular interest payments. Choice *B* is incorrect because the US Treasury does not issue agency securities. Choice *C* is incorrect because agency securities are less liquid than treasuries; therefore, agency securities pay a higher interest rate than Treasury securities. Choice *D* is incorrect because GSE securities are not formally backed by the "full faith and credit" of the United States, so they have default risk and credit risk. However, holders of GSE securities expect them to be paid with no default.

26. A: Choice *A* correctly specifies the MSRB rule that states that municipal bond orders must be filled in the order stated by the issuing municipality unless that municipality allows exceptions. Choice *B* specifies a reporting requirement for bond issues with preference to retail investors. Choice *C* is a FINRA

This material is provided for exam preparation purposes only and does not indicate an endorsement of any specific scientific, political, or religious point of view. © TPB Publishing. You have been licensed one copy of this document for personal use only. Any other reproduction or redistribution is strictly prohibited. All rights reserved.

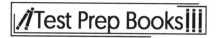
rule rather than a MSRB rule. Choice *D* requires municipal advisors serving in an advisory capacity on a competitive municipal security sale to obtain an identifying (CUSIP) number for the issue.

27. B: Choice *B* is correct because FINRA Rule 2122 – Charges for Services Performed specifies that charges for services provided are to be fair and consistent among customers. There is no exception for long-time customers. Choice *A* is incorrect because FINRA Rule 2121 – Fair Prices and Commissions lists relevant factors that may affect setting the price for services, and "type of security" is included in that list. Choice *C* is incorrect because when a broker-dealer acts as a principal on a transaction with an institutional customer, the broker-dealer is not necessarily required to disclose the terms of the trade in advance. However, if the broker-dealer's customer is a non-institutional investor, the broker-dealer must provide disclosure regarding terms of the transaction. Choice *D* is incorrect because FINRA Rule 2121 – Fair Prices and Commissions provides various methods for disclosing net transactions to an institutional customer, and a negative consent letter is one of those methods. A negative consent letter clearly describes the situation and allows the institutional customer with reasonable opportunity to object.

28. A: Choice *A* is correct because a non-discretionary order may leave the selection of price to the representative. Choice *B* is incorrect because the selection of which asset (security) to buy or sell qualifies the transaction as discretionary. Choice *C* is incorrect because the selection of the amount (quantity) to buy or sell qualifies the transaction as discretionary. Choice *D* is incorrect because the selection of action (whether to enter an order or not) qualifies the transaction as discretionary.

29. B: Choice *B* is correct because when a stock split occurs, old shares are exchanged for new shares, and the quantity of new shares exceeds the quantity of old shares, such as in a two-for-one split. Choice *A* is incorrect because a buyback occurs when a corporation purchases its own stock on the open market to lessen the number of shares among whom ownership will be shared and to whom dividends will be paid. Choice *C* is incorrect because a reverse stock split results in fewer new shares in exchange for more old shares. Choice *D* is incorrect because a tender offer is a publicly announced offer to purchase shares for a certain price if a certain quantity of shares is provided in acceptance of the offer.

30. A: Choice *A* is correct because a registered representative is authorized, because of being registered, to receive a transaction-based commission when a customer acts on the representative's advice. Choice *B* is incorrect because registered representatives may not charge for their advice unless they are also registered investment advisor representatives. Choice *C* is incorrect because registered investment advisor representatives may charge for their advice even if no trade is made. Choice *D* is incorrect because, with proper disclosures, registered investment advisor representatives may charge for their advice and receive a transaction-based commission if the transaction is appropriate for the client.

31. B. Choice *B,* the Municipal Securities Rulemaking Board (MSRB), has jurisdiction over banks that handle municipal securities. Choice *A,* FINRA, does not have jurisdiction over banks that handle municipal securities transactions. Choice *C,* FDIC, supervises banks and examines banks and savings associations for sound financial processes and solvency. Choice *D,* the SEC, is an agency established by law and is not an SRO.

32. B: Choice *B* is correct because the penny stock risk disclosure document does not include any guarantee to indemnify the customer for market declines. Choices *A, C,* and *D* are incorrect because these represent items in the penny stock risk disclosure document.

This material is provided for exam preparation purposes only and does not indicate an endorsement of any specific scientific, political, or religious point of view. © TPB Publishing. You have been licensed one copy of this document for personal use only. Any other reproduction or redistribution is strictly prohibited. All rights reserved.

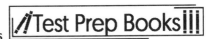

33. A: Choice *A* is correct because the trend in the percentage of female students enrolled is not perceived as affecting the school's ability to provide debt service for education bonds as much as the school's ability to attract students, receive government assistance, and increase tuition. Choice *B* is incorrect because if tuition is not increased as much as costs, the ability to provide debt service for education bonds could be impaired. Choice *C* is incorrect because government actions regarding educational aid could impact the ability to provide debt service for education bonds. Choice *D* is incorrect because the school's reputation may affect the level of enrollment, which would affect its ability to provide debt service for education bonds.

34. A: Choice *A*, direct rights offering, has no backstop purchaser. This means some rights may not be exercised, resulting in the issuer receiving less than the maximum proceeds of the issue. Choices *B*, *C*, and *D* refer to a rights offering in which a backstop purchaser contracts to purchase all rights that are not exercised. This is called an insured or standby rights offering.

35. C: Choice *C* is correct because the investor expects to sell the security for a higher price at some point in the future. Choices *A* and *B* are incorrect because a long purchase would not necessarily be accomplished in anticipation of a halt in trading. Choice *D* is incorrect because a long purchase is not necessarily done in anticipation of a stock split. An expected rise in the stock price, for whatever reason, would be the main reason to make a long purchase.

36. D: Choice *D* is correct because options traded on an exchange (listed options) are guaranteed. Options traded in the over-the-counter market (unlisted options) are not guaranteed. However, such unlisted options may have negotiated terms not available with options listed on the exchanges. Choice *A* is incorrect because options that are not guaranteed are traded in the over-the-counter market, and some characteristics may be negotiated. Choice *B* is incorrect because an option that is not guaranteed (unlisted option) does have risk of non-performance by the writer of the option. Choice *C* is incorrect because options traded in the over-counter-market have few trades, potentially making the process of identifying a counterparty lengthier and more costly.

37. B: Choice *B* is correct because SEC Rule 17f-2 – Fingerprinting of Securities Industry Personnel directs that, unless an exemption applies, the following firms must have each partner, director, officer, and employee fingerprinted: every broker, every dealer, every registered transfer agent, and every registered clearing agency. Choice *A* is incorrect because FINRA Rule 3110(e) – Responsibility of Member to Investigate Applicants for Registration provides that each member firm will have a documented process to use for background checks, before it asks to register a person with FINRA, to determine that the applicant has integrity and other characteristics appropriate for activity in the securities industry.

Choice *C* is incorrect because the Securities Exchange Act of 1934 Section 3(a)(39) – Definitions and Application of Title (Statutory Disqualification) refers to several possible situations in which a firm may not hire an individual, such as the persons having been subject to disciplinary action taken by such organizations as an SRO or a corresponding foreign regulatory organization, securities exchange, Commodity Futures Trading Commission, or foreign financial regulatory authority. Choice *D* is incorrect because the Securities Exchange Act of 1934 Section 3(a)(39) – Definitions and Application of Title (Statutory Disqualification) refers to several possible situations in which a firm may not hire an individual, such as if the individual had a conviction of any certain offenses, including a felony, within 10 years prior to an application for membership or participation.

This material is provided for exam preparation purposes only and does not indicate an endorsement of any specific scientific, political, or religious point of view. © TPB Publishing. You have been licensed one copy of this document for personal use only. Any other reproduction or redistribution is strictly prohibited. All rights reserved.

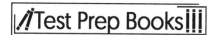

38. A: Choice *A* is correct because DPPs are investments different from those that the unsophisticated general public investor generally chooses. Choice *B* is incorrect because DPPs are often "unlisted" and not traded on national exchanges such as the NYSE. Choice *C* is incorrect because they may invest in asset classes whose values will likely not correlate with the fluctuations of the markets for stocks and bonds. Choice *D* is incorrect because investors who are interested in DPPs, as well as broker-dealers and representatives who consider offering DPP-related services to investors, should understand their characteristics and the associated SEC and FINRA regulations.

39. C: Choice *C* is correct because an alternative contact is only required for an account holder who is a natural person. Choices *A*, *B*, and *D* are incorrect because these are all required items of data that the broker-dealer firm is required to keep.

40. A: Choice *A* is correct because a published quote must be a bona fide price, so the investor can rely on it, make a choice to enter an order, and actually buy at the ask price or sell at the bid price. Choice *B* is incorrect because the quotes must provide actual prices available, which may be different from the buy or sell price of the most recent buy or sell transaction. Choice *C* is incorrect because FINRA Rule 6438 requires the same set of prices to be published in each market, not the most recent purchase or sale price. In some cases, an exception to the rule may be made for a customer limit order. Choice *D* is incorrect because FINRA Rule 5220 requires that a member broker-dealer firm may only make an offer to buy or sell if the member will fulfill an order as stated in the offer. The last buy or sell transaction is not always the appropriate quote.

41. A: Choice *A* is correct because market value of common stock is affected primarily by anticipated growth in earnings, which is affected by the general economic climate, the type of industry (whether cyclical, defensive, or growth), and the issuer's dividend policy. Choice *B* is incorrect because market value of non-convertible preferred stock is affected primarily by dividend yield as compared with the prevailing interest rates, as well as the credit-worthiness of the company, the company's industry, and the general economic environment. Choice *C* is incorrect because market value of stock rights and warrant rights generally tracks with the intrinsic value, which is the market value less the exercise price, plus item value. This may include a discount for dilution caused by an increase in the total shares outstanding, unless anticipated growth in earnings is proportionate to the increase in outstanding shares. Choice *D* is incorrect because while the market value of American Depositary Receipts (ADRs) may be affected by the credit rating of the issuing foreign company, its market value generally tracks similarly with common stock.

42. C: Choice *C* is correct because years to maturity is used. Choice *A* is incorrect because current yield is the nominal interest rate divided by the market value of the bond. Choice *B* is incorrect because the nominal yield is the coupon interest rate stated in the bond issue. Choice *D* is incorrect because the calculation does not use years to call, call premium, and call value.

43. A: Choice *A* is an indirect method for the Federal Reserve to manage monetary policy. Choice *B* refers to adjusting the federal funds rate or the discount rate. Choice *C* does not refer to activities performed by the Federal Reserve. Choice *D* refers to releasing statements to the public that are intended to influence investors' activities without the Federal Reserve having to take action.

44. D: Choice *D* is correct because stock received by exercising stock rights receives dividends when declared and paid. Choice *A* is incorrect because stock rights typically expire if not exercised within a specified period of time; expired stock rights receive no voting rights. Choice *B* is incorrect because

This material is provided for exam preparation purposes only and does not indicate an endorsement of any specific scientific, political, or religious point of view. © TPB Publishing. You have been licensed one copy of this document for personal use only. Any other reproduction or redistribution is strictly prohibited. All rights reserved.

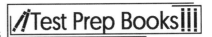

expired stock rights receive no dividends. Choice *C* is incorrect because expired stock rights receive no monetary value upon liquidation of the company.

45. D: In the event of liquidation, common shareholders, Choice *D,* would receive financial value after all other stakeholders. Choice *A* would be in line after debtors with collateral loans and before holders of subordinated debentures (also known as junior securities). Choice *B,* also known as holders of junior securities, would be after senior bondholders and before stockholders. Choice *C* would be after all debtors but before common shareholders.

46. A: Choice *A* is correct because a long sale is the sale of a security that is owned. These are securities that were purchased with the expectation of selling after the market price had risen. Choice *B* is incorrect because a long sale has no relation to the quantity of shares in the transaction. Choice *C* is incorrect because a long sale is unrelated to whether the settlement occurs in T+2 (by two business days after the trade date). Choice *D* is incorrect because a long sale has no relation to whether the seller is an individual or a group.

47. B: Rule 144 is under the Securities Exchange Act of 1934, which is Choice *B.* For fairness, some securities are restricted or controlled securities with conditions under which they may be sold to the public. Rule 144 sets those conditions. Choice *A* governs the initial issuance of securities. Choice *C* protects corporate bondholders by structuring the manner in which corporate bonds are issued and the proceeds are used. Choice *D* established investment companies.

48. D: Choice *D* correctly notes that some characteristics of OTC transactions are private. Choice *A* is incorrect because the securities are received from an issuer in the primary market. Satisfaction is not guaranteed in neither the primary market nor the over-the-counter market. Choice *B* is incorrect, as OTC activity is reported and affects prices on exchanges, and vice versa. Choice *C* is incorrect, as broker-dealers are typically involved in OTC transactions.

49. A: Choice *A* is correct because a variable contract typically has an option to invest in an equity sub-account similar to an equity mutual fund. An equity-indexed contract (EIC) typically has an option to receive a minimum guaranteed rate of return, along with upside potential linked to increase in an equity index, but no more than the maximum set in the contract. Choice *B* is incorrect because an EIC typically offers an option to receive a minimum guaranteed rate of return. Choice *C* is incorrect because both contracts may offer a choice that includes the S&P 500 Index, either as an equity index choice, a large company "value" fund or sub-account in the variable contract, or a selection that approximates the return of the S&P 500 Index when the increase in the index price is within the minimum and maximum limits. Choice *D* is incorrect because equity subaccounts of variable annuity contracts typically do not have a predetermined maximum positive return. However, EICs typically do have a predetermined maximum positive return.

50. D: Choice *D* is correct because with cumulative voting, a common shareholder may use all their votes to vote for a candidate for director. This empowers minority shareholders. Choices *A, B,* and *C* have no vote unless they also are common shareholders.

51. D: Choice *D* is correct because the investor sold the security for a higher price than it was previously purchased for. Realized profits would be reduced by commissions paid to a broker-dealer to handle the transactions. Choice *A* is incorrect because the counterparty buyer could have made a long sale at the same time. Choice *B* is incorrect because a broker-dealer does not typically participate in the gain or loss

This material is provided for exam preparation purposes only and does not indicate an endorsement of any specific scientific, political, or religious point of view. © TPB Publishing. You have been licensed one copy of this document for personal use only. Any other reproduction or redistribution is strictly prohibited. All rights reserved.

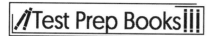

of a client investor. Choice C is incorrect because the quantity of shares will not change, except in the case of a stock split or reverse split.

52. C: Choice C is correct because a mortgage bond is one example of a secured bond, which is secured by mortgages on real estate. In case of liquidation, the mortgage bond would have a claim to monetary value based on the liquidation of the collateral. Choice A is incorrect because a debenture is an unsecured bond. Choice B is incorrect because a convertible unsecured bond would be convertible to stock under certain conditions, but it would not be considered a secured bond. Choice D is incorrect because convertible preferred stock is neither a debt security nor is it secured by collateral. It would be convertible to common stock under certain conditions, but it would not be considered a secured bond.

53. D: Choice D is correct because FINRA provides notices for OTC shares. Choice A is incorrect because an exchange handles notices for shares traded on that exchange, assuring its deadline is met. Choice B is incorrect because approval of corporate actions by the board of directors is required before notices are provided. Until the board of directors votes its approval, the corporate action does not exist, and no notice is appropriate. Choice C is incorrect because FINRA, not the NYSE, provides notices for OTC shares.

54. D: Choice D reflects public comment by the Federal Reserve, which may influence investors to adjust their behavior without the Federal Reserve needing to take action. Choice A is an example of open market activity by the Federal Reserve. Choice B describes activity the Federal Reserve does not generally undertake, as the Federal Reserve buys or sells government securities through open market activity. Choice C is an example of adjusting interest rates, which is different from releasing a public comment.

55. D: Choice D is correct because a derivative derives its market value from the market value of its underlying security. Choice A is incorrect because common stock does not receive its market value from an underlying security. Rather, it receives its market value from the perceived value of the issuing company. Choice B is incorrect because a stock index option is a derivative. It receives its value from the current value of an index. Choice C is incorrect because a derivative's value is intrinsic value plus time value.

56. D: Choice D is correct because UITs, closed-end investment management companies, and open-end investment management companies are diversified investment vehicles that are all governed by the Investment Company Act of 1940. A UIT has an indenture that guides how the sponsor selects a set of income-producing investments and receives units of ownership that are priced by an evaluator so that it then may be sold to the public. The indenture also specifies an entity, typically a trustee, who holds the investments, keeps record of ownership, and provides financial and tax reporting requirements. Choices A, B, and C are incorrect because they are not characteristics of UITs.

57. A: Choice A is correct because Sec. 2 (a) states "specific charges shall be brought." Choice B is incorrect because the person or member firm who is the subject of the process receives an opportunity to speak or have someone, such as an attorney, speak to the accusation. Choice C is incorrect because a record of the process is kept. Choice D is incorrect because any determination states the following: the act that violated a rule, regulation, or law, which rule, regulation, or law was violated, how the violation was determined, and the penalty.

58. C: Choice C correctly states that the deadline for providing a prospectus is no later than the time the security is bought, but it may be provided earlier. Choice A refers to hedge funds domiciled outside the

This material is provided for exam preparation purposes only and does not indicate an endorsement of any specific scientific, political, or religious point of view. © TPB Publishing. You have been licensed one copy of this document for personal use only. Any other reproduction or redistribution is strictly prohibited. All rights reserved.

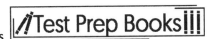

US, which provide an offering document describing the way the fund purchases and disposes of assets. Choice *B* is incorrect, as the financial strength of the issuer is included in the prospectus. Choice *D* is incorrect, as it must be approved by the SEC prior to being provided to potential purchasers.

59. C: Choice *C* is correct because the investor typically asks a broker-dealer to complete a buy order. The broker-dealer contacts a clearing broker, who works with a market maker, who offers an ask price. Choices *A* and *B* are incorrect because the investor's broker-dealer is the introducing broker-dealer who contacts a clearing dealer. The clearing broker works with a market maker who offers an ask price. Choice *D* is incorrect because the clearing broker works with a market maker who offers an ask price.

60. A: Choice *A* reflects the addition of a country's goods and services produced and exported to the GDP to calculate the GNP. Choice *B* is not always correct, depending upon the situation. Choice *C*, exchange rates, refers to the proportion of one nation's money that can be exchanged for another nation's money. Choice *D* is incorrect, as a country can become dependent upon foreign capital, which would not be in the country's best interest.

61. D: Choice *D* is correct because the Firm Element is a systematic instruction process, developed by each member firm. The following associated persons are generally required to fulfill this requirement:

Registered persons having communication with customers
Registered operations professionals
Research analysts
Immediate supervisors of the above persons

Every year, each firm assesses its needs and organizes its process in a document. Choice *A* is incorrect because this element must be fulfilled within 120 days after the second anniversary of registration and within 120 days of every third anniversary after that. Choice *B* is incorrect because not necessarily every person having communication with customers must complete the Firm Element. Choice *C* is incorrect because Firm Element training is developed by each member firm.

62. D: Choice *D* is correct because the rule does not require that the representative's continuing education scores be provided to customers. Choices *A*, *B*, and *C* are incorrect because the rule does require these items to be provided annually to each customer.

63. C: Choice *C* reflects the broad stock market's preference for lower interest rates. These typically spur eventual economic expansion and a broad stock market advance in anticipation of economic growth. Choice *A* generally occurs when interest rates increase, which occurs during expansion of the economy. Choice *B* refers to stocks that follow the business cycle, which would be in retreat during contraction when interest rates generally decline. Choice *D* refers to stocks of essential industries such as food, beverages, and utilities, which generally advance during all parts of the business cycle.

64. B: Choice *B* is correct because Treasury receipts are bonds created by brokerage firms and backed by government securities. They make no interest payments before maturity but are purchased at a discount to par. Choice *A* is incorrect because T-bills make no interest payments before maturity. They are purchased at a discount to par. Choice *C* is incorrect because, similar to corporate bonds, T-notes pay a fixed interest rate in semiannual payments. Choice *D* is incorrect because T-bonds pay a fixed interest rate in semiannual payments.

65. A: Choice *A* is correct because a discretionary order is an order for which the representative chooses a characteristic of the order other than the price or timing. The chosen characteristic could be which

This material is provided for exam preparation purposes only and does not indicate an endorsement of any specific scientific, political, or religious point of view. © TPB Publishing. You have been licensed one copy of this document for personal use only. Any other reproduction or redistribution is strictly prohibited. All rights reserved.

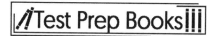
security to buy or sell (asset), the quantity to buy or sell (amount), or whether to enter an order or not (action). Choices *B* and *D* are incorrect because the representative's changing the timing of the order does not make it a discretionary order. Choice *C* is incorrect because the representative's changing the timing and price does not make it a discretionary order.

66. C: Choice *C* is correct because the maximum possible loss is the purchase price of the stock less the premium received from selling the option. The sale of a covered option is intended to reduce risk and increase income. Choice *A* is incorrect because the writer is obligated to sell the stock when the option is exercised. Choice *B* is incorrect because the writer may not change the quantity of shares, which is stated in the stock call option contract when written. Choice *D* is incorrect because the writer may not change the expiration date, which is stated in the stock call option contract when written.

67. A: Choice *A* is correct because GO bonds account for a little less than one third of all municipal bonds sold. Revenue bonds make up about two thirds of those sales. Choice *B* is incorrect because transportation bonds are typically revenue bonds. Choice *C* is incorrect because private activity bonds are revenue bonds. Private activity revenue bonds do lower interest rates for companies. Choice *D* is incorrect because moral obligation bonds are revenue bonds, not GO bonds.

68. C: Choice *C* is correct because a municipal fund security is made up of a collection of securities, while a municipal bond is a single security. Choice *A* is incorrect because 529A plans are municipal fund securities. These are also called 529 ABLE Plans, established by the Achieving a Better Life Experience (ABLE) Act. Choice *B* is incorrect because LGIPs are municipal fund securities. These assist state and/or local governments to manage their cash reserves more efficiently. Choice *D* is incorrect because 529 college savings plans are municipal fund securities.

69. D: Choice *D* is correct because the goal is to sell when the market rises to a target price at which the investor would be pleased to sell. Choice *A* is incorrect because a buy limit order is typically set at a favorable price below the current market at which price the investor would be pleased to buy. Choice *B* is incorrect because a sell limit order is typically set at a price above the current market where the investor would be pleased to sell. Choice *C* is incorrect because the investor's selected price typically is a specific price, not a percentage above the current market.

70. C: Choice *C* is correct because closed-end investment companies do not continually issue shares like open-end investment companies do. Choice *A* is incorrect because their shares are traded during the day, unlike open-end investment companies. Choice *B* is incorrect because the market value for closed-end investment company shares fluctuates throughout the day in accordance with supply and demand. In order to trade the shares, buyers and sellers typically pay a commission to a broker-dealer firm. Choice *D* is incorrect because closed-end investment companies may issue preferred stock and bonds, similar to a typical public company.

71. D: Choice *D* is correct because IDR bonds assist in financing a facility of one or more private companies. Such a facility could be a stadium, factory, or industrial park. Choice *A* is incorrect because utility bonds benefit a public utility's facility, such as an electric power plant. Choice *B* is incorrect because education bonds assist with public colleges and universities, which would typically operate in publicly owned buildings. Choice *C* is incorrect because housing revenue bonds typically provide financing for private single-family or multi-family homes.

72. C: Choice *C* is correct because one purpose of MSRB Rule G-37 is to provide objectivity between issuers of municipal securities and the firms and individuals who advise them and assist with placement

This material is provided for exam preparation purposes only and does not indicate an endorsement of any specific scientific, political, or religious point of view. © TPB Publishing. You have been licensed one copy of this document for personal use only. Any other reproduction or redistribution is strictly prohibited. All rights reserved.

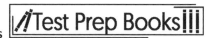
of bond issues. Choice *A* is incorrect because if a firm is assisting, or seeking to assist, an issuer with its municipal securities issue, the firm and its MFPs are not allowed to request political contributions or assist persons associated with the issuer in obtaining political contributions. Choice *B* is incorrect because payments to non-political accounts are regulated in a way similar to payments to political accounts. Choice *D* is incorrect because political contributions by a PAC administered by the firm or its persons are overseen by the MSRB, just as political contributions by the firm or its persons are.

73. A: Choice *A* is correct because no-load funds may have a 12b-1 fee of up to 0.25% per year. Choice *B* is incorrect because a load fund may have a 12b-1 fee up to 0.25% of the fund's net assets per year for shareholder service. Choice *C* is incorrect because 12b-1 fees are deducted from the NAV on a daily basis. Choice *D* is incorrect because management companies selling no-load funds typically sell them directly to the public with no soliciting representative involved.

74. C: Choice *C* is correct because the purchaser has no obligation to exercise the option. If the option is not exercised, the premium paid for the option is the maximum possible loss. Choice *A* is incorrect because a profit will only be realized if the call option is "in the money," meaning exercising the option will result in a profit after selling the underlying security. If the option is "at the money" or "out of the money," no profit will be made, so there would likely be no reason to exercise the option. Choice *B* is incorrect because the ODD, also named "characteristics and risks of standardized options," is provided to each person before buying or selling an option. Choice *D* is incorrect because the buyer of an option must either sell or exercise the option in order to realize a profit.

75. C: Choice *C* is correct because securities regulation intends that an investor make an informed decision, and the decision is carried out as intended by the investor. Choice *A* is incorrect because securities laws are intended to result in investors' decisions to purchase or sell securities being carried out in a manner that matches what the investor wanted to occur. Choice *B* is incorrect because the size of the order should not affect the time sequence of order execution unless an order of a certain quantity cannot be fulfilled. Choice *D* is incorrect because the intention of securities regulation is not that every security transaction be completed even if the specific security is not available. Generally, a substitution can only be made if the investor has provided discretion to the broker-dealer, and this should be indicated on every order in which discretion is exercised by the registered representative.

This material is provided for exam preparation purposes only and does not indicate an endorsement of any specific scientific, political, or religious point of view. © TPB Publishing. You have been licensed one copy of this document for personal use only. Any other reproduction or redistribution is strictly prohibited. All rights reserved.

Series SIE Practice Tests #4 & #5

To keep the size of this book manageable, save paper, and provide a digital test-taking experience, the 4th and 5th practice tests can be found online. Scan the QR code or go to this link to access it:

testprepbooks.com/bonus/sie

The first time you access the tests, you will need to register as a "new user" and verify your email address.

If you have any issues, please email support@testprepbooks.com.

This material is provided for exam preparation purposes only and does not indicate an endorsement of any specific scientific, political, or religious point of view. © TPB Publishing. You have been licensed one copy of this document for personal use only. Any other reproduction or redistribution is strictly prohibited. All rights reserved.

Index

This material is provided for exam preparation purposes only and does not indicate an endorsement of any specific scientific, political, or religious point of view. © TPB Publishing. You have been licensed one copy of this document for personal use only. Any other reproduction or redistribution is strictly prohibited. All rights reserved.

This material is provided for exam preparation purposes only and does not indicate an endorsement of any specific scientific, political, or religious point of view. © TPB Publishing. You have been licensed one copy of this document for personal use only. Any other reproduction or redistribution is strictly prohibited. All rights reserved.

This material is provided for exam preparation purposes only and does not indicate an endorsement of any specific scientific, political, or religious point of view. © TPB Publishing. You have been licensed one copy of this document for personal use only. Any other reproduction or redistribution is strictly prohibited. All rights reserved.

Dear Series SIE Test Taker,

Thank you for purchasing this study guide for your Series SIE exam. We hope that we exceeded your expectations.

We strive to make our practice questions as similar as possible to what you will encounter on test day. With that being said, if you found something that you feel was not up to your standards, please send us an email and let us know.

We would also like to let you know about this other book in our catalog that may interest you.

Series 7

This can be found on Amazon: amazon.com/dp/1637751745

Series SIE Flash Cards

This can be found on Amazon: amazon.com/dp/1637756070

We have study guides in a wide variety of fields. If the one you are looking for isn't listed above, then try searching for it on Amazon or send us an email.

Thanks Again and Happy Testing!
Product Development Team
info@studyguideteam.com

This material is provided for exam preparation purposes only and does not indicate an endorsement of any specific scientific, political, or religious point of view. © TPB Publishing. You have been licensed one copy of this document for personal use only. Any other reproduction or redistribution is strictly prohibited. All rights reserved.

FREE Test Taking Tips Video/DVD Offer

To better serve you, we created videos covering test taking tips that we want to give you for FREE. **These videos cover world-class tips that will help you succeed on your test.**

We just ask that you send us feedback about this product. Please let us know what you thought about it—whether good, bad, or indifferent.

To get your **FREE videos**, you can use the QR code below or email freevideos@studyguideteam.com with "Free Videos" in the subject line and the following information in the body of the email:

   a. The title of your product

   b. Your product rating on a scale of 1-5, with 5 being the highest

   c. Your feedback about the product

If you have any questions or concerns, please don't hesitate to contact us at info@studyguideteam.com.

Thank you!

Made in United States
Orlando, FL
27 August 2023

36472848R00109